STUDIES IN THE
LUTHERAN CONFESSIONS

IN THIS DIVERSITY OF TRUE
OPINIONS LET TRUTH ITSELF
BEGET CONCORD.

The Confessions
of St. Augustine

STUDIES IN THE
LUTHERAN CONFESSIONS

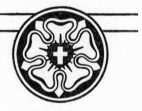

WILLARD DOW ALLBECK

 MUHLENBERG PRESS • PHILADELPHIA

PREFACE

The continued adherence of Lutherans to their confessional writings is an observable fact. The doctrinal article in synodical constitutions is ample evidence of this loyalty. It is the common bond among Lutherans, distinguishing them from other communions.

A consequence as well as a cause of such confessionalism is the continued study of the symbolical writings. Students in Lutheran theological seminaries find that they are required to complete courses in Lutheran symbolics. Pastors restudy the confessions for sermonic purposes or in the preparation of doctrinal papers. Others who would understand Lutheranism must become acquainted with the *Book of Concord.*

This book is published as an aid to such study. For seminary students it is intended to be a guide and an analysis. The student is expected to read the *Book of Concord* with it. He will find here an account of the historical occasion in which each of the symbolical writings had its origin. Each document must be understood in the light of the purpose for which it was written; each has its distinct characteristics.

The analysis of the contents of the *Book of Concord,* presented here, gives a running account of the argument contained in the symbolical writings. Attached to the outline are occasional comments calling attention to characteristics of the doctrinal treatment, or to its importance, or to criticisms of it. In this sense this book is a companion to the *Book of Concord.*

A comment on bibliography is given in the Introduction. But it is proper to note at this place the author's indebtedness to the work of Professor J. L. Neve. The first edition of his studies was published in 1917 under the title, *Introduction to Lutheran Symbolics.* When republished in 1926 it bore the name, *Introduction to the*

Symbolical Books of the Lutheran Church. It has had extensive use as a handbook for those beginning the study of the Lutheran symbols. Not only Dr. Neve's writings, but also his encouragement in theological study and the guidance of his mature theological insights are herewith gratefully acknowledged.

In the preparation of this book much encouragement was given by Dean Edward C. Fendt of the Theological Seminary of Capital University. Professor Paul H. Buehring of the same institution read the manuscript and offered helpful criticism. President Abdel Ross Wentz of Gettysburg Theological Seminary and President Paul J. Hoh of the Philadelphia Theological Seminary granted permission to consult works in the libraries of their institutions. Dean E. E. Flack of Hamma Divinity School of Wittenberg College also has contributed to the preparation of the manuscript by suggestions, and by permitting the reading of his unpublished manuscript, *History and Analysis of the Lutheran Confessions.* Pastors who participated in a seminar on "The Lutheran Confessions" also made their contribution. To all these persons the author expresses his sincere thanks.

Permission to quote from copyright material was granted by: Concordia Publishing House, from *Concordia Triglotta,* 1921; The Macmillan Company, from Gustav Aulén, *Christus Victor,* 1931, F. J. Badcock, *The History of the Creeds,* 1938, and Anders Nygren, *Agape and Eros,* 1932-39; Meador Publishing Company, from Charles L. Hill, *The Loci Communes of Philip Melanchthon,* 1944; and the Wartburg Press, from J. L. Neve, *Introduction to the Symbolical Books of the Lutheran Church,* 1926.

TABLE OF CONTENTS

Preface v

Introduction ix

    I. Lutherans and the Book of Concord 1

    II. The Ecumenical Creeds 16

    III. The Origin of the Augsburg Confession 46

    IV. Articles I-VI of the Augsburg Confession 58

    V. Articles VII-XIII of the Augsburg Confession . . . 78

    VI. Articles XIV-XXI of the Augsburg Confession . . . 97

    VII. Augsburg Confession Articles on Abuses 117

    VIII. The Origin of the Apology 137

    IX. Outline of the Apology (Articles I-VI) 145

    X. Outline of the Apology (Articles VII-XXI) 158

    XI. Outline of the Apology (Articles on Abuses) . . . 174

    XII. The Origin of the Smalcald Articles 187

    XIII. Outline of the Smalcald Articles 194

    XIV. The Catechisms 213

    XV. Outline of the Large Catechism 223

    XVI. The Origin of the Formula of Concord 239

    XVII. Outline of the Formula of Concord (Chapters I-VI) . . 254

    XVIII. Outline of the Formula of Concord (Chapters VII-XII) 272

Bibliography 292

Index 295

INTRODUCTION

In the four hundred years since Luther's death, those who have been designated "Lutherans" have had repeated occasion for testifying concerning their doctrine. In the sixteenth century imperial efforts were made to Romanize it, and when Calvinism was making large gains there were those who attempted to "Calvinize" Lutheran doctrine. In the seventeenth century the Pietistic movement was an effort to moralize it. The Enlightenment of the eighteenth century was determined to rationalize it. And the nineteenth century was marked by vigorous plans to unionize it.

Whenever there has been a determination to uphold the scriptural doctrines reaffirmed by Luther, there has also been recourse to the confessional statements of the Reformation age. The outstanding, though not the only, materials in this field are those found in the *Book of Concord*. Virtually all its contents have been under attack from one side or another, or have fallen into disuse at some time or other. But a revived and consistent Lutheranism has found them indispensable, and has restored them to use.

It was inevitable that a body of documents of such importance should attract extensive study. The dogmaticians in the century following Luther's death built their systems upon the confessional books. Presently there appeared historical introductions and explanatory treatments of the symbolical writings. Written in Latin and in the mood of the dogmaticians, they interpreted the *Book of Concord* to the seventeenth century. An example is the *Isagoge in libros ecclesiarum lutheranarum symbolicos* by John Benedict Carpzov in 1665.

Treatises on Lutheran symbolics were published also in the eighteenth century. They continued to be largely dogmatic with a gradual increase in interest in the historical approach. By the end of that century and with the opening of the nineteenth, there came a full-blown movement to make an objective, historical investigation of the Lutheran symbolical writings. From that time to the present there has been intensive, scholarly research of the highest kind directed in this field with rich results.

The details concerning the works on Lutheran symbolics previous to his day are given by Edward Köllner in the introduction to his *Symbolik der lutherischen Kirche,* published in 1837. More recent works, or an encyclopedia article, will give a bibliography for the nineteenth century.

It will suffice here to note the more important works consulted in the preparation of this volume. Students who read the works in German will find ample bibliographies in the books listed below.

In celebration of the four-hundredth anniversary of the Augsburg Confession there was published at Göttingen in 1930 *Die Bekenntnisschriften der evangelisch-lutherischen Kirche.* It is a new edition of the confessional writings critically prepared in an effort to recover their original form. Footnotes indicate changes made in the various editions as well as deviations from the original manuscripts. There are also footnotes to clarify obscure phrases in the text. For each of the confessional writings there is provided a historical introduction. The work, which is in two volumes, was produced by a group of eminent German scholars. It has been the primary source used in this book.

Of outstanding importance also is the *Concordia Triglotta* published in 1921. Prepared by members of the faculty of Concordia Theological Seminary in St. Louis, under the editorship of F. Bente, it presents the *Book of Concord* in German, Latin, and English in parallel columns. The historical introductions are the most extensive of any in English, and there are ample indexes.

The Book of Concord edited by Henry E. Jacobs and issued first in 1882-83 is a standard work. The first volume contains an English translation of the symbolical writings. The second volume is made up of historical introductions, related Reformation documents, and indexes. The Schwabach, the Marburg, and the Torgau Articles, as well as Eck's Four Hundred Four Theses are in this volume in later editions.

The account of the origin of the confessional writings, as given in the books mentioned, may be compared with the *Historische Ein-*

leitung written by Theodor Kolde for the tenth edition of *Die Symbol-ischen Bücher* prepared by J. T. Müller. The three-volume *Creeds of Christendom* by Philip Schaff covers similar data. *The Confessional History of the Lutheran Church* by J. W. Richard, with its lack of friendliness toward the Formula of Concord, and *The Confessional Principle and the Confessions of the Lutheran Church*, by T. E. Schmauk and C. T. Benze, which is an answer to Richard, provide profitable insights and source material in English. Further documents in English translation are found in *The Augsburg Confession, A Col-lection of Sources with an Historical Introduction*, by J. M. Reu.

References to the works and letters of Melanchthon have been compared with originals in the *Corpus Reformatorum* edited by C. G. Bretschneider, as well as in *The Loci Communes of Melanchthon* by C. L. Hill. Luther's *Larger Confession on the Holy Sacrament* of 1528 is found in volume twenty-six of the Weimar edition of *D. Martin Luthers Werke.* Translations of other of his writings are found in the Philadelphia edition of *The Works of Martin Luther.*

The study of the ecumenical creeds is aided by A. C. McGiffert's *The Apostles' Creed* which uses with some independence the older German studies. F. J. Badcock, in his *The History of the Creeds*, has a fresh approach with interesting results.

There is an abundance of material on the Augsburg Confession. *Einleitung in die Augustana* by Gustav Plitt is a two-volume work which provides many interesting insights. *Quellen und Forschungen zur Geschichte des Augsburgischen Glaubensbekenntnisses* by Wil-helm Gussman is a publication of this century containing much de-tailed information in its two volumes. A brief, but lively, commentary on the Confession is found in *Der Wille der Reformation im Augs-burgischen Bekenntnis* by Leonhard Fendt.

For the four-hundredth anniversary of the Smalcald Articles there was issued *Luthers Glaube und Theologie in den Schmalkaldischen Artikeln* by Johannes Stier. It is a brief but careful study of that document.

Luther's catechisms have evoked a large literature. Valuable material has been found in *Die Evangelischen Katechismusversuche vor Luthers Enchiridion* by Ferdinand Cohrs. Writers in this field make use of the *Historischer Kommentar zu Luthers Kleinem Kate-chismus* by Johannes Meyer. Another book by the same author is

Luthers Grosser Katechismus. Published in 1930 was Karl Thieme's *Die Augsburgische Konfession und Luthers Katechismen.* M. Reu in his *Luther's Small Catechism* has provided a wealth of scholarly data.

An old, but standard work on the *Formula of Concord* was written by F. H. R. Frank under the title *Die Theologie der Concordienformel.* A brief account is given by G. J. Fritschel in his book entitled, *The Formula of Concord, Its Origin and Contents.*

The research concerning the *Book of Concord,* of which these titles give only a small reflection, indicates the continuing interest in Reformation theology both from a historical and from a practical point of view. A more thorough understanding of the thought of the Reformation era is desirable for our day when the modern mood and the trend of world events may distort it. Lutheran churches which still make confessional use of the documents in the *Concordia* need continually to study and teach the doctrines contained therein. Preaching that is vigorously Lutheran finds strength there.

The following abbreviations are used in this book:

ANF, The Ante-Nicene Fathers

Bek., Die Bekenntnisschriften der evangelisch-lutherischen Kirche

C.R., Corpus Reformatorum

Conc. Trig., Concordia Triglotta

MSG, Migne, Patrologiae Series Graecae

MSL, Migne, Patrologiae Series Latina

NPNF, A Select Library of the Nicene and Post-Nicene Fathers

NSH, The New Schaff-Herzog Encyclopedia of Religious Knowledge

PRE, Realencyklopädie für protestantische Theologie und Kirche

W.A., Weimar Ausgabe, D. Martin Luthers Werke

Chapter 1

LUTHERANS AND THE BOOK OF CONCORD

A book celebrating a half-century of Lutheran testimony appeared officially from the printshop of Matthes Stöckel and Gimel Bergen in Dresden on June 25, 1580. It was celebrating the fiftieth anniversary of the public presentation of the Augsburg Confession to Emperor Charles V. It was the *Concordia,* or *Book of Concord,* in the German language.

Printing had been begun as early as the summer of 1578, when the task of setting type for the Formula of Concord was undertaken. By the spring of 1579, copies were off the press, though they were incomplete in some matters. In the meanwhile, men commissioned by the civil authorities toured the country presenting the Formula of Concord to the clergy for their inspection and signatures. Some of the commissioners were not very prompt in the matter, and as late as March, 1580, had to be urged to report.

But finally the list of signatures was complete, and the volume including them could appear for the anniversary. It was "by unanimous agreement and command of the said Electors and Estates put into print for the instruction and warning of their lands, churches, schools, and descendants." The preface carries the authorization of seventy-six electors, counts, dukes, and cities. Schaff says, "The Elector Augustus celebrated the completion of the work, which cost him so much trouble and money, by a memorial coin representing him in full armor on the storm-tossed ship of the church."

That same year a Latin edition appeared, printed at Leipzig. The translation of the Formula of Concord from the German had been

1

done by Lucas Osiander. But it was inaccurate in some parts, and was revised in 1582 by Selnecker. The next year it had further revision by a group of clergymen under the leadership of Martin Chemnitz, and this revision was published in the *Book of Concord* in 1584, becoming the official Latin text.

The *Concordia* is more than a book; it is actually a thick volume consisting of several books. It is a collection of doctrinal writings—a *corpus doctrinae*. Such collections had appeared during the sixteenth century, the first being the *Corpus Doctrinae Christianae Philippicum* of 1560 containing only works by Melanchthon. It was official for electoral Saxony and several other areas. Territories that desired to include writings by Luther or others prepared their own collection during the years that followed.

When the *Concordia* appeared with general approval, it overshadowed the local collections. Here was a *corpus doctrinae* that united the Lutherans in common faith, in contrast either to the Romanists or the Calvinists. It expressed convictions that were clearly Lutheran in distinction from those that had become ambiguous or cloudy under the teaching of Melanchthon.

Though accepted or acknowledged with varying enthusiasm in the many Lutheran territories, the *Book of Concord* was most appreciated in the German areas where discord had been most painful. The Scandinavian countries, relatively untouched by the controversies that produced the Formula of Concord, have been less likely to expect subscription by their clergy to the entire *Book of Concord*.

Some parts of the Lutheran Church in America have gone through a struggle on this matter. Those Lutheran bodies that trace their history back to the colonial period went through a more or less extended time of uncertainty concerning their acceptance of the whole *Book of Concord*. They felt the influence of rationalism in the years following the War of Independence.

As they became Anglicized and lost their ties with Europe, they tended to imitate other English-speaking denominations in revivalistic and nonliturgical practices. In one important instance, viz., the General Synod, there was even antagonism to most of the *Book of Concord*. The details of the confessional struggle must be read in a history of Lutherans in America.

At present, however, Lutherans in America, with few exceptions, give official approval to the *Book of Concord.* It is studied and professed with an understanding and a conviction that indicate a great area of unity of doctrine. Even where all the documents in it are not officially named, its doctrines are professed and its importance for the Lutheran Church is acknowledged.

The same was true of the Lutheran World Convention, now reorganized as the Lutheran World Federation. The statement agreed upon at Copenhagen in 1929 declares: "The Lutheran World Convention acknowledges the Holy Scriptures of the Old and New Testaments as the only source and infallible norm of all church doctrine and practice, and sees in the Confessions of the Lutheran Church, especially in the Unaltered Augsburg Confession and Luther's Small Catechism, a pure exposition of the Word of God." [1]

Lutherans look upon their official doctrinal writings in the *Book of Concord* as confessions rather than as theological treatises. The Lutheran Church in Germany and her offspring in America have been described as being too doctrinal. Such a misconception arises when the critics think of the confessions as a textbook in dogmatics. Their theological character is seen out of proportion to other features. Lutherans are sometimes to blame, particularly if they write about the confessions in a dry, dull, and dreary way, or if they preach their doctrines in the dispassionate mood of a laboratory.

Instead, the confessions must be seen as the expression of convictions. A living faith pulsates through them. They are testimonies. They affirm publicly what is believed by individuals united in the church. Their theological dress must not disguise their vital structure. They are professions before the public, not for the purpose of scholastic dispute but to give evidence of unalterable convictions.

In the Augsburg Confession the oft-repeated phrase, "Our churches teach . . ." clearly indicates that the sermons in the parishes were dealing with living issues. The Saxons were scarcely prepared to place themselves in jeopardy merely for matters of opinion. Only considerations of the greatest weight would induce them to risk the dangers involved in facing the empire and the papacy.

---

[1] *The Second Lutheran World Convention* (Philadelphia: United Lutheran Publication House, 1930), p. 202.

The instructions given Luther by the elector in preparation for the Smalcald meeting indicate quite clearly the confessional quality of the Smalcald Articles. What was to be said therein was to be said in the shadow of possible martyrdom. Nowhere could the confessional characteristic be clearer.

In the Formula of Concord one might expect a different spirit, since this document grew out of controversy. Yet in the introduction one finds immediately the confessional emphasis. There is evident the desire to acknowledge before the non-Lutheran world what Lutherans believed. Lutheran convictions in opposition to Rome and Crypto-Calvinism were expressed. The Formula disavows any interest in theological dispute for its own sake. It actually condemns useless and unnecessary controversy. But it notes that convictions must be maintained, even at the risk of controversy, as the Scriptures teach.

The confessions are thus seen as expressions of the live faith of Christians. They are an indication of the present life of the church. As expressed by T. E. Schmauk, "The Confessions are Scripture digested, assimilated, and beating in the life pulses of the Church." [2] Charles D. Williams used another figure when he wrote, "Creeds are not fences to keep our straying feet within the narrow paddocks of approved orthodoxy; they are rather flags to follow." [3] And T. A. Kantonen, contemplating present uses of the products of former days, wrote: "Dogmas are like coal-beds. They are the deposit of light and life in the past ages. But coal is not something to be admired and cherished and handed on; the energy in it must be released for present needs." [4]

It may be that many Lutheran pastors use their *Book of Concord* only as a reference work on some doctrinal point. When they need a sentence to clinch a point with authority, they seek it in a confessional writing. In the preparation of a sermon, some aspect of a doctrine is confused in their minds, and they turn to the confessions for guidance. Stated briefly, the *Book of Concord* is thought of as some-

---

[2] T. E. Schmauk and C. T. Benze, *The Confessional Principle and the Confessions of the Lutheran Church* (Philadelphia: General Council Publication Board, 1911), p. 9.

[3] *A Valid Christianity for Today* (New York: The Macmillan Co., 1909), p. 151.

[4] *The Lutheran*, December 6, 1939, p. 4.

thing academic, intellectual, and dogmatic—a thing for the library and the classroom.

However true this may be, there is more to be said. The *Book of Concord* can be thought of also as a thing of the pulpit and the prayer desk. The juice in it is not only printer's ink but also heart's blood. It bears the vivid marks of the earnest anxiety in God's name to make a good confession. It seeks to avoid—in fact, it renounces—interest in purely speculative and academic discussions.

Considerations of faith and life are everywhere primary in the confessions. Does the discussion of the Lord's Supper become involved in an analysis of the various kinds of presence? It is only that those kneeling at the communion rail may have an unwavering faith in the real presence of Christ in the sacrament. Does the treatmen of Christology become scholastic in its delineation of the *communicatio?* The purpose is not pedantic, but personal. The Christ in whose name we pray in our family devotions still wears the humanity with which he was born at Bethlehem. In these, as in other instances, the words of the confessions presume or prepare for worship.

It is still true in the Lutheran Church that the confessions express the inner conviction and life of the church. It is an inner conviction that is positive without being pugnacious. Worship carries the aroma of it. That which constitutes the vital stuff of Christian faith is here spelled out for others to see. Like Luther at the Diet of Worms, Lutherans in their confessions are saying, "Here we stand!"

However, it would be a mistake to think that the confessions are built upon Lutheran experience in finding God. They are not preeminently some sixteenth-century examples of religious empiricism. There is always about them the assumption that they are dealing with donations, not discoveries; with an Evangel, not simply an experience. They everywhere presume revelation. They are preeminently biblical. One of the two claims frequently made by the confessions for their reliability is that their doctrines are founded upon Scripture, and are supported thereby.

"Scriptural" means something more than quoting the Bible. All parties to the Reformation controversies did that. Romanist quotations were quite as ample as the Lutheran. Romanist theologians were not ignorant of Scripture by any means. Too frequently we have assumed that before Luther the Bible was an unknown book. Too much has been made of Luther's experience with the chained Bible at Erfurt. M. Reu has shown quite conclusively how much Scripture Luther had to memorize as a schoolboy, how much he had to learn as a student, how much he had to read as a priest and study as a teacher.[5] His was not an uncommon experience in the Roman Catholic Church. The Romanists knew their Bible and quoted it extensively. One needs only to read the Confutation to get an impression of their copious use of Scripture.

The Lutheran contribution was not in the use of more Bible and less of the writings of scholastics such as Thomas Aquinas. It was in a more discriminating use of the Bible, and in a more careful exegesis. Repentance was read not as "doing penance" but as a change of mind that left sin and clung to Christ in faith. Sacrifice in Scripture is found to be both vicarious and eucharistic. The Romanist theologians had failed to make this distinction, and therefore were entangled in the confusion of the sacrifice of the mass. Thus, when Melanchthon in the Apology examined their scriptural quotations, he showed them to be utterly untenable.

As may be expected, the longer treatises, namely, the Apology and the Formula of Concord, make the most extended use of the Bible. The Large Catechism comes into this category also. But biblical quotations are not lacking in the other writings. Valid exegesis underlies them all. The distortions of the Latin Vulgate and the misinterpretations of scholasticism are excluded.

Something more is involved than the use of the Bible as a source of quotations. The Lutherans wanted to get to the heart of the Scripture, to find the central theme, to discover what was basic and fundamental. The conclusion reached was that at the center is God's love revealed in Jesus Christ, his work, and the salvation he made available for mankind. The harmony of Scripture was found in this fact, the authority of Scripture in this gospel.

Luther, whatever his incidental comments on some books of the Bible, was vehement in his assertion that the Scriptures, conveying Christ to us, are truly and actually the Word of God. The confessions

---

[5] *Luther's German Bible* (Columbus: Lutheran Book Concern, 1934). pp. 75 ff.

everywhere assume that it is the Word of God which they are attesting, that it is this fundamental evangelical theme of Scripture which they are vindicating. Whatever may be the problem with regard to separate verses of Scripture and the analogy of faith, it must be said that, with regard to the central redemptive theme of the Bible, the confessions everywhere exhibit the confidence of declaring it, of interpreting it, and of being guided by it.

The confessional writings contain the conviction that God has given his Word. Those who accept them show themselves to be neither too proud nor too self-sufficient to receive God's gift. That they do not understand it completely does not cause them to refuse it. What God has given is too precious to be lost or jeopardized by false doctrine or practice. It is to be believed and cherished and preached.

That the confessions display Lutheran testimony concerning the gospel is the chief fact. But connected with it is the further fact that it is a united testimony. It is a mistake to think that the Reformation made its most important contribution by asserting the right of private judgment in matters of religion. It is a distortion of the Lutheran movement to interpret it as giving a man a Bible and telling him to formulate his own doctrines. Such an excessive individualism is foreign to the Lutheran Church.

The confessions are the expression of a united faith. They meant that those were together as Lutherans who believed together. They had a great devotion to the church, and desired earnestly to be included in it. As the body of believers they expressed what they found together in the Word. Their confessions were their Christian consensus.

It is in the Formula of Concord that the spirit of unity moves significantly, after the heat of controversy had abated. Two things in that document, namely, truth and unity, were the aims of the writers. The loss of either would be a disaster to the church, and therefore to the individual believer. Thus it was that the Formula became a renewed confession of faith. Almost a half-century had passed since the Diet of Augsburg, but there still were those ready to espouse the faith "which pure teachers and hearers confessed with heart and mouth."

Christian faith and worship are not only communion between the believer and God—their vertical dimension. They also form a fellowship between believers, which is a horizontal dimension constituted of Christian unity. The Formula declares itself to be based upon the doctrines of the Augsburg Confession. Therefore, in the introduction to the Solid Declaration it says: "We have declared to one another, with heart and mouth, that we will neither make nor receive any separate or new confession of our faith, but acknowledge as confessional the public common writings which always and everywhere were received in all the churches of the Augsburg Confession as such symbols or public confessions." [6]

With such interest in unity and common testimony, the Formula of Concord received the signatures of approval of about eight thousand leading persons in Lutheran areas. Princes and pastors had previously indicated their acceptance of other confessional writings by signing their names to them. The catechisms had been less used in this way. But in the *Book of Concord* they are accepted.

Thus it has long been Lutheran custom to indicate approval and acceptance of the confessions by formal signature. There have been times when there was criticism of confessional subscription. Even now, outside Lutheran circles, there is to be found the attitude that creeds and confessions are limitations on intellectual freedom. It is presumed that religious views are the product of human discovery, that no truth is final, and that progress is made by discarding the past. The only loyalty is to freedom and the future.

Lutherans do not think of confessional subscription as a bondage. Creeds are like highways. The motorist drives his automobile only where there are roads; he could make little progress through fields and woods. Because he can go only where there is a road, he would be moronic to consider roads a limitation to travel. It must be perfectly obvious that highways facilitate travel. The confessions likewise facilitate religious thinking. They have been made by those who with much labor have surveyed the terrain, avoiding the impassable mountains of the unrevealed and purely speculative, and skirting the disastrous swamps of error.

---

[6] *The Book of Concord,* ed. H. E. Jacobs (Philadelphia: United Lutheran Publication House, 1908), I, 535.

In former years there was much discussion of confessional subscription, distinguishing between kinds of subscription. Some advocated *quatenus* subscription, meaning that they approved the confessions in so far as they agree with the Word of God. Such a position was criticized as being a weak adherence. The subscriber was thought to have mental reservations. There was always the suspicion that he disagreed with some doctrine in the confessions. S. A. Ort once wrote: "A qualified subscription is the making of a qualified confession, and a qualified confession is a breaking away from historic doctrinal connection and development, and this is ecclesiastical suicide." [7]

That which is in use among Lutherans is the type of subscription indicated by the word *quia*. In this sense, the confessions are signed because they agree with the Word of God. It is presumed that pastors have satisfied their minds on this matter; that they have examined the confessions carefully and are prepared to declare the doctrines contained therein as their faith. They make the choice freely, but they have come to have convictions and are quite willing to profess them. As J. L. Neve wrote, "The subscription of a servant of the church must be a real confession; not anything evasive, but positive." [8]

It is *quia* subscription, as Neve has indicated, which is used in the *Book of Concord*. In the "Comprehensive Summary" of the Solid Declaration of the Formula of Concord, either the word *quia* is used or its meaning implied. The Unaltered Augsburg Confession was accepted "because (*quia*) it has been derived from God's Word, and is founded firmly and well therein." The Apology was confessionally accepted "because (*quia*) in it the said Augsburg Confession is not only sufficiently elucidated and guarded, but also confirmed by clear, irrefutable testimonies of Holy Scripture." The same scriptural and confessional character is acknowledged for the Smalcald Articles and the catechisms, though expressed in other words.

Moreover, the contents of the *Book of Concord* need to be seen in their status as church documents. To think of them in terms of individual subscribers is to fail to recognize their use in the fellowship of

---

[7] *Selected Sermons and Addresses* (Seattle: H. C. Stafford, 1914), p. 138.

[8] *Introduction to the Symbolical Books of the Lutheran Church* (2nd ed.; Columbus: Lutheran Book Concern, 1926), p. 32.

faith. Their service is in the community of believers. They are common testimonies.

The creeds certainly have had that character. Since ancient times a creed has been known as a "symbol." It was not only the profession of the faith of a candidate for baptism; it was also the faith of the church to which he was being admitted. A symbol was a token, badge, or password of membership—the mark by which Christians were recognized.

The confessions also were testimonies of groups of persons who because of some occasion were under the necessity of declaring their faith. Their common convictions were the basis of their unity. Their confessions were the evidence of the unity, their avowed and subscribed profession of it. They were their understanding of Scripture to be used in their congregations and transmitted to posterity.

That does not mean that the church or the subscribers are bound to every aspect of the theological proof. The Lutheran Church does not guarantee the accuracy of every patristic quotation, though mistakes of that kind are rather few. Variations in wording in the various texts and editions (except for the *Variata* edition of the Augsburg Confession) are not matters of concern, even when they add to or subtract from the argument. The basic doctrine remains. Even the historic form in which the doctrines are expressed has its value, and is therefore accepted.

That is to say that the confessions are historic documents which must be seen in the light of history. They must be read in terms of for whom, by whom, and against whom they were written. Since each had a specific occasion, each has distinctive characteristics.

The Augsburg Confession had to meet the political situation of a strong Roman Catholic emperor at the height of his power. It had also to meet the polemical situation raised by the Theses of Eck who tried to identify Lutherans with radical movements of the Reformation era. Under such circumstances the Augsburg Confession was irenic, rather than polemic, toward Romanism; it was ecumenic rather than partisan; it was scriptural rather than scholastic, and more popular than academic.

The Apology faced a changed situation. Neither the emperor nor the pope would yield. Lutheran faith and scholarship had been

10

impugned. Therefore the Apology is explicitly Lutheran rather than merely ecumenical. It is scholarly, verging on scholastic, rather than popular. It is composed of lengthy discussion instead of summarizing statements. Against Rome it takes a vigorous polemical attitude.

Much the same situation existed when the Smalcald Articles were written. There was the same expressed hostility to the papists. But a council was in prospect, and something less lengthy than the Apology was needed. Hence the Smalcald Articles present their polemic in brief, incisive terms, and give in barest outline their ecumenical and evangelical doctrines.

The catechisms were issued to overcome the distressing ignorance of the people. The situation for which they were prepared would make them didactic rather than polemical. In their historical setting they were understandably popular and plain instead of scholarly and academic. Their interest is more practical than theological.

When the Formula of Concord was completed Luther had been dead thirty-one years, and Melanchthon seventeen. In a considerable part of Germany Lutheranism was the legal religion. The problems were chiefly within rather than outside the Lutheran Church. The controversies among Lutherans had brought the issues into sharp focus and had given clear-cut faces to the terminology. They had been the debates of theologians with their academic distinctions.

Hence the Formula of Concord is scholastic, theological, and long. It is interested in unity and peace, dealing firmly though gently with dissenting Lutherans and refusing to condemn Melanchthon by name. It is not so irenic toward Calvinists and other non-Lutherans. It is, therefore, a document of specific Lutheranism.

This historic character of the confessions is not a liability; it is simply a fact. Historic qualities are liabilities only to those obsessed with modern science. The multiplication table is not outmoded, however ancient. Nor is historic quality necessarily an asset. The golden age is not always in the past. History inevitably involves limitations.

Yet this historic character of the confessions is something always to be recognized. Statements in the confessions are to be seen in the light of the occasions which called them forth. Quotations from any one of them can be misleading if they are severed from their historic context. There are varying emphases and distinct purposes

11

to be observed, and when these are noted, the understanding of the confessional doctrines is aided rather than impeded. A further implication is this, that for a full appreciation of the Lutheran position all of the confessions must be studied; one of them alone is not enough.

In addition to its historical features, the *Book of Concord* has a definitely theological character. Those who are not afraid of some theology in their religious fare will not find this objectionable. Only those who wish to keep Christian thinking in an infantile state will object to a theology. W. E. Garrison once remarked that "those who think they have no theology usually have a poor one."

To say that the *Book of Concord* is theological is to say that Lutherans have given what seems to them to be a coherent and consistent statement of scripture teaching. They have seen the rich variety in biblical teaching and have desired to state their understanding of its meaning in contrast to the erroneous interpretations of it. To say that it is coherent is to say that it is systematic. It has found a central principle in justification for Christ's sake through faith. That is the heart of the gospel, and what subverts it cannot be accepted. Such a theology is not eclectic but has the unity of an organism.

This also is the feature of its consistency. There is a loyalty to the basic revelation comprising the gospel. It is not a consistency whose chief instrument is logic. The theology of the confessions is willing at times to lay aside logic and to take up paradox. It is willing to incorporate into its documents some matters which are above logic and which are accepted simply as mysteries of faith to be accepted even when not understood. On the other hand, some teachings of Zwingli which were essentially logical were completely rejected and some Roman practices set up for rational purposes were condemned because contrary to the gospel. Their logic could not save them.

The *Book of Concord* has also an ecumenical character. It is the oft-repeated assertion of the confessions that they are fully in accord with the ancient church. They assert that their positions may be substantiated by reference to the church fathers and the documents of the ecumenic age. They declare that both the Scriptures and the early church, exhibiting the original Christian and apostolic message, support their views. To have accepted any other position would have been tantamount to acknowledging that they were heretical.

There is no need to examine each of the confessions for examples of patristic quotations. Even a casual reading reveals them. In *Die Bekenntnisschriften der evangelisch-lutherischen Kirche* there is an index of citations from ecclesiastical and profane writers which by its very size indicates the extensiveness of quotations from the fathers.

However, this claim to ecumenical character needs some qualification. The Lutheran doctrines would not have stood the test of the yardstick proposed by Vincent of Lerins: *semper, ubique, et ab omnibus*. On the doctrines of God, Christ, and the Trinity there could be no question. But the Lutheran claim to ecumenicity for their doctrine of original sin was challenged by the Romanists. Says Seeberg, "The Confutators were, from their viewpoint, right in objecting to the 'born without the fear of God, without trust in Him' as a definition of original sin. . . . The deliberate hostility of the critics should not blind us to the fact that a difference in point of view is here revealed." [9]

When it comes to Article IV on Justification in the Augsburg Confession, a doctrinal position is discovered which certainly was not the one commonly accepted in the ancient church. It is with justice that Seeberg speaks of it as "the new doctrine." [10] None of the sacerdotal, legalistic, Semi-Pelagian views common in the ancient and medieval church is tolerated in the Lutheran documents. In these respects the Lutherans were not ecumenical; they knew it, and so did the Romanists.

It is evident from the history of doctrine that the church fathers were neither always clear nor unanimous in their views on all doctrines. Hence they could be quoted approvingly by both Lutherans and Romanists. This was a problem even among the Evangelicals. It seems that when Melanchthon was convinced by Oecolampadius that church fathers could be quoted against Luther's view of the Lord's Supper, he regarded the Calvinist view with more favor.

The conclusion must be reached that in the doctrines of God, the Trinity, the person and natures of Christ—the positions indicated in the ecumenical creeds—Lutherans had not departed from the teach-

---

[9] R. Seeberg, *Text-book of the History of Doctrines*, C. E. Hay (Philadelphia: Lutheran Publication Society, 1905), II, 336.

[10] *Ibid.*, p. 332.

ing of the ancient church. But in the doctrine of salvation, upon which the ancient church was not clear, the Lutherans made an advance consistent with and built upon the ecumenical doctrines, but developing a theological system markedly different from that which had developed within Catholicism, whether Eastern or Latin.

The fact is that the *Book of Concord* is specifically evangelical. It depicts a distinctive type of Christianity in which the grace of God— pardon freely given—is central. Stirred into action by the Romanist doctrine of repentance, the evangelical thinkers geared every doctrine to that of justification.

Because of circumstances at Augsburg, the Confession went far in presenting a friendly face. But the imperial party and the papal representatives correctly sensed that here was a movement basically antithetical to Romanist doctrine and practice. The differences were irreconcilable, as subsequent conferences showed. Whatever the Confession might say, the Lutheran movement was not simply a reformed Catholicism; it was evangelical. The correspondence between the Tübingen faculty and the patriarch of Constantinople in the 1570's and later revealed the same thing. Aside from a common antipathy to Rome, Lutherans had nothing else in common with the Eastern Orthodox in theological outlook. Both Rome and the East were catholic, that is, they taught the meritoriousness of works. Lutherans in that sense were not catholic, but evangelical.

The outcropping of the evangelical emphasis in each of the confessional writings will be observed as they are examined. In this doctrinal symphony the evangelical motif is everywhere in evidence. The length at which it is discussed in the Apology indicates its importance. Nothing can be clearer than the decisively evangelical character of the confessions. Compared with it, Romanism has a decidedly different texture.

Finally, the *Book of Concord* must be seen as something of practical value. If it is opened as a biological specimen, it will be found that it is not something preserved in formaldehyde, but that life is pulsating in it. Quite in contrast to the dry scholastic stuff of Thomas Aquinas, this work talks about religion in life. It does not talk about Lutherans' thoughts in religion, but declares that this is what "we believe and teach."

For example, the Smalcald Articles steam with the heat of Luther's vigor. He was continually facing the practical issues of life. He described the wickedness of his day in vivid terms. In such realistic spirit he sat down to write his articles. When he took up the doctrine of the merit of Christ and the righteousness of faith, he did not write it like an article for an encyclopedia. Instead, he said that this is what "we teach and practice. Therefore we must be sure concerning this doctrine, and not doubt; for otherwise all is lost." [11]

Now observe the first application which he made of this doctrine. He turned at once to the chief worship of the church, viz., the mass, or the communion. Using the material principle of the Reformation as a red pencil, he underscored the erroneous doctrines and the distorted practices of papist worship. These are things, he said, which "we cannot tolerate, but we are compelled to condemn, in order that we may retain the holy sacrament pure and certain, according to the institution of Christ, employed and received through faith." [12] It was no academic dispute for Luther, but one vital to piety.

The Apology also sees itself as related to living religion. Melanchthon acknowledged that it is a theological document, composed in answer to the Roman Confutation.[13] Yet, of its contents he said, "I have comprised the chief arguments that there might be among all nations a testimony concerning us, that we hold the Gospel of Christ correctly and in a pious way." [14]

And he closed the German edition of the introduction with this prayer: "Lord Jesus Christ, it is Thy holy Gospel, it is Thy cause; look Thou upon the many troubled hearts and consciences and maintain and strengthen in Thy truth Thy churches and little flocks, who suffer from the devil, anxiety, and distress. Confound all hypocrisy and lies, and grant peace and unity, so that Thy glory may advance, and Thy kingdom, strong against all the gates of hell, may continually grow and increase." [15]

---

[11] *Book of Concord* (Jacobs), I, p. 312.
[12] *Ibid.*, p. 317.
[13] *Ibid.*, p. 74. *C. R.*, XXVII, 419.
[14] *Ibid.*, p. 74. *C. R.*, XXVII, 421.
[15] *Ibid.*, p. 75

Chapter II

THE ECUMENICAL CREEDS

There are three creeds which have wide Christian acceptance. In general they represent the consensus of the doctrinal views of the ancient church, and form the foundation of the doctrinal teaching of most of modern Christendom. They are commonly designated as the Apostles', the Nicene, and the Athanasian creeds.

The Formula of Concord in its Solid Declaration calls these creeds "ecumenical" and the Epitome speaks of them as "the unanimous, universal Christian faith." They constitute the agreement of the ancient church in rejecting heresies which had arisen. They state in creedal form the trinitarian faith of the apostolic church.

The universal character of these creeds is to be acknowledged even if they are not officially professed by some groups. The Protestant Episcopal Church, for example, does not give official adherence to the Athanasian Creed. Some groups, such as the Disciples of Christ —followers of Alexander Campbell—formally profess no creed. But in so far as they are trinitarian, they agree with the ecumenical creeds.

Likewise the universal character of these creeds is recognized, even if there are variations in the text as accepted here or there. For example, the Eastern Orthodox churches reject the *filioque*—"and the Son"—in the statement that the Holy Ghost "proceedeth from the Father and the Son." In some groups there is a modification or even rejection of the statement, "He descended into hell." These few exceptions in details do not disqualify the creeds as universal trinitarian professions of ancient Christian faith.

16

THE APOSTLES' CREED

The text of the Apostles' Creed incorporated in the *Book of Concord* is the one customarily used in the Roman Catholic Church since the middle ages. It formed part of the baptism liturgy. It corresponds to the text found in the *Rituale Romanum* of 1614.

The Creed originated amid the obscurities of ancient church history. The most careful research has failed to discover the exact story. Parts of the history are now known but there are large gaps still unfilled.

The known facts begin with the period of the writing of the New Testament. In the apostolic church there were concise sentences used as expressions of faith or as parts of worship. An early baptismal formula is that in the great commission in Matthew 28:19—"baptizing them in the name of the Father and of the Son and of the Holy Ghost." A similar trinitarian formulation is the benediction at the end of II Corinthians.

But there are statements of faith that concern only Christ. Such was Peter's confession, "Thou art the Christ, the Son of the living God" (Matt. 16:16). St. Paul wrote, "No man can say that Jesus is the Lord, but by the Holy Ghost" (I Cor. 12:3). The declaration in Romans 10:9 is "If thou shalt confess with thy mouth the Lord Jesus, and shalt believe in thine heart that God hath raised him from the dead, thou shalt be saved." Of a similar nature is I John 4:15, "Whosoever shall confess that Jesus is the Son of God, God dwelleth in him, and he in God." Also I John 5:5, 10. The Ethiopian eunuch's baptismal creed was, "I believe that Jesus Christ is the Son of God" (Acts 8:37). Evidently baptism also was only in his name. Concerning baptisms at Ephesus it is recorded that "they were baptized in the name of the Lord Jesus" (Acts 19:5).

There are passages in the New Testament that have the appearance of liturgical formulas or of fragments of creeds. In I Peter, the latter part of the third chapter gives the impression of creedal material. The same is true of Philippians 2:5-11. Even more striking is I Corinthians 15:3, 4—"For I delivered unto you first of all that which I also received, how that Christ died for our sins according to the scriptures; and that he was buried, and that he rose again the third day according to the scriptures." Similar passages are found in

17

the epistles of Ignatius written early in the second century.

Sometimes the creedal statement includes God and Christ. Thus I Corinthians 8:6, "But to us there is but one God, the Father, of whom are all things, and we in him; and one Lord Jesus Christ, by whom are all things, and we by him." St. Paul in II Timothy 4:1 wrote, "I charge thee therefore before God, and the Lord Jesus Christ, who shall judge the quick and the dead at his appearing and his kingdom," etc.

The trinitarian form, however, came to prevail in the church. The First Epistle of Clement asks, "Have we not one God and one Christ and the Spirit of grace poured out on us?" (46:6). Justin Martyr in his First Apology stated that baptism was in the name of the Trinity.[1] But in his Dialogue with Trypho he wrote this statement used in exorcism which speaks only of Christ: "This very Son of God—who is the Firstborn of every creature, who became man by the Virgin, who suffered, and was crucified under Pontius Pilate by your nation, who died, who rose from the dead, and ascended into heaven." [2]

Irenaeus, writing "Against Heresies" in the latter part of the second century, said the church believes "in one God, the Father Almighty, Maker of heaven and earth and the sea and all things that are in them; and in one Christ Jesus, the Son of God, who became incarnate for our salvation; and in the Holy Spirit, who proclaimeth through the prophets the dispensations of God, and the advents, and the birth from a virgin, and the passion, and the resurrection from the dead, and the ascension into heaven in the flesh of the beloved Christ Jesus, our Lord," etc.[3]

In Tertullian's writing, "On the Veiling of Virgins," occurs this passage: "The rule of faith, indeed, is altogether one, alone immovable and irreformable; the rule, to wit, of believing in one only God omnipotent, the Creator of the universe, and His Son, Jesus Christ, born of the Virgin Mary, crucified under Pontius Pilate, raised again the third day from the dead, received in the heavens, sitting now at the right (hand) of the Father, destined to come to judge quick and

---

[1] *Apol.* I, 61. *ANF* I, 183. *MSG* VI, 428.

[2] *Dial.* 85. *ANF* I, 241. *MSG* VI, 696.

[3] I, 10, 1. *ANF* I, 330. *MSG* VII, 549 f.

dead through the resurrection of the flesh as well (as of the spirit)." [4]
Similar passages may be found in his writing "Against Praxeas" and
"On Prescription Against Heretics." [5] His writings come from about
A.D. 200.

The "rule of faith," of which Tertullian thus gives a paraphrase,
was the church's statement of its doctrine, part of which was the baptismal confession of faith. But the "rule of faith" (*regula fidei*) was
not uniform for all areas. In fact, there was considerable diversity both
in the "rule of faith" and in the baptismal creed. The form which has
been reconstructed from the "Church Order" of Hippolytus resembles
the Apostles' Creed. Yet in Egypt and elsewhere there was in use a
statement which simply said, "I believe in God, the Father, Creator
of all, and in Jesus Christ, His only-begotten Son, our Lord, and in
the Holy Ghost, the holy church, the resurrection of the body." It is
uncertain whether this is a rudimentary form or an abbreviation.

Some have thought that back of these various rules of faith there
was one which was the mother of them all, and which existed in the
New Testament period. Scholars (A. Seeberg and Feine) [6] have reconstructed statements of what such a primitive "rule of faith" might
have been. Other scholars have been of the opinion that there was
no such primitive apostolic rule, but that the various rules grew up
somewhat independently of each other, especially in the East, though
all seem to have had a common pattern and core.

The next problem is to trace one or several of these early formulations and see how it developed into the Apostles' Creed. On this
matter there is no agreement. One view is widely held because of the
scholarship of Harnack. It was his thesis that Rome was the center
of Western influence and that the Apostles' Creed must be traced
through that city. Another view is that the development is to be
traced to France, northern Italy, and the Balkans, where the dominant
creedal influences were Eastern. The provinces influenced Rome,
rather than the reverse.

---

[4] Chap. I. *ANF* IV, 27. *MSL* II, 937.

[5] Translations are from *The Ante-Nicene Fathers*.

[6] A. Seeberg, *Der Katechismus der Urchristenheit* (1903). Paul Feine,
*Die Gestalt des Apostolischen Glaubensbekenntnisses in der Zeit des Neuen
Testaments* (1925). Cited in *Bek.*, I, xii.

According to the view of Harnack,[7] there came into use in Rome a baptismal confession which is important for the history of the Apostles' Creed. The confession is known as the "Old Roman Symbol." It was taught orally and seldom committed to writing. The oldest known text of it is in Greek rather than Latin. It was written about A.D. 340 by Marcellus, Bishop of Ancyra (modern Angora in Turkey), who for a time had been a refugee in Rome, and who on his departure wrote a letter including a creed presumably Roman. About sixty years later, a priest of Aquileia, named Rufinus, wrote down the creed used in his city, indicating in it the words not found in the Old Roman Symbol. The Roman creed obtained by subtracting Aquileian words differs only slightly from the text of Marcellus.

According to Ambrose and Rufinus, the Old Roman Symbol as the official creed in Rome was preserved with great care. No changes were permitted in the wording. How long it had been in use in Rome is not clear. Since Augustine, who lived 345-430, wrote expositions of it, there was use of it then in North Africa. Fragments from the writings of Bishop Dionysius of Rome seem to refer to it about the year 250. The passage quoted from Tertullian may indicate that it was well known by A.D. 200. Some authorities think that it was in existence as early as the end of the first century.

It seems that during the Gothic invasions the Roman creed was dropped from most of its accustomed use. The invaders were Arians. To emphasize their Catholic faith, the Romans brought into use the Nicene Creed with its specifically anti-Arian phrases. Such is the proposed explanation.

Meanwhile the Old Roman Symbol was being used in the provinces where modifications were made to it during the passing centuries. In what is modern Yugoslavia, Bishop Nicetas of Remesiana about A.D. 400 wrote his creed which is nearly identical with the Apostles' Creed. Of special importance is the development made in parts of Gaul—areas of modern southern France. The creed of Faustus of Riez about A.D. 460 shows some changes. Even more are found in the text included in a sermon by Caesarius who was bishop of Arles, 503-43. Two centuries later, the Apostles' Creed was complete as it is now used. The text is found in the Old Gallican *Missale* of the eighth

---

[7] *"Apostolisches Symbolum,"* PRE I, 741 ff. NSH I, 240 ff.

century. It is also in the writings of Pirminius, an abbot of Reichenau.

With this development of the creed through the years there was continued the tradition that it had been written by the Apostles. The changes had been very gradual. They were made on the basis of creedal statements long in use in the East and founded on the New Testament. Therefore they caused no apparent trouble. And it seems that when the church in Rome, now free of Arian pressure, returned to the use of a creed other than the Nicene, it accepted this Gallican form with its tradition of apostolic authorship. The reasons are not clear why this Gallican form was taken rather than one of the many others in existence. There may be some significance in the fact that the creed began to be used in Rome at the time when the kingdom of the Franks was strong and was exerting influence there.

The history thus far presented assumes with Harnack that the Roman influence in the earlier centuries was decisive. The other view takes nearly the same facts, but by adding further evidence arrives at a different result. Some of the facts are given another form. It is argued, for example, that Marcellus nowhere claims that the creed written in his letter is the Roman creed; actually it shows signs of being Eastern. Nor can the Roman creed be determined with entire accuracy from the creed of Rufinus, even after the subtractions have been made. Moreover, the peculiarities of the Aquileian creed show Eastern affinities.

The evidence indicates that baptismal creeds both of the East and of the West have much in common. The basic framework is the same, whether in Rome or in Syria. In Rome there was great reluctance to add to the framework, whereas in the East there was greater liberty and variety in the additions. The influences, therefore, which developed the baptismal confession into the Apostles' Creed—a development which occurred in areas north of Rome—are most likely Eastern.

Much commerce traveled over the imperial highways extending from Constantinople westward through Greece, the Balkans, into the Lombardy plains, and thence across the Alps either into the valley of the Rhone or that of the Rhine. Missionary effort had come into Gaul from the East where Christianity was strongest. Just as Irenaeus came from Asia Minor to live at Lyons, so the theology, liturgy, and creeds of Gallican areas show traits received from the East.

Moreover, almost all the phrases which appear in the completed Apostles' Creed are found earlier in creeds of Asia Minor, or of cities along the highway such as Sirmium. Remesiana was also on the highway, and the creed of Bishop Nicetas fits into the picture. The full text of the Apostles' Creed is found in the manuscript from the monastery at Bobbio in northern Italy and in the Gallican *Missale* of northern Gaul. Badcock therefore concludes that the complete text of the Apostles' Creed (*textus receptus*) originated in the territory near Lake Constance in the seventh century.[8]

The imperial highway, to which Badcock calls attention, was not a one-way road, yet the flow of doctrinal influence was from the cultural centers in the East to the northern and western frontiers. Rome was not the dominant force in the West for several centuries, and ideas from the East passed it by on the North. Even Harnack in his investigations recognized that phrases such as "Maker of heaven and earth," "descended into hell," and "catholic" are of Eastern origin.[9] He also had called attention to the close relations between Gaul and the East.

If the situation at Rome is investigated, the evidence indicates a great reluctance to make any changes in the creed. When it was modified, the change was the result of heavy pressure. Perhaps during the earliest years the candidate for baptism was asked only this:

Do you believe in God?

Do you believe in Jesus Christ?

Do you believe in the Holy Ghost?

During the second century the conflict with Gnosticism and Marcionism may have made necessary the addition of certain words, so that by A.D. 225 the questions would be:

Do you believe in God the Father Almighty?

Do you believe in Jesus Christ, His only Son, our Lord, having been born and having suffered?

Do you believe in the Holy Ghost; the holy Church, the forgiveness of sins, the resurrection of the flesh?

---

[8] F. J. Badcock, *The History of the Creeds* (London: S.P.C.K., 1938), p. 157.

[9] *PRE* I, 746. *NSH* I, 242.

This was exactly the interrogatory form found in the Gelasian Sacramentary several centuries later.

By the end of the fourth century the declaratory form of the creed had picked up a substantial increment. Badcock would make Bishop Damascus responsible for it between A.D. 371 and 380. The creed of Rome of that date as derived from (1) a comparison with Western creeds, (2) from identity with the creed of Milan, (3) from the *Explanatio symboli* attributed to Ambrose, and (4) from Augustine's sermons, is here compared with the Old Roman Symbol as presumably given by Rufinus.

ROMAN CREED	OLD ROMAN SYMBOL
Credo in Deum Patrem	*Credo in Deum patrem*
omnipotentem;	*omnipotentem;*
Et in Jesum Christum,	*et in Christum Jesum,*
Filium Ejus unicum, Dominum	*filium ejus unicum, dominum*
nostrum,	*nostrum,*
qui natus est de Spiritu	*qui natus est de Spiritu*
Sancto,	*Sancto*
ex (or *et*) *Maria virgine,*	*et Maria virgine,*
passus sub Pontio Pilato,	*qui sub Pontio Pilato*
crucifixus, et sepultus,	*crucifixus est et sepultus,*
tertia die resurrexit a	*tertia die resurrexit a*
mortuis,	*mortuis,*
ascendit ad (or *in*) *caelos,*	*ascendit in coelos,*
sedet ad dexteram Patris,	*sedet ad dexteram Patris,*
inde venturus est judicare	*unde venturus est judicare*
vivos et mortuos;	*vivos et mortuos;*
Et in Spiritum Sanctum;	*et in Spiritum Sanctum,*
Sanctam ecclesiam;	*sanctam ecclesiam,*
Remissionem peccatorum;	*remissionem peccatorum,*
Carnis resurrectionem.[10]	*carnis resurrectionem.*[11]

The differences are seen to be slight, but are made full use of by Badcock to support his view. When the Apostles' Creed in its full text is found in Rome four centuries later, it has been imported from

---

[10] Badcock, *op. cit.*, p. 118.

[11] A. C. McGiffert, *The Apostles' Creed* (New York: Charles Scribners Sons, 1902), p. 43.

the kingdom of the Franks. Charlemagne, whose influence in Rome was sufficient to effect liturgical changes, may have induced the Roman Church to accept this creed from his territories also.

Which of these two accounts of the history of the Creed may be most acceptable remains to be seen. At any event, the Apostles' Creed is acknowledged to be a Gallican creed of the seventh or eighth century, which had almost reached its final form by the beginning of the sixth century. That it was written by the Apostles, each of whom contributed a sentence, is evidently not true, even though a tradition to that effect occurs in the *Explanatio* ascribed to Ambrose in the fourth or fifth century, and therefore is very ancient. The Apostles' Creed is definitely Western in its final development. It was known for a long time in the West before traces of it appear in the East.

Even though not written by the Apostles, the Creed is none the less apostolic. It professes the doctrines which the Apostles taught. It confesses a trinitarian faith characteristic of the apostolic church. Its phrases are close to or identical with those used by the Apostles whose words are recorded in the New Testament. Perhaps, if the Apostles had written it, the Creed would have included some phrases not now found in it and might have omitted others. Yet in no sense are the phrases of the Apostles' Creed antagonistic to the doctrines of the Apostles.

The uses of the Creed have to some extent determined its form. Its liturgical use was of great, if not primary, importance. It was an expansion of the formula for baptism, and became the confession of faith made by the person to be baptized. For this reason, if for no other, the Creed has a trinitarian pattern. The connection of the Creed with baptism is ancient and well established. It was part of the worship of the church.

This liturgical use of the Creed is sufficient reason for the fact that it retained its character as a statement of personal conviction. The other uses to be noted were not without their influence on the form of the Creed. But however shaped, the Creed continues to have the character of a confession of what "I believe." It gives formal and objective expression to the contents of subjective faith.

A second use may be called catechetical. As an expansion of the formula used in baptism, it became the basis for the instruction of the candidate for baptism. It was the substance of what he was to know and understand. It became the outline for many sermons and expositions, and therefore was a guide for much of the teaching done in the church. In this use the doctrinal aspect of the Creed becomes prominent. The appeal is to thought as well as to assent. There is the assumption that faith may follow as well as precede knowledge.

The polemical use has usually been assumed to have determined the inclusion of some of the phrases of the Creed and even the form in which others were expressed. Those who professed Christian faith were expected also to renounce what was not in accord with it. They were not only to reject the devil and paganism; they were also to oppose heretical and perverted Christian doctrines.

The attack on pagan and heterodox views is obviously only by inference. It is never specific. The Creed is so clearly scriptural that it might be used a long time without any awareness that its words specifically exclude the doctrines once taught by marginal sects. Only as the history of the church reveals the climate in which the Creed arose does the full significance of its phrases appear. The Christian faith, under attack by those who opposed or misunderstood it, vigorously and successfully asserted itself in the convictions of the Creed.

In addition to these three uses (which Köllner suggests)[12] the Creed has had or been proposed for an ecclesiastical use. It not only excludes those without; it also unites those within. The suggestions for its use as a basis for church union must be recognized as being subject to limitations. Nonetheless, the Apostles' Creed expresses the common convictions and the united testimony of Christian believers. It is a bond uniting all those who profess Christian faith in baptism unless by unevangelical interpretations or additions they distort its doctrines. In its function of uniting Christians in fellowship, the Creed therefore is seen in its church use, its service of Christians in their corporate totality. It is not only a personal profession of faith; it is also a church creed.

The contents of the Apostles' Creed deserve a brief review. It is scarcely possible to outline the Creed, for it in itself is really an outline. Its brevity is such as to preclude further condensation. If

---

[12] Eduard Köllner, *Symbolik der lutherischen Kirche* (Hamburg: F. Perthes, 1837), p. 20.

anything, the phrases need expansion to make their full meaning obvious. The following paragraphs, therefore, examine the Creed in comparison with the Old Roman Symbol as reported by Rufinus. Also they will study it as consisting of three articles—the form in which it occurs in the *Book of Concord*.

The first article of the Creed may not have been necessary for Jewish converts to Christianity who needed to add faith in Christ to their Old Testament belief in God. But the conversion of pagan Gentiles and the trinitarian formula for baptism called for an expression concerning God.

It may have been that the ancient church used the word "God" instead of "Father" in the formula of baptism. The passage quoted above from Clement is typical of such usage. McGiffert says, "The collocation 'God, Jesus Christ, and the Holy Spirit' is much commoner in the literature of the late first and early second centuries than 'Father, Son, and Holy Spirit.'" The benediction in II Corinthians 13:14 speaks of "God" rather than "Father."

Whether the word "God" was added to "Father" in the formula of Matthew 28:19, or whether the reverse was true cannot be determined. The word "God" has rich connotations from its use in the Old Testament and in the Christianized use of the Greek equivalent, *Theos*. Some Eastern creeds, desiring to oppose the polytheism surrounding them, spoke of "one" God.

The word "Father" carries with it the Christian thought of God as indicated in the Lord's Prayer. Without it the thought of God can easily have a coloring which is chiefly philosophical, and which is lacking in the warmth of redeeming love. But to Christians God is "our Father" (Rom. 1:7). Among some early Christian writers the term had the significance of "Creator," in the phrase "Father of all" (Eph. 4:6). In some instances the term is seen in its trinitarian setting as the "Father of our Lord Jesus Christ" (Rom. 15:6).

The attribute "almighty" calls to mind the divine majesty continually guiding and sustaining the world. It is an attribute commonly used in the Old Testament. It carries with it the sense of God's eternal governing, as well as his limitless power. Some of the ancient creeds added other attributes. For example, the creed of Aquileia inserted the words "invisible and impassible" in opposition to those

who taught that Christ was simply visible God, instead of truly
human, and that in his death God the Father suffered. These views
were known as Sabellianism and Patripassianism.

The phrase "Maker of heaven and earth" was not in the Old
Roman Symbol, but occurred in some of the rules of faith, and in the
writings of Irenaeus and Tertullian. It was used in opposition to the
Gnostics and Marcion who did not believe that God was creator of
all things. It expresses faith in the work of God as stated in Genesis
1:1. When "Father" is understood in relation to the Son, Jesus Christ,
rather than as the source of all human life, this phrase adds clarity to
the first article.

At the beginning of the second article, the phrase, "and in Jesus
Christ, His only Son, our Lord," expresses the basic conviction of the
apostolic church. The reading "Christ Jesus" in the creed of Aquileia
apparently was of Eastern origin, for Latin creeds consistently have
the other order. The words are names, not titles, and as used together
express the unity of his Person. At the same time he is identified as
Son of the God named in the first article, and accepted as Lord. Some
of the ancient creeds say "only-begotten" instead of "only."

The Old Roman Symbol continues with the words, "Who was
born of the Holy Spirit and the Virgin Mary." The distinction between
the conception and the birth developed later in the Gallican forms.
The ancient creeds were interested in affirming the genuineness of
the incarnation. The Virgin Mary was so named as a historical person,
although the *Explanatio of* Ambrose emphasizes her virginity. The
birth of Jesus Christ was a reality, an occurrence in history. This was
asserted against those who denied that he was ever really born or
had a truly human body.

The same interest carries the Creed on to its statements concerning his sufferings and death. Had there been some other purpose,
the Creed might have included notice of his baptism, works, and
teaching. But the Creed is interested in the further evidence of his
humanity as seen in the fact that he suffered, was crucified, died, and
was laid in a tomb. The Old Roman Symbol noted only the crucifixion
and burial. These were evidences of a genuine humanity. The mention of the name of Pilate further establishes the fact in history.

The descent into hell was not included in the Old Roman Symbol, but was mentioned in the creed of Aquileia and was known elsewhere in the fourth century. Based on I Peter 3:19, Colossians 2:15, and Ephesians 4:9, the doctrine asserts Christ's triumph over the powers of evil. No polemical reason for the phrase has been discovered.

The resurrection of Christ was a central part of Christian faith from the beginning of the church. The New Testament and the early Christian literature all give ample attention to it. It was as certain and definite as the specific "third day" on which it occurred. That they had a living Lord was the conviction of all Christians.

The ascension also was part of the triumph of Christ affirmed in ancient creeds, and therefore to be expected in the Apostles' Creed. The Old Roman Symbol then reads, "and sitteth on the right hand of the Father." But Gallican additions of "God" and "Almighty" made the expression conform to the first article. Christ's return for judgment, together with the preceding phrases, are so prominent a part of apostolic conviction that it is most natural to expect them to be included in the Creed.

The third article concludes the trinitarian confession by expressing faith in the Holy Ghost. The baptismal formula, rather than any heretical opposition, would account for this phrase. The New Testament church was so close to the guiding of the Holy Ghost that an expression of this faith would be expected, and is quite ancient.

Sanctam ecclesiam catholicam is the reading in the Latin version of the Creed. The *catholicam* was not in the Old Roman Symbol, but occurs in another creed of the fourth century and appears thereafter in Gaul. The word first is found in the writings of Ignatius.[13] Later it is used in Eastern creeds and in Christian writings of both East and West, being taken over from the Greek into the Latin. Originally it meant "universal" but in the course of time came to be synonymous with "orthodox." Instead of "Catholic" Luther preferred the word "Christian" as others before him had done, since it covers the same thought, but in a word more commonly understood.

The "holy church" is an expression familiar in early Christian writings. As in the Old Testament the Hebrews were God's chosen peo-

---

[13] *Ad. Smyrn.*, p. 8. *ANF* I, 90.

ple, so in the New Testament Christians are his holy assembly (I Pet. 2:9). It is holy because it is cleansed by Christ (Eph. 5:25-26), it is his body (Eph. 5:30, 32), and it consists of saints (I Cor. 14:33).

The words, "communion of saints," appear in the creeds of Nicetas and Jerome. The reason for their insertion in the Apostles' Creed is not clear. According to Roman Catholic interpretation, the words indicate fellowship with the saints in heaven (Heb. 12:23). The view that the words represent the church of true believers, who are nourished in it by God's grace, was advocated by Luther, though not original with him.

"The forgiveness of sins" is so scriptural a teaching that its place in the ancient creeds seems quite natural. McGiffert suggests that the statement on forgiveness and that on the church are related and that they appear in the Old Roman Symbol because of controversy. A conflict arose in Rome over the question whether or not a Christian guilty of grievous sin might be forgiven and restored to fellowship. The practice which came to prevail acknowledged the right of the church to grant forgiveness. The statements in the Creed accordingly were in contrast to those who rejected both the forgiveness and the church possessing such power.

The ancient creeds affirm faith in "the resurrection of the flesh." The English translation, "body," instead of "flesh," dates from the time of Henry VIII. Resurrection, or resurrection of the dead, was always part of Christian faith. But the use of the word "flesh" indicates an interest in opposing the Gnostics and others who taught that the physical body was inherently evil. Christians believed that God would restore to life what he had once created; therefore it must not be polluted by immorality.

The Old Roman Symbol had no statement on life everlasting, though other creeds of that and later times contained it. Cyprian quoted the question asked at baptism, "Do you believe in the forgiveness of sins and eternal life through the holy Church?" [14] Our Lord had so much to say about eternal life that this final phrase in the Creed seems to be both a necessary part of our faith and a fitting climax to it. The closing thought is of the consummation of all of God's promises and of mankind's hopes.

---

[14] *Ep. to Januarius*, LXIX, 2. *ANF* V, 376.

The Apostles' Creed seen in its entirety has obviously great values. It may be evaluated with reference to its form. Both its brevity and its inclusiveness are important. As Schaff says, "It is by far the best popular summary of the Christian faith ever made within so brief a space." [15]

Or it may be evaluated from the standpoint of its use. In many respects it is superior to all others for catechetical and liturgical purposes. As an outline for instruction, it gives attention to the elemental items of Christian faith. And its brevity fits it admirably for use in baptism and other services of worship.

If valued for its content, it is seen to be both simple and profound. Its language consists of phrases familiar in Scripture and easily understood by the common people. Yet its phrases have a theological substratum that is solid and impressive. Many volumes are required to state fully what the Creed affirms simply.

But the Apostles' Creed also has limitations. It is inadequate for all the phases of systematic theology. There is, for example, no mention of the sacraments. A further limitation is due to its age. It could not be expected to say anything about doctrinal development after it was formulated. Other confessional writings are needed for that purpose. This calls attention to a further limitation, namely, that it is insufficient for purposes of church union. Reunion only on the basis of the Apostles' Creed would repudiate the doctrinal affirmations of the Reformation.

There is no need to overestimate this Creed. It is sufficient if we appreciate the greatness of its simple, elemental structure, and profess it as an expression of our earnest Christian conviction.

THE NICENE CREED

The Creed which is known as Nicene has a history more definite than that of the Apostles' Creed. It also has a more definitely polemical purpose. Its name is in part misleading, as its history will indicate.

The occasion for the Nicene Creed was the rise of Arianism, especially in the East. Arius, a presbyter in Alexandria in Egypt, came into conflict with his bishop about A.D. 318 because of his views con-

[handwritten left margin: *Polemic = Purpose for refutation of errors*]

---

[15] Philip Schaff, *The Creeds of Christendom* (New York: Harper & Brothers, 1899), I, 15.

cerning Christ. His doctrines spread and were popularized in songs.

The conflict became so acute as to make necessary the First Ecumenical Council, which was held in Nicaea in 325. There Arianism was condemned. A creed was adopted which contained expressions completely excluding the Arians. A creed in use in the East was modified to give it this specifically anti-Arian character.

It has usually been said that the creed of Caesarea served as the basis for the new formulation. There is not only the word of Eusebius, the bishop of Caesarea, testifying to this fact, but a comparison of the creeds themselves tends to support it. However, on the basis of more recent investigations,[16] the view has been advanced that some other creed formed the basis of that of Nicaea, and that other cities, such as Alexandria, Jerusalem, and Antioch, must have greatly influenced the result.

The changes in the Creed consisted of omissions, substitutions and additions. They omitted those phrases concerning Christ which were capable of abuse by the Arians and others. When they made substitutions, it was for the purpose of using phrases unequivocally orthodox. Thus, instead of Christ being identified as "the Word of God," he is called the "Son of God, begotten of the Father." The "Word" (*Logos*) was a term that the Arians had twisted to their peculiar interpretation.

The Arian view was that Christ was a creature, even though the highest and best of creation. So, instead of saying "firstborn of all creation," the revised Creed said, "begotten of the Father before all worlds." More than this, the orthodox party was interested in affirming the essential deity of Christ. Hence it inserted the words, "of one substance with the Father, God of God," etc. In addition, it anathematized all who denied both Christ's eternity and his essential divine nature.

During the many years of conflict that followed the Council of Nicaea until the orthodox doctrine was completely victorious, the Creed of Nicaea exerted influence in several ways. In some instances its distinctive expressions were incorporated in local creeds. In other instances it was used in a modified form—the result of omitting such parts as the anathema, or of inserting phrases popular in some areas.

---

[16] Badcock, *op. cit.*, pp. 180 ff.

There were also places where the Creed of Nicaea was used without change.

At the Second Ecumenical Council, held at Constantinople in 381, the Creed of Nicaea was ratified. But it seems that a modified form of it, or one including Nicene phrases, appeared there also. The traditional view was that at Constantinople the Council revised the Creed of Nicaea, and made official the form thus revised. Harnack declared that the weight of historical evidence is against this tradition.[17] It cannot even be proven that the revised Creed appeared at Constantinople, much less that it was adopted. How it came to the attention of the church is not known. Because of the tradition, this form is known as the Niceno-Constantinopolitan Creed. It omitted the anathema and had a longer third article than the Creed of Nicaea.

At the Fourth Ecumenical Council, meeting at Chalcedon in 451, the form of the Creed which was ascribed to Constantinople received official approval, gradually supplanting the other. A half-century later it was in general theological use, and soon was in liturgical use as well.

According to the researches of Harnack,[18] Bishop Cyril of Jerusalem amended the creed of his city by inserting the characteristic anti-Arian phrases of Nicaea. His modified creed corresponds to the Constantinopolitan form. Whether he or someone else brought it to the attention of the council at Constantinople is not known. Neither is it clear why it was acted on at Chalcedon.

Even more significant is a creed written in 374 by Epiphanius, a converted Jew and a bishop on the Island of Cyprus. His creed is virtually identical with the one which seems to have appeared at Constantinople, except that it included the Nicene anathema.

Against the foregoing theory of Harnack, it is urged by Badcock[19] that the manuscript of Epiphanius gives evidence of interpolations by a later hand, and that therefore its importance is reduced. Moreover, there is an accumulation of allusions from the fifth century pointing to the fact that the Council of Constantinople did actually revise the Creed of Nicaea. There are allusions also in the writings of Nestorius and in the records of the Council of Chalcedon.

---

[17] *"Konstantinopolitanisches Symbol,"* PRE XI, 16. "Constantinopolitan Creed," *NSH* III, 258.

[18] *Op. cit.,* PRE XI, 22. *NSH* III, 299.

[19] *Op. cit.,* pp. 186 ff.

Moreover, there is no apparent reason why Cyril's Creed of Jerusalem should have received approval. But there are several reasons why the Creed of Nicaea should have been reaffirmed, and additions made which would be acceptable to Constantinople, the host city. And if the Niceno-Constantinopolitan Creed exercised little authority before 451, the reasons, as recognized by Harnack,[20] lie in the rivalries between the great cities, including Rome. For it was a long time before the authority of the Council of Constantinople was generally acknowledged. There are valid grounds, therefore, for retaining the traditional view that the Creed of Nicaea was revised at Constantinople into its longer form.

The Niceno-Constantinopolitan form, with slight changes, is the Nicene Creed of our day. The Western church came to use the singular personal pronoun instead of the plural, saying "I believe," rather than "We believe." In the Latin another change was made by restoring the words, "God of God," which had been dropped from the Constantinopolitan form.

The change which produced controversy had to do with the *filioque.* Augustine[21] had contended that the Son, being equal with the Father, shares in his acts. Hence it is correct to say of the Holy Spirit that he proceeds from the Father *and the Son.* In the East, John of Damascus[22] opposed this teaching, saying that God is the only Source; the Holy Spirit proceeds from Father through Son.

Augustine's doctrine prevailed in the West, gaining such general acceptance that the *filioque* was inserted in the Creed by the action of the Council of Toledo in 589. Thereafter it won its way into general Western use, but not without struggle. The church in the East, however, continued to reject it, so that it became one of the disagreements leading to the break between the two parts of the church in 1054.

Though the Creed in the strictest historical sense is not the original Creed of Nicaea, nevertheless it is entitled to the name "Nicene" in view of the fact that it truly represents Nicene doctrine. It is the faith of the apostolic church formulated so as to guard the truth of its

---

[20] *Op. cit., PRE* XI, 24. *NSH* III, 259.
[21] *De trin.* IV, 20, 29. *NPNF* III, 84.
[22] *De fide orth.* I, 12. *NPNF* IX, 15.

teachings against Arianism. It is an ancient local creed amplified with theological phrases so as to give a more exact statement of Christian teaching. In registering its conviction that Arianism is a distortion of Christian thought, it professes its firm faith in the full deity of Jesus Christ.

Its uses are quite similar to those of the Apostles' Creed. Its liturgical use is important. Both in the East and in the West it has long been the major creed used in connection with the Lord's Supper, and so continues in Episcopal and Lutheran services.

The Roman Catholic and Protestant churches have made little use of it for catechetical instruction. But it has been the basis of instruction to a considerable extent in Eastern Orthodox areas. It is incorporated in The Orthodox Confession, in the Longer Catechism of Philaret, and in other catechisms. Related to its use as an outline for the instruction of the young is its use as a doctrinal guide for preaching and teaching. In this function it has been accepted in all these groups.

The polemical use has been noted in connection with the account of its origin. It had official status in its various forms as adopted by the councils, and was used against its opponents. And because the church had the support of the emperor, those who were adjudged heretics by its standard suffered the weight of civil penalties.

Like the Apostles' Creed, the Nicene has ecclesiastical use in that it presents a universal Christian consensus. It has official standing in the Eastern Orthodox churches such as the former does not have. In this sense it is the most ecumenical of all the creeds, and therefore is superior to the Apostles' Creed as a basis for reuniting Christendom.

The contents of the Nicene Creed need attention only in so far as they differ from those of the Apostles' Creed. In both instances the pattern is trinitarian. Both are developments of primitive rules of faith based upon the baptismal formula. The Apostles' Creed, in so far as it is traced through the Old Roman Symbol to the second or third century, formed its phrases in contrast to Judaism, paganism, Gnosticism, and certain distortions of Christian teaching. The Nicene Creed, with its roots in the fourth and fifth centuries, shows anti-Arian as well as anti-Apollinarian and anti-Macedonian features.[23]

---

[23] Apollinaris taught that in the humanity of Christ the Logos replaced the spirit. Macedonians denied the full deity of the Holy Ghost.

The first article corresponds largely with that of the Apostles' Creed and affirms the same point of view. It expresses faith in "one" God, stressing monotheism, as certain Eastern creeds were accustomed to do. It expands somewhat the idea of creation in the words, "and of all things visible and invisible." This phrase was in the Creed of Cyril; but the Creed of Eusebius and that of Nicaea, which also contain it, do not include the words, "heaven and earth." The phrase is intended to indicate that everything came into being by the creative power of God, "for by him were all things created, that are in heaven, and that are in earth, visible and invisible," etc. (Col. 1:16.) Philaret in his Catechism says that the word "invisible" means "the invisible or spiritual world, to which belong the angels."

Without any doubt this first article expresses faith in the creative activity of God who is transcendent above all. Somewhat less prominent, but no less real, is the conviction expressed in the words "Father Almighty," that he is immanent, guiding and directing the affairs of his creation. For the Greek equivalent of "Almighty" (*pantokratora*) has the significance, not so much of possessing all power, as of exercising all power and rule.

The second article is about twice the size of that in the Apostles' Creed. Here occurs the wording declaring the pre-existence and essential deity of Christ. Here are the anti-Arian phrases.

As all Christians accept Jesus Christ as Lord, so does the Nicene Creed, and it indicates his uniqueness by the word "one." He is the only Saviour. Then follows the statement of his divine Sonship. The Creed of Eusebius spoke of him as "the Word of God." But that phrase had been acceptable to Arian thinking, and for it was substituted at Nicaea the phrase "the Son of God." With it was included the word "only-begotten" and thus it appears in our Creed.

This also is a testimony to Christ's uniqueness. The Arians also were willing to accept his uniqueness, but the Creed pushes on to identify his nature as truly divine, rather than as a part of creation. Therefore the phrase of Eusebius, "the firstborn of every creature," even though it originates in Colossians 1:15, could not be retained because the Arians had spoiled it with their interpretation. But it was quite acceptable to retain his phrase, "begotten of the Father before all worlds (aeons, ages)." And at Nicaea were added the

35

words, "begotten, not made," thereby definitely excluding the Arian opinion.

Not only the source, but also the nature of his being was involved. The creed of Eusebius spoke of him as "God of God, Light of Light, Life of Life." At Nicaea they omitted the last phrase, but placed in front of the other two phrases the words, "of the essence (*ousia*) of the Father," and inserted after them "very (true) God of very God" and "of one substance with the Father." Here is the *homoousia* famous in church history.

The phrases thus heaped up are designed to assert incontrovertibly the true and absolute deity of Christ. The interest in the Apostles' Creed was to defend his true humanity, and subsequent phrases in the Nicene Creed make the same defense. But it is the declaration of faith in the divine nature of Christ which is distinctive of the Nicene Creed. It not only calls him "true God" and speaks of him as "Light" thereby indicating his holiness, but it also ascribes to him, as Eusebius had done, participation in the divine work of creation—"by whom all things were made" (the Creed of Nicaea adding "both in heaven and on earth").

Moreover, Christ has another, a distinctive divine work. He is our Redeemer. This faith was the chief interest of those opposing Arius. Whatever might be their theological or speculative interests, they were impelled to combat Arianism because its doctrine of Christ jeopardized our salvation. Their experience in Christian faith gave them no alternative.

Eusebius indicated that "salvation" was Christ's objective, but his statement of the incarnation and suffering of Christ was brief. The form adopted at Nicaea is somewhat fuller, while the complete form of the creed adds further particulars. The creed declares (as the form at Nicaea did not) that he came "from heaven," that he was incarnate "by the Holy Ghost of the Virgin Mary," that he "was crucified for us under Pontius Pilate," that he "was buried," that he rose "according to the Scriptures," that he "sitteth on the right hand of the Father," that he will come "again with glory," and that his "kingdom shall have no end."

These are numerous additions. It is difficult to account for the inclusion of all of them. There is evidence that the phrase "of the

Holy Ghost and the Virgin Mary" was inserted to combat Apollinari-anism. For the rest the most likely explanation seems to be that they were parts of other creeds, e.g., of Antioch or Jerusalem. They had developed in this form to combat those who denied either Christ's true humanity or his redeeming work, or both, and because the church found them useful in dealing with fourth-century problems. The dominant redemptive interest is indicated by the words "for us men, and for our salvation" and "crucified for us."

It will be observed that this Creed has no statement on the "*descensus.*" The phrases on the resurrection and the sitting at the Right Hand are simpler than in the Apostles' Creed. On the other hand, the eschatological phrases are expanded beyond those of the Apostles' Creed. Christ's coming "with glory" represents the enthusi-astic faith of the church in the second advent. And the sense of triumph continues in the words "Whose kingdom shall have no end." This phrase expresses conviction in the final victory of the faith.

The third article is much fuller than that in the Apostles' Creed. The creeds of Eusebius and Nicaea merely said "and in the Holy Ghost." Later heresies made necessary the full article found in the Constantinopolitan form.

The article completes the trinitarian profession of the Creed by expressing faith in the Holy Ghost. It also includes the Third Person of the Trinity in the divine creative work by calling him "the Lord and Giver of life." Moreover the effect is to identify him as a *Person* of the Trinity, rather than as merely a sort of impersonal divine energy.

The relation of the Holy Ghost to the other Persons of the Trinity is indicated by the concept "procession"—"who proceedeth from the Father and the Son." Here is the *filioque* which the Eastern Church omits. Tertullian in his writing "Against Praxeas" speaks of the "Spirit from God and the Son." [24] It was Augustine who fully developed the doctrine of the equality of the Persons in the Trinity. Though the *filioque* was approved at Toledo, Spain, in 589, it was long in winning wide use. Under Charlemagne its inclusion in the Creed became more prevalent. The doctrine of "double procession"—from the Father

---

[24] *Adv. Prax.*, 8. *ANF* III, 603. *MSL* II, 179.

and the Son—is regarded as an insolent Latin heresy by the Eastern Orthodox churches.

The Holy Ghost shares in divine honors. He is "with the Father and the Son together worshiped and glorified." Here is ascribed to him the veneration and exalted esteem reserved for Deity alone.

The Creed thus has indicated those respects in which the Holy Ghost shares with the Father and the Son the divine work of creation, the divine nature, and the divine worship. On the other hand, it also indicates the respects in which he is distinct, i.e., in name, in a particular phase of creation, and in "procession" rather than being begotten. One more item is added to his uniqueness, viz., that he is the agent of inspiration—"Who spake by the prophets." This doctrine is expressed in II Peter 1:21, "For the prophecy came not in old time by the will of man: but holy men of God spake as they were moved by the Holy Ghost."

The fullness of the Creed's statement concerning the Holy Ghost indicates both a religious faith and a theological development. At the Council of Constantinople were condemned the Macedonians who rejected the deity of the Holy Ghost. Harnack expressed the judgment that if this Creed was actually formulated at Constantinople, it would have expressed more explicitly the *homoousia* of the Holy Ghost, and would have added phrases similar to "very God of very God." Since this article of the Creed appears lacking in polemical fire, he concludes that it could not have been the product of that council.[25]

To this it is answered that the words of the third article are quite sufficient to establish the deity of the Holy Ghost. It is distinctly significant that the Creed calls him "Lord" and ascribes to him divine works and honors. The words of the article are a precise answer to the details of the Macedonian doctrine. The gentle and devout tone of the article recalls the statement of Rauschenbusch: "The doctrine of the Holy Spirit is one of the most religious of all Christian doctrines. It is not primarily a product of reflection, but of great religious emotions and experiences."[26]

---

[25] *Op. cit.*, PRE XI, 21. *NSH* III, 258.

[26] *A Theology for the Social Gospel* (New York: Macmillan, 1917), p. 188.

The phrase concerning the church calls attention to four characteristics—two more than are noted in the Apostles' Creed. That there is "one" church is an expression of its unity. Of what that unity consists there is no indication except what may be inferred from the other characteristics, i.e., it is united in holiness, universality, and apostolic faith. The marks, "holy" and "catholic" have had attention in connection with the Apostles' Creed.

The fourth mark, "apostolic," looks backward in history and sees the continuity through the years of the faith taught by Christ to his disciples. Perhaps apostolic doctrine was uppermost in the minds of those engaged in doctrinal battles; but apostolic sacraments and practices were involved also. The church is apostolic in the sense that it has what the church of the first century had. If it is apostolic, the church of any century is the church of all centuries since Christ.

In the Creed the believer acknowledges "one baptism for the remission of sins." The word "one" emphasizes kind, not number. It is not a question of baptism once, in contrast to repeated baptisms, although Christian doctrine declares that a person needs to be baptized but once. Instead, the word stresses the fact that only Christian baptism is availing for the remission of sins; all other baptisms are valueless.

At the end of time will come the "resurrection of the dead" which the Christian confidently expects. The question of the allegedly evil character of the "flesh" was no longer prominent; hence the Creed returns to the phraseology of Scripture. Associated with the resurrection is the "life of the world to come" or of "the future age." Since that future life is to be endless, the words of this Creed are likely equivalent to the "everlasting life" of the Apostles' Creed. There is no further attempt to describe the future; that life is an item of faith, as firm and real as it is indescribable.

After inspecting the Nicene Creed in detail, it is important to see it once more in its totality. The careful workmanship in the parts contributes to an appreciation of the eminence of the whole structure. Estimated from the standpoint of its form it is seen to be nearly the maximum in size for liturgical or catechetical use. There is conciseness in some items, but otherwise there is a solid fullness in treatment. More could scarcely be expected in a usable creed.

As to its use, attention has already been called to the fact that in terms of official acceptance it is the most ecumenical of the creeds. It is the creed of the mass in both the Eastern Orthodox and the Roman Catholic churches, and is the communion creed of the Anglican and Lutheran churches. In this respect it is the major church creed, presenting the faith of the church in both full and well-rounded form.

As for its content, it is valued as expressing precise trinitarian faith. It is a valuable guardian of orthodox faith concerning the divine nature of Christ and the divine personality of the Holy Ghost. It is justly high in the esteem of Christians because it has clarified theological thinking by presenting words and phrases specifically applicable to certain Christian concepts. The product of rich theological thought and of religious speculation, not all of which was orthodox, it nevertheless is a popular statement of certain, profound Christian insights.

It also has its limitations. Being less simple than the Apostles' Creed, it is therefore more difficult for some minds. There are many persons to whom only the plainest, most childlike statement of the faith can be useful. Furthermore, even to cultivated minds the Creed appears to be unnecessarily metaphysical and theological. The discussion of "essence" appears to hark back to a Greek type of thought no longer current. A practical age prefers to think of God in terms of his acts, rather than of his inner nature. Finally, there is for the Nicene, as for the Apostles' Creed, the limitation of age. There are issues which became vital during the Reformation, but which are not given attention in this Creed. It therefore needs to be supplemented by evangelical declarations.

Nevertheless the Nicene Creed retains its force. It is the victorious monument of a great doctrinal struggle in the past. It still carries with it the echoes of battle as it serves the present age in a declaration of full-blooded Christian faith.

THE ATHANASIAN CREED

The names of the two previous creeds have been shown to be not precisely accurate. To call this the "Athanasian" Creed is clearly a mistake. It is better to use the other name applied to it—*Symbolum*

Quicunque. It is so called because the Latin text begins with the words, *Quicunque vult salvus esse*, etc.—"whosoever will be saved," etc. "Athanasian" is the traditional name given because Athanasius of Alexandria was thought to have been the author.

In the thinking of the ancient church a creed was a profession of faith which ordinarily was connected with baptism. The *Symbolum Quicunque* first appears as a theological composition or canticle sung daily at Prime—the first of the canonical hours—during the reign of Charlemagne. None of the earliest records refers to it as a creed. But in the popular mind a doctrinal composition thus used liturgically was thought to be creedal, and by the thirteenth century it was so named. Alexander of Hales about the year 1230 said that in England "there are three symbols, one of the Apostles; one of the Fathers which is sung in the Mass; and the third, the Athanasian, which is sung at Prime." [27] In the strict sense, therefore, this Creed is not only not Athanasian, but it is not even a creed.

The first to demonstrate that it is not Athanasian was Gerhard Voss in 1642.[28] The reasons are decisive. Roman Catholic scholars along with others accept the verdict. The first argument is that of the silence concerning the Creed in the age of Athanasius. There is no reference to it in the writings either of Athanasius, or of his contemporaries, or of his biographers. Nor is there mention of it in the councils of Constantinople, Ephesus, or Chalcedon, which were closest to his time. In fact, the latter two councils forbade anyone to compose any creed other than the Nicene.

There is also the argument from its contents. It is not a Greek creed, as it would have been if written by Athanasius, but it is a Latin one. It does not contain his favorite term, *homoousia*, but it does contain the *filioque* and the doctrinal development of Augustine. Moreover, all the evidence points to the fact that it had its origin in Latin areas, for the oldest Greek copies are obviously translations. As Schaff reports, there was a legend that Athanasius had composed the Creed while he was an exile in Rome, and that the *filioque* is in the Creed either as a Latin interpolation, or because Athanasius was drunk at

---

[27] Quoted by Loofs in "Athanasian Creed," *NSH* I, 338.
[28] *Dissertationes tres de tribus symbolis, apostolica Athanasiana et Constantinopolitana*, Amsterdam, 1642.

the time he wrote it.[29] But to return from fiction to fact, the name of Athanasius is not uniformly connected with the Creed in the oldest manuscripts extant. Indeed, sometimes other men are named as the author.

Since Athanasius was not the author, the manuscripts must be examined in an effort to determine the composer. The almost complete text of the Creed appears as a canticle about the year 870 in a prayer book of Charles the Bald. There is a dispute concerning the age of another manuscript, Loofs dating it about 800, and Lietzmann putting it at 700 or earlier. About 670 a council at Autun decreed, "If any priest, deacon, subdeacon, or cleric does not receive the creed which has been handed down from the Apostles as inspired by the Holy Spirit and the creed of Bishop Athanasius without criticism, he is to be condemned by his bishop." [30] This is also likely the Creed referred to in the records of a synod at Toledo in 633.

This would push the origin of the Creed near to the end of the sixth century or earlier. Phrases parallel to those in the Creed are found in writings of the fifth century. And some authorities would trace the Creed back to Ambrose in the fourth century. Badcock presents a considerable list of quotations similar to phrases of the Creed from Caesarius of Arles, Vincent of Lerins, Augustine, and Ambrose.[31] But similarity of phrases is not conclusive evidence; it may mean instead that these phrases came into current use and were utilized in the formulation of the Creed. It does not necessarily mean that they are quotations from the Creed.

No definite conclusion can be drawn, therefore, concerning the age of the Creed. It is evidently as old as the seventh century, but how much older than that cannot be determined. In view of the fact that phrases parallel to those of the Creed are found in numerous instances in southern Gaul, that area may well have been the place of its origin. Yet it is possible that Milan may have been its birthplace.

Nor is there any agreement as to the identity of the author. Many names have been suggested, but none with general satisfaction.

---

[29] *Op. cit.*, I, 35, n. 2.

[30] Mansi, XI, 125. Quoted by Loofs, *NSH* I, 341.

[31] *Op. cit.*, pp. 227 ff.

Harnack and others have suggested that it had more than one author.[32] The chief evidence is the fact that a manuscript in Paris contains only the second part of the Creed. Hence it was inferred that the first part originated in one place as an elaboration of the Apostles' Creed, and that the second part was written elsewhere to express Christological doctrine, and that sometime later someone combined the two. But the Paris manuscript shows signs of being a copy of a fragment, and therefore its evidence is not conclusive. The Creed could very well be the work of a single author; and Ambrose may have been the man, as Seeberg argued.

The most apparent use of the Creed has been liturgical. Besides its use at Prime in Roman Catholic practice, it is used in other offices during Advent and Lent. In the Church of England the Book of Common Prayer directs that it shall "be sung or said at Morning Prayer instead of the Apostles' Creed" on thirteen Feasts. The Eastern Orthodox churches commend it (without the *filioque*) for devotional use as an appendix to the Hour Offices. Other churches make no liturgical use of it.

But some do use it as a doctrinal guide, as is the case in the *Book of Concord*. Among the Reformed it is accepted specifically by the Second Helvetic, Belgic, and Gallican confessions, and by the Thirty-Nine Articles of the Church of England. Other than this it has had little official recognition.

The Creed quite evidently consists of two parts. The first is concerned with the Trinity, the second with Christology. Each part opens and concludes with the statement that this faith is necessary to salvation. The second part is about half the length of the first.

The first part sees both the trinity and the unity of God, and insists on holding them together. The unity does not obliterate the distinction of the Persons, nor does the identity of the Persons sever the unity of essence (or substance). Each Person is identified by name.

The word "Person" is to be understood in its historical theological sense, as the Augsburg Confession observes. "Person" or *hypostasis* is used to designate a focus of personality within Deity in whom there are three such foci. The word does not mean an entirely discrete or

---

[32] Cf. Loofs, *op. cit.*, PRE II, 185. NSH I, 340.

separate individual as when used to indicate a human being. Instead, it represents a real distinction in the Trinity, though the exact nature of the distinction is not understood. The Creed is thus presenting a developed and mature doctrine of the Trinity, the result of centuries of thought. In this it is superior to the Apostles' and Nicene creeds.

Beginning with the sixth verse the Creed declares the equality of the Persons in every respect. Every form of subordinationism is rejected. There is equality in essence (Godhead), in glory, in eternity, in being uncreated, in being immeasurable, eternal, and almighty. Thus each of the Persons is truly God.

These attributes are familiar and acceptable to the thinking of those accustomed to the Old Testament concept of God. But Arians, and anti-trinitarians generally, refused to apply them to the Son and the Spirit. But if all three Persons are truly God, all these attributes must belong to each of them equally. Or, put the other way, if these attributes belong to each of the Persons, each one must be God. The attribute translated by the English word "incomprehensible" since 1548 has the significance of being without bounds or limits, transcending every measure, infinite.

If "almighty" is understood in this Creed as in the others as "all-governing" and referring to Providence, the indication may be to a work, rather than to an attribute, of God. In that case, the Creed, beginning with verse thirteen, views the Trinity from the standpoint of work: Almighty, God, and Lord, i.e., Provider, Creator, and Ruler. Yet each Person of the Trinity participates in each of these works; for the works are performed by the Unity.

There is a further distinction of the Persons noted, beginning with verse twenty (according to the numbering in the *Book of Concord*). The Father is "unbegotten," the Son is "begotten" and the Holy Ghost "proceeds" from the Father and the Son (*filioque* doctrine). The Creed carefully repudiates any distinction which suggests inequality—in age (before or after) or authority (greater or less). All three Persons are equal, and together constitute a Unity.

The second part of the Creed, in discussing doctrines of Christology, affirms the fact of Christ's two natures. Each of these natures is complete and perfect. They are united, however, in one Person, yet without loss of identity or without being fused into a third nature.

In these particulars the Creed repeats the doctrinal positions affirmed at the Council of Chalcedon. It thereby rejects Apollinarianism which considered his human nature incomplete, Nestorianism which taught that the union of the two natures was not intimate, and Eutychianism which believed that the union of the natures meant the loss of the identity of the human nature.

Beginning with verse thirty-six, the Creed repeats the thoughts and even the words of the other creeds concerning the suffering and subsequent events of Christ's life. It includes the *descensus.* It makes a further statement concerning the effort of the general judgment, indicating that the bliss and the punishment will be everlasting, as taught in Matthew 25:46.

It will be observed that whereas the Nicene Creed is interested in Christ's pre-existence as an aspect of his true deity, this Creed in its second part looks more at the incarnate Christ both on earth and in glory. Moreover, its interest is redemptive; what Christ did, he did for "our salvation." The Creed's phrases are not for purposes of idle speculation but for an expression of faith.

It is in this sense that the orthodox sentences standing at the beginning and end of each part are to be understood. To say that this is the faith necessary for salvation does not mean that every layman must be a theologian, or that every simple-hearted Christian must know all the theological implications of devout trust in Christ. But it does mean that theological opinions opposed to these doctrines do stand in the way of true faith in Christ, and therefore of salvation. Those who deny that Jesus Christ is the Son of God and the Saviour of the world cannot have saving faith in him. The Creed presents in logical fashion the biblical truths, guarded against errors which had arisen. The doctrines contained therein are the ripe fruits of Christian thought and experience under the grace of God.

✻ line #40

Chapter III

THE ORIGIN OF THE AUGSBURG CONFESSION

Emperor Charles V was young and vigorous. He was having continued success in meeting the problems besetting his reign. Though the military forces allied to the pope had suffered defeat, and imperial troops from Spain and Germany had looted Rome, Charles had been reconciled to the pontiff and been crowned at his hands. The king of France also had been defeated, and a treaty had been made with him.

Victorious and powerful, Charles was prepared to deal with the troubles in Germany. Therefore on January 21, 1530, a diet (*Reichstag*) was called to convene on the eighth of April in the city of Augsburg, not far from Alpine country. The summons was phrased in what appeared to be remarkably conciliatory terms. After mentioning the threat of Turkish invasion, it declared that the purpose of the diet was "to allay divisions, to cease hostility, to surrender past errors to our Saviour, and to display diligence in hearing, understanding, and considering with love and kindness the opinions and views of everybody ... so that we all may adopt and hold one single and true religion; and may all live in one communion, church, and unity, even as we all live and do battle under one Christ." [1]

In Saxony, where the summons arrived on March 11, the prospect of a diet held both hopes and dangers. Perhaps for the sake of justice and peace in the empire some concessions would be made by the emperor to the rising demand for reforms. Perhaps, remembering the loyalty of the Saxon elector to him, Charles would allow some tolera-

---

[1] *Concordia Triglotta* (St. Louis: Concordia Publishing House, 1921), Hist. Intro., p. 15.

tion of the modified church practices prevalent in Lutheran areas. And yet, the victories and the Catholic faith of the emperor must not be forgotten. In Saxony they had not yet learned that Charles had promised the pope to wipe out heresy.

It was the part of wisdom that the Saxons have ready for the Augsburg Diet a skillfully prepared statement of their position and their requests. Precisely what were the reforms they desired? In order that such a document might be ready, Elector John instructed Luther, Melanchthon, Jonas, and Bugenhagen to write a statement.

The members of this committee undertook their task with the understanding that they were to explain to the emperor the nature of their doctrine and the changes made in the practice of their congregations. They felt that it would be wise to defend the changes on the basis of Scripture and the church fathers. Modifications of church practice which could thus be justified ought to be permitted in the church and the empire.

Within a few days the manuscript had reached such a state that it could be submitted for the elector's inspection. They met him at Torgau and there gave him their document, which therefore is called the "Torgau Articles." The original manuscript for a long time had been lost. But in 1830 there was discovered at Weimar a document which generally is acknowledged to be the Torgau Articles.[2]

If the Torgau Articles had a sermonic text, it would be Acts 5:29, "We ought to obey God rather than men." For its theme was that the abuses in the church were introduced by human authority, whereas the reforms put into effect by the Lutherans were on the basis of God's Word. The Torgau Articles deal chiefly with the correction of abuses, such as the celibacy of priests, one kind only in the Lord's Supper, the mass, confession, and so forth. They are the topics discussed in the articles on abuses in the Augsburg Confession (XXII-XXVIII). There were other matters also, such as singing in German instead of Latin in public worship, and many practices offensive to gospel doctrine.

The Saxons arrived in Augsburg on May 2, more than a month ahead of the tardy emperor. Luther had come with them only as far as Coburg, where he had to remain safe in Saxon territory because he

---

[2] An English translation is given in Volume II of Jacobs, *Book of Concord*, pp. 105 ff.

was still technically an outlaw under the ban of the empire. Even if he had been safe in Augsburg, it would have been unwise to irritate the emperor by his presence there. The elector and his party found in Augsburg a considerable interest in their cause among the people. But they found also something else that was profoundly disturbing.

There was being circulated in Augsburg a pamphlet written by Dr. John Eck, the Romanist theologian. He had gathered a large number of quotations from Luther, Zwingli, Melanchthon, and others, and these with statements of his own formed his "Four Hundred Four Theses." Some of them were extreme statements of Luther, made to sound worse by being taken out of their context. For example, "The Mass has been changed into a sacrifice of Satan" (274). "The celebrants of the Mass are idolators" (276). "The kingdom of the pope is nothing but tyranny, the realm of Antichrist" (353).

Most of the statements were not so inflammatory. But the purpose in every case was to show that the Lutherans were wild radicals whose views were identical with those of recognized heretics. Eck saw to it that a copy of his theses reached the emperor on his way to Augsburg.

Here was a situation too dangerous to ignore. The Lutherans, consulting together, agreed that their document must defend them against such unjust accusations. The prejudices raised against them by Eck would make impossible any fair consideration of their petitions. A further defense must be written.

That such was the situation is attested by Melanchthon: "Some papal scribblers had disseminated pasquinades at the diet which reviled our churches with horrible lies, charging that they taught many condemned errors, and were like the Anabaptists, erring and rebellious. Answer had to be made to his imperial majesty, and in order to refute the pasquinades, it was decided to include all articles of Christian doctrine in proper succession, that every one might see how unjustly our churches were slandered in the lying papal writings." [3]

Melanchthon in the midst of the work of editing the Torgau document turned to the task of reorganizing it. He must do more than justify before the emperor the Lutheran correction of church abuses. He must also defend the orthodoxy of the Lutheran faith. The emperor must be convinced that the Lutherans in their doctrines had not departed from

---

[3] *C.R.* IX, 929. Trans. in *Conc. Trig.*, Hist. Intro., p. 16.

those of the ancient church. Reasons must be given why their teachings are to be tolerated in the church and the empire. The label of heresy must be removed.

Besides the Torgau Articles which contained some doctrinal inferences, Melanchthon could use two other statements of Lutheran doctrine prepared the year before: the Schwabach Articles and the Marburg Articles.

The first of these had been written for the elector by Luther, Melanchthon, and others, in the summer of 1529. Attempts were being made then to form a united front of evangelical states, and Elector John desired a doctrinal statement upon which they could agree. Luther's articles, in which the others had shared, were presented at a conference at Schwabach, but failed to win the approval of the southern Germans. There were seventeen of these articles. They set forth Luther's distinctive views, particularly on the Lord's Supper.

The Marburg Articles had been written by Luther at the end of the famous colloquy between him and Zwingli with their associates at Marburg. That colloquy also had been a failure so far as unity between Lutherans and Zwinglians was concerned. But the fifteen articles expressed evangelical conviction on the chief points of doctrine. They had passed through the crucible of theological criticism, and had found phrases for expressing both the consensus and the disagreement between Lutherans and Zwinglians. Both sets of articles in their finished form were valuable formulations for Melanchthon's purpose, though he made greater use of the Schwabach Articles.

Back of these documents was Luther's writing, *Concerning Christ's Supper,* of 1528, at the end of which is his creedal statement of faith.[4] In it he had given an outline of doctrine, and indicated the contrast with the Roman Catholic teachings. In the Schwabach Articles he used the same material, but somewhat rearranged it and deleted most of the anti-Roman parts. Back of these documents also were the doctrinal sections of the *Articles* and the *Instruction* for the visitations made in some Lutheran areas in 1528.

By the eleventh of May, Melanchthon had proceeded far enough that he could send a draft of his manuscript to Luther at Coburg. In his letter to Luther he wrote, "Our *Apologia* has been sent to you,

---

[4] *W.A.,* XXVI, 499 ff.

though it is more properly a confession. For the emperor will not have time to hear long discussions. Nevertheless I have said those things which I thought would be especially profitable and appropriate. With this purpose I have included about all the Articles of Faith, because Eck has published the most diabolical slanders against us. Against these I wished to present a remedy. Determine in regard to the whole writing in accordance with your spirit." [5]

Luther approved what had been written. He wrote, "I have read over Master Philip's *Apologia*. It pleases me very well, and I know of nothing therein to improve or change; nor would it be proper, for I cannot tread so gently and softly. Christ, our Lord, grant that it may bear much and great fruit as we hope and pray." [6] Apparently Luther did not see any later forms of the articles before they were read at the diet. There is no basis, however, for thinking that he rejected the Confession in the form presented to the Emperor. In fact, after he had read the Confession in its final form, he wrote in a letter of July 3 that "it pleases me very much."

Melanchthon continued to work on the manuscript almost up to the day of its presentation. At the end of May the representatives from Nürnberg sent to their authorities a copy of the articles as they had developed by that date. The copy was found in 1905 in the Nürnberg archives and is the oldest form of the articles in existence. Another copy, this time of the articles in the middle of June, also found in Nürnberg, shows that by that time the Confession was virtually in its final form. Melanchthon worked on the Latin and German versions together. Sometimes he wrote a part in the Latin text and translated it into German, sometimes the reverse.

The articles thus being prepared were the special declaration of the Saxons. But at Augsburg while waiting for Charles to arrive it became evident that it would be highly desirable for all the Lutherans to present a common statement. Melanchthon's document was examined by the representatives from other states to see if they could accept it. It was for this reason that the Nürnberg representatives had sent a copy to their authorities.

---

[5] *C.R.* II, 45. Trans. in J. W. Richards, *The Confessional History of the Lutheran Church* (Philadelphia: Lutheran Publication Society, 1909), p. 54.

[6] *W.A., Briefe*, V, 319. Trans. in Schmauk, *op. cit.*, pp. 358 f.

When it became evident that the Lutherans could unite behind this document, a change had to be made in the preface. That which Melanchthon had written, and which was lost until the Nürnberg manuscript was found, had been a fulsome statement concerning the loyalty and uprightness of Elector John. Its purpose had been to reassure Charles concerning the elector's integrity and motives, and to assert that no heresy was tolerated in Saxony. But when the articles were to become the Confession of all Lutherans, Melanchthon's preface was discarded, and a new one was written by the Saxon chancellor, Dr. Brück. It is the preface of the Augsburg Confession.

Charles reached Augsburg on the fifteenth of June, and soon after the opening of the diet he was prepared to receive the Lutheran document. He wanted it handed to him without a public reading, but the Lutherans insisted upon having it read. Somewhat unwillingly Charles consented. But in order to exclude the populace, the place of meeting was to be the smaller episcopal palace rather than in the large council room where the diet usually met. There on the twenty-fifth of June the Confession was read in German by Dr. Christian Beyer in such a clear voice that the people in the courtyard could hear.

At the conclusion of the reading two copies of the Confession were handed to the emperor. The story that he gave the German copy to the Elector of Mainz to be deposited in his archives, and that later it was taken by Eck to the Council of Trent, is not based on primary authorities. All trace of it has been lost. The Latin copy was first deposited in Brussels. But in 1569 Philip II instructed Duke Alva to bring it to Spain that it might be destroyed. A receipt at the Brussels Archives shows that Alva got the copy.

The story of the action which resulted from the presentation of the Confession properly belongs to the account of the origin of the Apology of the Augsburg Confession. At this point it will suffice to observe that a committee of Roman Catholic theologians prepared an answer called the "Confutation." There were conferences between the theologians of the two sides in an effort to reach a common ground but without success. Whereupon Melanchthon began writing his defense, or "Apology," of the Confession. The emperor, however, declared that the Lutherans were effectively answered in the confutation and must submit by April 15—something less than seven months away.

During the diet, in spite of the emperor's prohibition, the Confession found its way into print. One Latin and six German editions were issued privately. In 1531 Melanchthon published the Confession with the Apology in Latin and German. This is the *editio princeps* which quite properly is regarded as authoritative, even though Melanchthon had made editorial changes in the language of the text. It is the text found in the *Book of Concord*. However, for the German *Book of Concord* of 1584, the editors sent to Mainz to get the original German copy. It was not there, so someone sent instead another manuscript copy. The editors thought they had received the original and used it in their edition.

After 1531, editions of the Confession continued to appear in print, frequently with slight changes in the phraseology. In the edition of 1540, however, the changes were such as to involve the doctrinal position, particularly in the article on the Lord's Supper. On this doctrine Melanchthon had modified Luther's position to the degree that he approached Calvinism. His edition of 1540 therefore phrased the article on the Lord's Supper in such an ambiguous way that either Lutherans or Calvinists could see their interpretation in it.

When a controversy arose between strict Lutherans and those secretly Calvinistic (Crypto-Calvinists), the difference in language became apparent and important. The Crypto-Calvinists insisted on using the 1540 changed edition—therefore called the *Variata*—whereas the Lutherans adhered to the 1531 edition—the *Invariata* or "Unaltered Augsburg Confession." Strictly speaking, of course, there is no published "unaltered" Confession, for every edition has some editorial changes from the text given the emperor. But these changes are unimportant, whereas the differences between the *Variata* and the *Invariata* are of confessional significance.

It is this confessional significance which to Lutherans is the foremost aspect of the Augsburg Confession. Though at first it had been intended as a petition against abuses, it had come to be a creed, a statement of faith. It was not a mere academic document of theologians' quibblings or scholastic hair-splitting. Instead it was the conviction arrived at by Bible study and Christian life in the parishes. In every instance the doctrine set forth is that which "our churches teach." It therefore had meaning for the whole Lutheran Church, clergy and laity alike.

The confessional position is quite clearly portrayed in ecumenical light. The Lutherans stressed the point that they had not departed from the faith of the ancient church. "Nothing has been received on our part against Scripture or the Church Catholic," says the conclusion. They were even willing to say at the end of the doctrinal articles that their teaching in no way "varies from the Scriptures, or from the Church Catholic, or from the Church of Rome as known from its writers" (Fathers).

It was not only that they wanted to repel the charge of heresy. More than that they wished to show their positive loyalty to such universal doctrines as that of the Trinity, or of the incarnation. It was a living faith in the triune God, such as Luther put into words in his Small Catechism, and which they expressed in common with the apostolic church. Devoid of sectarian narrowness, it is an expression of Christian catholicity, of universal Christian faith.

But the Lutherans at Augsburg did not permit the catholic aspects of their faith to obscure its evangelical nature. The doctrine of justification by faith, recovered from the rubbish of Romanism, is stated clearly and concisely. It colors the other articles. Like the needle of a compass, it gives direction to the other declarations. There can be no question but that it presents a doctrine of salvation in accord with the New Testament. In its phrases Paul speaks again.

In this respect it is opposed to Romish doctrine. And the pope's representatives knew it. One needs only to look at the Confutation to see how well they understood the situation. They knew that the doctrine of the Confession would be fatal to the Romish system. They were aware of the consequences to their whole scheme of meritorious works, monastic orders, and hierarchical exactions if the faith of this Confession were to prevail. They had no misconceptions about the theological color of this document. They were not misled by its moderate statements, its lack of anti-Roman polemic.

When one remembers the historical occasion which called forth the Confession, the absence of attack on Roman Catholic positions can be understood. The purpose of the Lutherans at Augsburg was to convince the emperor that as his loyal subjects they were Christians in the best sense of the term, not dangerous heretics; and that therefore they should be permitted to continue their reformed practices and doctrines in their territories. It was not their primary purpose to convince Charles that he should set up these reforms throughout his empire. They were simply defending their right to hold pure, scriptural doctrine within their territories.

The lack of anti-Roman polemic is to be accounted for also by their conception of the church. Lutherans were not heretics; neither were they schismatics. They held earnestly to the unity of the church. In their thinking there could be but one church. It was their hope that by friendly dealing in frank, face-to-face conference the truth might prevail and the unity of the church be preserved. The preface, echoing the words of the emperor's summons, expresses the hope that "these matters may be settled and brought back to one perfect truth and Christian concord, that for the future one pure and true religion may be embraced and maintained by us, that as we all serve and do battle under one Christ, so we may be able also to live in unity and concord in the one Christian church."

If the historical occasion were forgotten, it would seem surprising that the Confession is phrased in such moderate tones. It is mild in comparison with much that had been written against the papacy. Compare it, for example, with Luther's *An Exhortation to the Clergy Assembled at the Diet at Augsburg* in which he speaks of Romish penance as a "hellish blasphemy of Christ." [7]

The Confession passes by in silence several disputed topics. Nothing is said about the papal claim to rule by divine right. There is no mention of purgatory or of transubstantiation. The painful question of indulgences is neglected. The treatment of rites and usages, and of the mass, is designed to show that the departure from Catholic usages has been as little as possible. Luther wrote, "The devil still lives, and he has noticed very well that your Apology (the Confession) steps softly, and that it has veiled the articles of purgatory, the adoration of the saints, and especially that of the Antichrist, the pope." [8]

---

[7] *W.A.*, XXX, Part 2, 289. Philadelphia ed., IV, 341.

[8] *W.A.*, *Briefe*, V, 496. Trans. in *Conc. Trig.*, Hist. Intro., p. 20.

The brevity and lack of anti-Roman distinctions make it necessary that, for a full understanding of the Lutheran position, the other confessional writings be utilized. Without them it is possible to get an imperfect impression of the Confession. With them as a context the Confession is seen in its true light. It is by no means semi-Roman. The papists understood well enough that it breathed a spirit foreign to them. But the distinctions between Lutheran and Roman doctrine become fully explicit only in the other symbolical writings. The Confession by itself, therefore, is not enough; the rest of the *Book of Concord* is needed to make the picture complete.

The positive Lutheran character of the Confession is clear enough. It stands distinctly opposed not only to the Anabaptists with their radicalism but also to the Zwinglians with their humanistic view of the sacraments. The former are repudiated by name, the latter by inference. The Confession shows that the Lutherans were unwilling to be identified with them.

It also shows no evidence of modifying Luther's doctrine, as was done later in the *Variata.* In 1530 Melanchthon and Luther stood together in doctrine. At Augsburg, Melanchthon, who was often an appeaser, saw the mighty power of the empire and the terrible danger confronting the Lutherans. As his negotiations with the emperor's secretary, Valdes, show, he was willing to go far in making concessions. Yet pressed by the sturdy convictions of his elector and colleagues, he wrote the doctrine which was unquestionably Luther's.

For the Diet of Augsburg the Confession was adequate. On that occasion it expressed clearly enough the orthodoxy of the convictions firmly held by the Lutherans. It was a classic expression of their faith. Signed by the rulers of important sections of Germany, it became the official standard of their belief. From that time on, wherever there were Lutherans, the Augsburg Confession was professed. Each Lutheran collection or body of official doctrinal writings (*corpus doctrinae*) was certain to include the Augsburg Confession. Thus it has had from the very beginning an official status as a symbolical writing.

Remembering the purpose of the Confession, it is not to be expected that it be a systematic treatise in dogmatic theology. There was no intention that it should be, like Melanchthon's *Loci Communes,* a book for the schools. Neither was it designed to be a church constitution, forming the framework for an ecclesiastical organization. Its purpose was to be a witness of earnest, scriptural faith. It is not to be criticized if it is not more than that. It was sufficient that it sounded the keynote of Lutheran faith, allowing the other writings to elaborate on the theme.

Since it had such official acceptance, standing first in time and prominent in its historic occasion, it became the basic creed, the *Grundbekenntnis*, of the Lutheran Church. It has been customary in some areas to designate it as the primary symbol, and the other writings as secondary symbols of the Lutheran Church. Such a designation can be misleading if it is understood to disparage the other writings. Yet even where they are duly appreciated, the eminence of the Confession will be recognized—an eminence which the other writings freely affirm.

The Augsburg Confession does something more than outline the doctrines professed by Lutherans. It indicates also the mood of their movement. For it is an expression of their theological conservatism in contrast to radicalism. It shows their appreciation of historic continuity and apostolicity in contrast to novelty and modernism. And it commits the Lutheran Church to such an attitude. This does not necessarily mean a static theology. But it does mean that the Lutheran Church is to heed the lessons of the past while facing the problems of the present.

Finally, it must be observed that the Augsburg Confession had political significance. Evidence for the statement that it is also a political document is seen in the fact that it was presented at an imperial diet, not a church council. It was signed by public officials, not by theologians. It was addressed to the emperor, not to the pope.

When any settlement of the religious issues was attempted or made, the concessions granted were available to adherents of the Augsburg Confession. Such was the case in 1555 in the provisions of the Religious Peace of Augsburg. The Confession was the rallying cry of all Protestants seeking civil rights both before and after the Thirty Years' War, 1618-48. Many years passed before the adherents of other confessions had similar rights in the empire. On the continent of Europe, therefore, the Augsburg Confession was the first, and for a long time the only Protestant symbolical writing recognized by civil authorities of the empire.

In the perspective of four hundred years, the stature of the Augsburg Confession becomes apparent. The massiveness of its evangelical witness, united with ecumenical doctrine and founded on Scripture, is impressive. Its mood is stately and assured. Avoiding a petty sectarianism it bears aloft a majestic affirmation of faith. Even its moderation adds to its strength, for petty polemics signify littleness. Painstakingly prepared and bravely proclaimed, it is a fitting document to lead the faith of the great Reformation.

Chapter IV

ARTICLES I-VI OF THE
AUGSBURG CONFESSION

The preface of the Augsburg Confession was written by Gregorius Brück, the Saxon chancellor, a doctor of laws, and a man competent in affairs of state. In writing, he addressed Charles in proper terms of respect, recalling to his mind the purpose of the diet. In reviewing the plan proposed for dealing with the religious issues, Brück used almost the identical words of the imperial summons. The Lutherans, he wrote, have come promptly in obedience to the summons, and are prepared to negotiate frankly as the summons requested, in order that there may be religious unity.

The preface states that when the diet had opened on Monday, June 20, in accordance with the imperial edict a request was made for a statement of the religious issues in the German and Latin languages. On Wednesday, the 22nd, it had been decided to deal with religious problems before discussing the Turkish war, and Friday was appointed for hearing the Lutheran Confession. The postponement until Saturday is not mentioned in the preface.

Brück next indicated the Lutheran attitude. Obeying the imperial request, the Lutherans, both clergy and nobility, present their Confession based on Scripture. If others will do the same, the Lutherans are prepared to negotiate "as far as may be honorably done." Brück here diplomatically represents the Lutherans as a party not in opposition to Charles, but to other states, the emperor presumably being a neutral judge.

If, wrote Brück, the other states refuse to negotiate, the responsibility for the disunity must be theirs. Moreover, at both diets of Speyer, and elsewhere, Charles had encouraged the hope that a general council of the church would be held. If the religious issues cannot be decided at this diet, the Lutherans appeal to such general council. This appeal will not be withdrawn except on the basis of a satisfactory religious settlement at this diet.

With this preface Brück shows the legal basis for the Confession and for their appeal to a council. The Lutherans in conforming to imperial laws are not rebels. Nonetheless they are deeply in earnest in their religious convictions, and are prepared to exhaust every resource in their search for justice.[1]

ARTICLE I. OF GOD

Here, at the very outset, by naming the Council of Nicaea, the Confession seeks to create a favorable impression of its orthodox position on the basic doctrine of God. In this it was successful. Eck had quoted Luther as saying, "My soul hates the word *homoousion*"—the key word at Nicaea (Thesis 82). And again, "In the Holy Council of Nice, faith and the Gospel were lacking, and human traditions gained the upper hand" (Thesis 146).

But the Lutherans could not fairly be charged with heresy at this point. The Marburg Articles had cited the Nicene Creed and Council. Luther in his creed of 1528 accepted the trinitarian faith "as it is held both in the Roman Church and in the Christian Church throughout the world." [2] The Schwabach Articles affirmed the same trinitarian faith but without mentioning Nicaea.

The Romanists in their Confutation speak of this article with approval. It was agreed upon by both sides in the committee appointed by Charles to achieve harmony. And at the Conference at Worms, 1540-41, where an effort was made to reconcile Lutherans and Romanists, this article was passed over as not being in dispute.

The article quite obviously consists of two parts: what is affirmed, and what views are rejected. In both phases the position taken is

---

[1] In the *editio princeps* each of the articles did not have a caption. The headings are later additions, and are not always accurate.

[2] W.A., XXVI, 500.

ecumenical. The theological definitions and delimitations of the church through the centuries are accepted. Normal Christian doctrine, rather than its aberrations, is espoused.

In its positive phase the article is committed to monotheism. The possibility of polytheism is obviously excluded. Using a Platonic concept, the article thinks of God in terms of a distinctive divine essence. Every thing or person not God is less than and different from God in essence.

But tied to the divine essence are certain specific qualities or attributes—again a Platonic way of thinking. Those which are listed are: eternity, without body, indivisibility, omnipotence, omniscience, infinite goodness. That is to say that God is superior to human limitations and conditions.

Besides his attributes, the article cites the works of God: the creation and preservation of all things. These works are here assigned to the unity of God rather than to one of the Persons of the Trinity, as in the Nicene Creed. There is no sense in which the Creator-God somehow operates without the co-operation of the Saviour and Spirit.

The positive phase of the article is also trinitarian. Following the doctrinal thinking of Augustine, the three Persons of Deity are declared to be equal in nature, power, and eternity. Any other view is subordinationism. In this matter Lutheran teaching was in accord with Latin rather than with Greek thinking.

The distinctions in the Trinity are not of essence—a difference in kind; nor of ability—greater or less power; nor of time—a difference in age. The article blocks off these blind alleys. Nevertheless the distinctions in the Trinity are said to be real; they are distinctions that actually exist, however little they may be understood. "Word" and "Spirit" are not simply terms representing God by other names; they stand for genuine identities. The word "person" is thus given a special theological meaning, i.e., a self-subsisting entity.

The negative phase of Article I first of all rejects the views of those who taught a religious dualism. It specifically names the Manichaeans, whose doctrines were particularly subversive of Christianity. Their name is derived from Manes or Mani, a Persian religious philosopher who flourished about A.D. 250. He attempted to combine elements of

Christianity with phases of oriental philosophy. According to his teaching there are two eternal and antagonistic existences representing light and darkness. In this scheme it was impossible to believe in God as creator or as incarnate Saviour. Yet Manichaeism at one time was widely held, appealing to such great minds as Augustine.

Another dualism rejected was that of the Valentinians. In teaching a doctrine of emanations they resembled the Gnostics, with whom they are sometimes classified. Valentinus, who died about A.D. 160, taught at Rome. His was an attempt to unite Christian ideas with pagan philosophy in an effort to solve the deepest problems in metaphysics and theology. He taught that God and the material world are distinct and eternal—almost a ditheism. To understand the ultimate nature of things and the meaning of Scripture, one needs a superior wisdom or *gnosis,* according to his teaching.

Besides the dualists, the article rejects the various anti-trinitarians. The most noted of these within the realm of Christendom were the Arians. They derived their name from Arius who lived A.D. 256-336. Arianism is understood to teach that the Logos, created by God, is superior to men, but is not fully God—a sort of demigod. Arianism cannot believe in a God who is a Trinity of equal Persons. Traces of Arian views have continued in modern times among the Socinians and some Unitarians.

The Eunomians condemned in the article were a special brand of Arians. Eunomius of Cappadocia taught that the Logos did not even have a nature similar to the Father. He rejected trinitarianism as irrational.

Important as a powerful rival of Christianity in Mediterranean lands has been Islam. Mohammedans are absolute monotheists. In their teaching, Christ was simply a Hebrew prophet. In rejecting the incarnation of Christ, they deny other cardinal Christian doctrines also. These were the views of the fanatical Turks pressing the eastern defenses of Charles' empire.

Melanchthon named last the Samosatenes, and stated their doctrine. They accepted the teachings of Paul of Samosata who flourished about A.D. 260. He was a "Monarchian"—teaching that there is one Ruler, one God, not a Trinity. Jesus was a man divinely empowered. The Logos was not a personality, but something impersonal. The Holy Spirit was merely a divine agency. The "new" Samosatenes were those persons of Reformation times holding such views. One such, named Campanus, had challenged Luther to a debate while the elector and his associates were at Torgau on their way to Augsburg.

It will be recognized that this article gives religious answers to questions concerning God. It leaves untouched such philosophical problems as those of monism and pluralism. It gives the answer of faith in the personal and trinitarian nature of God in contrast to a scientific concept of a sum total of cosmic forces—proton-electron-continuum. Whatever may be the solutions proposed on the intellectual, i.e., philosophical and scientific, level, there is no conclusion on the religious level without faith.

ARTICLE II. OF ORIGINAL SIN

Two of Eck's theses may be cited as making this article necessary. He quoted Zwingli as saying that "original sin is no sin, but a natural defect, like stammering" (184). The Lutherans wanted to dissociate themselves from such a denial of original sin. Eck had quoted Melanchthon also as saying, "Original sin is an actual wicked desire; hence Scripture does not distinguish between actual and original sin" (185). These phrases, found in Melanchthon's *Loci*, may give a wrong impression because torn from their context.

In declaring acceptance of the doctrine of original sin, the Confession could claim connection with historic Christian doctrine. Tertullian was the first to use the phrase "vice of origin." [3] The doctrine had reached its fullest exposition under Augustine, even if part of his argument rested on a faulty Vulgate translation of Romans 5:12.

The article traces the history of human sinfulness back to "the fall of Adam." In other words, it was not part of human nature as created by God. Next, the article notes the extent of human sinfulness; it is found in "all men begotten according to nature," or, as the *Concordia Triglotta* translates it, "begotten in the natural way." [4] By this phrase, Jesus Christ alone is made an exception. In all others the universality

---

[3] *De anima*, p. 41.
[4] P. 43.

of sin is unbroken. "The Scripture hath concluded all under sin" (Gal. 3:22).

Next the article defines original sin. In a negative or privative sense it consists of being "without the fear of God, without trust in God." Since the righteous have reverence for and faith in God, the absence of these virtues marks a person as unrighteous, i.e., sinful. In a positive sense, original sin consists of concupiscence or what Melanchthon had called "actual wicked desire." The German text reads, "evil desire and inclination" instead of concupiscence. It is the perversity which loves the evil rather than the good. These two phases correspond somewhat to the "formal" and the "material" aspects named by Aquinas. In the German text of the article the order of the two phases is reversed.

The character of this condition is that it "is truly sin." The Scotists in the Roman Church defined original sin as a weakness, a deprivation, a loss of superadded gifts, but not really sin and guilt. In the Confutation the Romanists agreed that original sin is truly sin. But at the Council of Trent the conflict between the Thomists and the Scotists made an ambiguous statement necessary.

The consequences of original sin are named as condemnation and eternal death. Such disastrous results are felt "even now." The article concludes its positive section by indicating the remedy for original sin, namely, rebirth through baptism and the Holy Ghost.

The article repudiates doctrines opposed to these. The only errorists named are Pelagians who denied the sinfulness of this vice of origin. They asserted that any man can make himself righteous by his own efforts. The "others" referred to in the Article include without question the Semi-Pelagian Romanists who attacked the evangelical doctrine of man's entire spiritual inability and his absolute need of grace. Remembering Eck's quotation, it would seem that Zwingli also is thought of with "others."

In this article the Lutherans could justly claim connection with ancient Christian doctrine, particularly under Augustine. But it was certainly in conflict with a long Semi-Pelagian tradition in the Roman Church, and the Confutation surmised as much. This evangelical doctrine reflects influences from the doctrine of justification by faith— something which was lacking in the Roman doctrine. These two theologies, the one centering about faith, the other about works, are bound to define original sin differently. It is no wonder that at the conference at Worms, 1540-41, Melanchthon and Eck debated the topic for three days. The agreement they reached was purely verbal.

There are two aspects of the doctrine of original sin not touched in this article. They are free will, and the cause of sin. They are discussed in the supplementary Articles XVIII and XIX.

The doctrine of original sin as presented in this article is coherent with the doctrine of redemption through Christ. Leonhard Fendt says that "original sin belongs to holy history (*Heilsgeschichte*), not human or natural history." [5] Seen in the light of *solus Christus* no other interpretation of original sin is possible.

The Lutherans in this article do not describe exactly how original sin is transmitted. It is not necessary, nor yet forbidden, to draw a traducianist inference. It is not even stated or implied that human nature is a dichotomy—consisting of body and soul. What is certainly affirmed is the totality of the sinful involvement; all human nature is guiltily sinful. It will not do to think, as Augustine seemed to do, that concupiscence is essentially fleshly, physical, or sexual.[6] Evil desire is that, and much more. Luther wrote, *totum hominem esse carnem*—the entire man, in all that he is and does, is "fleshly." [7]

It is noteworthy also that this article sees the profound depths of sinfulness, rather than the apparently superficial nature of separate sinful acts. Plitt, whom Neve quotes, says that "Luther, in the special experiences of life into which God had led him, had begun to learn, not what sins are, but what sin is." [8] Melanchthon shared the same understanding.

Systems of thought which are based on reason, whether scientific or theological, reject the doctrine of original sin. They point to the difficulties inherent in the doctrine, and either deny the sinfulness of human nature, or explain it on other grounds. Thus Rauschenbusch said, "A theology for the social gospel would have to say that original

---

[5] *Der Wille der Reformation im Augsburgischen Bekenntnis* (Leipzig: H. G. Wallmann, 1929), p. 25.

[6] *De nupt. et conc.*, I, 24, 27. NPNF V, 273 ff. MSL XLIV, 429.

[7] *W.A.*, XVIII, 742.

[8] Gustav Plitt, *Einleitung in die Augustana* (Erlangen: Andreas Deichert, 1867-68), II, 104. Neve, *op. cit.*, p. 126.

sin is partly social." [9] Liberal theology is likely to accept the idea of "social heredity" as a substitute for original sin. Yet Rauschenbusch acknowledged that "the theological doctrine of original sin is an important effort to see sin in its totality, and to explain its unbroken transmission and perpetuation." [10]

ARTICLE III. OF THE SON OF GOD

On the doctrine of Christ, Eck had gathered statements by Zwinglians, Lutherans, and others, piling them together to give the impression that all their authors were heretics. Ascribed to Luther was the declaration that "Christ merited nothing for himself, but for us" (73). Also he was quoted as saying that "Christ did not have an intellectual soul, but in place of his soul had divinity" (79). The statement that "no satisfaction is required for sins, except the death of Christ" (265), is attributed to Luther, Melanchthon, and others.

Lutheran doctrine concerning the person and work of Christ was thoroughly ecumenical and orthodox. It accepted completely the doctrinal decisions in Christology made in the ecumenical councils beginning with Nicaea. Luther clearly taught the two natures of Christ, and that his humanity included body and soul. [11]

This article appears in the Confession not simply to refute false charges, but much more significantly to express the ardent faith in Christ which is at the heart of the evangelical doctrine of salvation. The warm attachment of Lutherans to Christ made them deeply resent the Roman doctrines and practices which in any way cast a shadow on his redeeming work. It made them sensitive also to certain Christological teachings of Zwingli, and at a later time of Calvin.

In the Confession, this article follows the one on original sin, reversing the order found in the Marburg and Schwabach Articles. Perhaps Melanchthon felt that the logical order was sin first, and then the Saviour. At any event his soteriological interest is seen in the fact that the following article treats of justification.

The article quite distinctly presents the incarnation and the work of Christ. The two are somewhat intertwined.

---

[9] *Op. cit.,* p. 61.
[10] *Ibid.,* p. 67.
[11] *W.A.,* XXVI, 503.

With regard to the incarnation, the article first affirms the fact of the two natures of Christ. He is "God the Son" (as the German text reads), or "the Word, that is, the Son of God" (according to the Latin text). The reference is to Article I which taught that the Son shared in the divine essence and attributes. Besides the deity of Christ, there is also his humanity expressed in the words "became man, born of the pure Virgin Mary" (German text). Without leaving it to inference, the article explicitly states that "there are two natures, the divine and the human." This in ancient times had been the first stage in Christological doctrine.

Next comes the relation of the two natures as the second stage of that doctrine. The article accepts the decision of the Council of Chalcedon as opposed to the views both of the Nestorians and the Eutychians. The union of the two natures is real and inseparable, not merely verbal or temporary as Nestorianism might say. Yet the identity of each nature is preserved, not lost as the Eutychians and Monophysites taught. Hence there is "one Person, one Christ, true God and true man."

The third point concerning the incarnate Christ has to do with the two states involved. The state of humiliation is indicated by the facts of his birth, suffering, death, and burial. The reality of his humiliation is underscored by the insertion of the word "truly," which is not found in either the Schwabach or the Marburg Articles at this place. It was evidently intended as a protection against any charge of Docetism, i.e., that Christ's body was not real, but was a phantom or mere appearance.

The state of exaltation is marked by the descent into hell, the resurrection, the ascension, and the reign at God's right hand. It was in keeping with Lutheran teaching, in contrast to the Reformed, that the descent into hell was regarded as the beginning of his triumphant exaltation. It was part of his conquest of the kingdom of the devil. The reality of the resurrection is also emphasized by a "truly." And the phrase, "the right hand of the Father," is used without any reference to the opinion of Zwingli which made it a fixed or limited location in space. Luther is quoted as saying that it "is nothing else than the almighty power of God, which fills heaven and earth." [12]

---

[12] *Book of Concord* (Jacobs), I, 629. W.A., XXIII, 133, 143.

Concerning the work of Christ, this article affirms the atonement. The Latin version reads that he suffered and died "that he might reconcile the Father unto us, and be a sacrifice, not only for original guilt, but also for all actual sins of men." The order in the German version is: "that he might be a sacrifice, not only for original sin, but also for all other sins, and propitiate (appease) God's wrath."

It is obvious that Melanchthon here intends an objective atonement—one which offers something to an offended God—rather than a subjective theory suggesting a change within men. However, at the very heart of evangelical doctrine is the conviction that redemption and salvation are produced by divine agency. God does it. Man neither does it, nor begins it, nor assists in it. Thus the core of the doctrine of the atonement is the propitiation of God by the divine Son whereby the divine agency might be fully released for salvation.

Nygren in his *Agape and Eros* italicized the sentence, *"Luther insists, in opposition to all egocentric forms of religion, upon a purely theocentric relation to God."* [13] The gospel is never a means whereby men may make themselves holy and thus win God's favor. It teaches us to look away from ourselves and see "what God hath wrought." Luther in his *Larger Commentary on Galatians* said, "For by Himself to overcome the world's sin, death, the curse, and God's wrath, this is not the work of any created being, but of almighty God." [14]

The use of the word "sacrifice" in the article is quite in keeping with Luther's usage. The thesis of Aulén in his book, *Christus Victor*, is that what he calls the "classical theory" was revived and deepened by Luther. It is quite in accord with his thesis that the "sacrifice" of the article is not an Anselmic payment of a debt—so much for so much. Instead, it is a means of triumph over death, sin, the devil, the law, and God's wrath. Aulén says, "It is God's act of victory, when Christ goes in under the Divine Wrath, and bears the burden of the punishment which on account of that Wrath impends upon men. Thus the Love of God breaks through the Wrath." [15]

---

[13] Anders Nygren, *Agape and Eros* tr. A. G. Hebert (London: S.P.C.K., 1932-39), II, 463.

[14] W.A., XL, Part 1, 441. Quoted in Gustav Aulén, *Christus Victor* (London: S.P.C.K., 1931), p. 122.

[15] *Op. cit.*, p. 131.

In the Marburg Articles Zwingli had agreed with Luther "that the same Son of God and Mary, the indivisible Person, Jesus Christ, was crucified for us . . ." But remembering Zwingli's inclination to ascribe suffering to the human nature of Christ only, Luther wrote in the Schwabach Articles, "One should not believe or teach that Jesus Christ as a man or in his human nature has suffered for us . . . but that God and Man, or God's Son, truly suffered for us." This is the view which quite clearly prevails in the article of the Confession.

The extent of the atonement is also indicated. In Romish thinking, the atonement covered original sin, leaving the actual sins to the individual to be atoned for by penance or the sacrifice of the mass. Lutherans were not content with such a partial atonement. What Christ had done was all that is needed. Luther expressed the comprehensiveness of it when he wrote in his Confession of 1528, "Jesus Christ has for us poor sinners suffered, been crucified, dead and buried, (and) therewith he released us from sins, death, and the eternal wrath of God through his guiltless blood." [16] The word translated "released" is from *erlösen*—to save, redeem, deliver, rescue.

The completion of the atonement is reflected in Christ's kingly rule. As to time, his reign is "forever." It extends over "all creatures." The purpose is that those whom he has delivered and who believe in him may be made holy, and be strengthened against the attempts of the devil to recapture them. Christ is not a Saviour of long ago only, but he is our constant Champion. And at the end of the age he will be the Judge of all mankind. This is apostolic faith.

It must never be forgotten that in discussing the incarnation we are dealing with a mystery wherein we move by faith, not by sight. The rise of heresies has made necessary some definition of Christian faith, even when that definition had to be in part a confession of ignorance. How Christ's divine and human natures could unite in one Person, without being two persons, is beyond our comprehension. A Platonist can think of human nature as an essence independent of any personality; the modern mind has difficulty in thinking of human nature apart from persons. But it is the best statement we have concerning a mysterious fact which we heartily accept. Melanchthon in

---

[16] W.A., XXVI, 502.

his *Loci* wrote, "The mysteries of divinity we have the more rightly adored than investigated." [17]

The same must be said for the doctrine of the atonement. The theories more often draw pictures than give explanations. The theological treatment of the doctrine will continue to propose problems to a living, growing theology. But the fact of the atonement, that he gave "his life a ransom for many" (Matt. 20:28), is at the center of our unswerving faith.

No errorists are named in the article as it appears in the *Book of Concord*. But the German *editio princeps* included the phrase, "and condemned are all heresies which are opposed to this article." The implied rejection of Zwinglian and Romish views has been noted.

ARTICLE IV. OF JUSTIFICATION

Eck was not misrepresenting Luther when he quoted him as saying, "Faith alone justifies, not works; because faith and works directly antagonize; hence works cannot be taught without injuring faith" (187). The Romanists correctly recognized that here was the line of cleavage. Luther made an antithesis between faith and works in the doctrine of justification. The Romanists made a synthesis of them. Luther saw salvation as solely the work of God in which man trusts. The Romanists regarded it as a work in which man co-operates.

At the beginning, rather than at the end of this article of the Confession, Melanchthon rejects an ancient heresy. It was a Pelagian view that men could be justified before God by their own strength, merit, or works. Eck could not accuse the Lutherans of that. The Confutation acknowledged as much. Following the statement on original sin in Article II, the rejection of Pelagianism was bound to be asserted.

Man's spiritual inability is expressed more explicitly in the German *editio princeps:* "and since mankind is born in sin, and neither keeps God's law nor can love God from the heart, it therefore is taught that through our works or satisfactions we cannot deserve the forgiveness of sins, and that also we cannot on account of our works be esteemed righteous before God."

---

[17] *C.R.*, XXI, 84. Also in C. L. Hill (tr.), *The Loci Communes of Philip Melanchthon* (Boston: Meador Publishing Co., 1944), p. 67.

The positive side of the article uses the word "freely" (*gratis, aus Gnaden*) to indicate the source of justification. It all originates and flows from the grace of God, his boundless, unmerited Love. Justification is the expression of the creative power of a loving God in the spiritual life of men. It introduces a new principle or force in human affairs, one which men of themselves could not produce.

The ground for justification is seen in the phrase "for Christ's sake" which occurs twice. Later the article adds concerning Christ, "who by His death hath made satisfaction for our sins." Here is the application to human need of the redemption accepted in the preceding article. On man's side there was no ground for fellowship with God; there existed only the estrangement and penalty of sin. But God in Christ established a ground in the Saviour's obedient suffering and death.

The Latin text uses the word "satisfaction" whereas in the German it reads "suffered for us." Aulén says, "With regard to Satisfaction, it is well known that Luther spoke very severely about the use of this word: we will not allow it, he says, in our schools or on the lips of our preachers, but would rather send it back to the judges, advocates, and hangmen from whom the pope stole it." [18]

Yet Luther did use it, as Melanchthon has done in this article, without making it the legalistic thing familiar in the Roman Church. It was not a satisfaction of merits mathematically measured or carefully calculated. It turned away God's wrath against sin adequately. Measurement and computation, such as prevailed in Roman legalism, are not involved.

The means whereby justification accrues to the individual is faith. The Romanists could consent in their way to God's grace and Christ's atonement, but faith with no mention of works was something objectionable to them. The gospel, as the Lutherans understood it, made faith the only way by which men could receive God's grace. That which God had originated, which God the Son had worked out, which could not be deserved or purchased, could therefore only be bestowed and received. And faith was the receiving. Here the Confession was on strong biblical ground, as Melanchthon was later to show in his Apology.

---

[18] *Op. cit.*, p. 134.

Because faith is dependence, it makes God rather than men the origin and center of salvation. Because faith is trust in the atonement, it honors Christ and clings to him. Since faith stands forth as the only means of justification and is the root from which all other virtues stem, the antithesis of faith, viz., unbelief, is the greatest of all sins. Faith is an open window into which God's sunshine streams from the sky where clouds have been removed.

The nature of justification is twofold: imputation and nonimputation. Imputation is the reckoning to one's account of the righteousness of Christ. Nonimputation means that for Christ's sake the believer's sins are not taken into account. This is the theme of the fourth chapter of Romans. The article speaks of the positive side as being "received into favor" by God. It is God's act. It removes a believer from among the unsaved into the category of the righteous. It is not that he is righteous, or that his faith is a virtue deserving such reward. But God sees Christ to whom the believer clings, and attributes to him Christ's righteousness.

If the credit side of man's ledger is empty until the merits of Christ are there written down, the debit side has plenty of entries. Yet in justification these are no longer charged to one's account, but are canceled. As the article says, "Sins are forgiven for Christ's sake." Man's bad credit-rating is obliterated. He is acquitted of crimes committed. As in Luther's famous phrase, the believer is *simul justus et peccator*—he is both a righteous man and a sinner.

Justification is not looking at salvation from man's side, as if seeing the transformation within a man—his regeneration, renewal, sanctification. It does not answer the question, "Is the believer good within?" It does answer the question, "Does God consider him good?" or "Is he saved?" It is looking at salvation from God's side with the theocentric emphasis typical of the Reformation. It simply means that for Christ's sake God reclassifies the sinner, reverses his judgment of him, includes him among those who receive the summons, "Come ye blessed!"

This article states the fact of justification without explaining how righteousness can be imputed. It is indeed a mysterious working of God presented in a figure of speech. No one believes that God literally keeps books or presides in a courtroom. We have no clear understanding of divine operations. Theologies based on reason have made this ignorance a basis for denying any imputation; because it does not fit into a logical framework, it is rejected. The article, however, accepts it as a matter of sincere faith.

Justification is related to regeneration and to sanctification in a vital way. This is discussed later. With all this profound trust in Christ, the believer must also have a high ethical sense. How can that be maintained? Justification by faith as a central doctrine in Lutheranism must not be permitted to lead to a complacent attitude, an easy religion devoid of spiritual struggle. This is a sensitive point in Lutheranism, as will be noted later.

One more question may be raised. Since part of justification is nonimputation (forgiveness of sins), and since forgiveness of sins occurs daily in the Christian's life, is justification a continuing action of God, or was it an act of God performed at the moment when the Christian became a believer and was "received into favor"? The article presents justification as an act of God which remits the sins of the believer and takes him into fellowship with God. It is a radical change in his relation to God. It is the beginning of the state of grace for the believer in which the forgiveness of sins is a continuing benefit.

This article of the Confession presents a doctrine of justification unfamiliar and intolerable to the Romanists. They had this to say of it at the Council of Trent:

If any shall say that men are justified either by the sole imputation of the righteousness of Christ, or by the sole remission of sin, to the exclusion of that grace and charity which is shed abroad in their hearts by the Holy Spirit which inheres in them, or shall say that the grace whereby we are justified is merely and only the favor of God: let him be accursed.

If any one shall say that justifying faith is nothing but confidence in the divine mercy remitting sin on account of Christ or that this faith is the sole thing by which we are justified: let him be accursed.[19]

Thus Rome clung to her doctrine of work-righteousness. Hers was the idea, "If I perform good deeds, God will save me." Therefore Luther brusquely remarked, "There is no difference between the Jew, the Papist, and the Turk." [20]

---

[19] Sess. VI, Canons 11, 12.
[20] W.A., XL, Part 1, 603. Quoted in Nygren, *op. cit.*, II, 470.

ARTICLE V. OF THE MINISTRY

In his Theses Eck tried to create the impression that Lutherans, Zwinglians, Anabaptists, and fanatics were all of a kind. Thus he quoted certain Zwickau fanatics as having said, "The New Testament has lost its power as well as the Old. Accordingly, we are to adhere to no Scripture, but only to the Spirit, according to the Eternal Gospel" (111). A little later he quoted Luther: "Faith alone is necessary; all other things are most free, neither commanded nor prohibited" (194). A religion of that kind would be purely subjective and lacking in objective means and ministry.

This article was prepared to meet that accusation. The title which has been traditionally given to the article is therefore misleading. Its aim really is to show how justifying faith is obtained. It presents a statement on the means of grace.

The article first indicates the bearers of the means of grace, namely, those in the office of the ministry. Theirs is a function, an office, not a priestly order.

In his Confession of 1528 Luther, in condemning "all orders, rules, cloisters, convents . . . with vows and duties" because they conflict with the doctrine of justification by faith, remarked that "the holy orders and true institutions established by God are these three: the priestly office, matrimony, and civil authority. All those who are found in the pastoral office or ministry of the Word, are in a holy, true, good, God-pleasing order and estate, since in it they preach and administer the sacraments, and oversee the treasury, the sextons, and messengers or servants. This is nothing else than a holy work before God." [21]

After stating that faithful parents and conscientious public officers also perform a work pleasing to God, he continued: "Beyond these three institutions or orders there is now the common order of Christian love"—feeding the hungry, and so forth.[22] It is evident from this that Luther did not set the ministers up as a special order above the laity. He looked at the ministry as a function, a divinely provided service with a distinct task, namely, preaching the Word and administering the sacraments. This is the thought Melanchthon expressed in this article of the Confession.

---

[21] *W.A.*, XXVI, 504.
[22] *Ibid.*, 505.

In the second place, this article names the means of grace: the Word and the sacraments. Their administration has made a ministry necessary. They have a divine origin. They are objective instruments in a visible church. According to Scripture they are the only means whereby God's grace can reach us. There is no need to supplement them with other rites and ceremonies. Neither must they be neglected and despised.

The article next specifies the function of the means of grace. Through them is given the Holy Ghost by whom justifying faith is developed. Romanist minds, on hearing the word "faith," were accustomed to think of it as a form of knowledge. To guard against such a mistake, Melanchthon, after writing the term, repeats in almost identical words the definition of justifying faith presented in Article IV.

When the Holy Ghost "worketh faith" in individuals, his activity is never independent of, but always connected with the gospel. The Word truly includes the law, and when it is preached repentance arises. But when faith is ignited, it is the gospel side of the Word which has been proclaimed, as Melanchthon says with fine discrimination.

The phrase, "hear the gospel," must not be interpreted too narrowly so as to mean listening to the reading of the Bible. The Latin version speaks of the ministry as a "ministry of teaching the gospel" (*ministerium docendi evangelii*). The German version calls it the "office of preaching" (*Predigtamt*). The Schwabach Articles described the "office of preaching" as "the oral Word, viz., the gospel." The Apology even includes reading under the hearing of the gospel. The Holy Spirit therefore accompanies any communication of the truth of the gospel. The Marburg Articles had agreed "that the Holy Ghost gives this faith or his gift to no one without preaching, or the oral Word, or the gospel of Christ preceding."

The phrase "where and when it pleases God" corresponds to the expression "how and where He will" in the Schwabach Articles, and the "how and in whom He will" of the Marburg Articles. Melanchthon was not intending a reference to predestination in these words. In a letter written to Brenz in 1531 he said, "In the entire *Apologia* I have avoided that long and inexplicable dispute concerning predestination." [23] Instead, the words indicate the fact that just as justification is the work of God, so also the details are in his hands.

Finally, the article repudiates the view that God's grace does not come through means, but directly to those who have made themselves ready for it. Those who believed that God spoke to them directly, independently of the Word, were guilty of erratic fanaticism. Believing in the immediacy of the Spirit, they disparaged the corporate church with its sacraments and worship. Such people were the Anabaptists of various kinds in the Reformation era. The "others" likely include such fanatics as Carlstadt and Schwenkfeld. Perhaps Zwingli was also intended, since he made the sacraments mere symbols. It may be that the Papists were included, because they made church laws equal to Scripture, and taught that men can prepare themselves for God's grace.

ARTICLE VI. OF NEW OBEDIENCE

Since the Lutherans taught that justification comes only through faith, Eck tried to accuse them of being entirely hostile to good works. A statement of this kind has been noted in connection with Article IV. Among the statements he quoted from Melanchthon are these: "All works of man, however praiseworthy in appearance, are altogether vicious and are sins worthy of death" (199). "After one has been justified no laws or ordinances bind him" (367).

In this article Melanchthon shows the relations of works to justifying faith. Later he added Article XX to discuss good works further. At this point the Confession, which has established itself upon the doctrine of justification by faith, and has clearly stated its exclusion of works from justification, seeks to avoid the charge of encouraging godless conduct.

Therefore, it first declares the necessity of good works as a fruit of faith. It is not a static or lifeless faith of which the Confession has been speaking. Instead, it is vigorous and dynamic, having continuing consequences in the believer's life. The Marburg Articles had said, "this faith . . . exercises good works through us, namely, love towards one's neighbor, prayer to God, and suffering all persecution."

---

[23] *C.R.,* II, 547.

Similarly the Schwabach Articles spoke of faith, which as "an efficacious, new and living thing, produces much fruit, is always doing what is good; towards God, by praise, thanksgiving, prayer, preaching and teaching, and towards neighbors, by love, serving, aiding, counseling, giving and lending and by suffering every sort of evil, even unto death."

Faith, if it has any reality, has vitality. "Living faith" is tautology; "dead faith" is a contradiction in terms. The necessity of good works is that of inner necessity, of things which belong together, in fact, cannot be separated. It is in contrast to a necessity composed of compulsion from without. There is nothing forced or artificial about the fruits of faith. They are the normal, natural evidences of life.

In the next place, the article identifies the good works. In the Roman Church there was much rubbish that was labeled "good works." Those only are to be accounted good works which are commanded by God, and are in accordance with his will. In the Large Catechism Luther took pains to point out that obedience to each of the Ten Commandments is a truly good work, in contrast to which the works of the monks were foolishness.

The identity of the good works carries with it also a certain necessity. It is the necessity of the divine order. The fruits produced by faith out of inner necessity correspond precisely with the requirements of God's kingdom. There is nothing arbitrary about that will of God yet we cannot go back of that will to ask why it is so. It is enough to know that it is a holy will.

Having shown the necessity and the identity of good works the article hastens to repeat the warning that they do not "merit justification before God." There is more to be said on this topic in other confessional writings. But at this point Melanchthon wanted to be sure that after meritorious works had been ejected from the front door they did not creep in through a rear entrance. Neither at the beginning of a man's life as a Christian, nor anywhere along its course, do his good works become the basis of his fellowship with God.

In support of this position the article presents a scriptural and a patristic quotation. The words of Christ in Luke 17:10 indicate that works can never rise to the place where they become meritorious. The patristic quotation, affirming justification by faith, comes from the commentary on I Corinthians 1:4 by Ambrosiaster, the pseudo-Ambrose who was identified with Saint Ambrose in the middle ages.[24]

This article shows us justifying faith both at its beginning and also in its fruition. It is the Lutheran conviction that faith must exist before there can be any fruitage. Something must have occurred within before there can be any outward manifestation, but when it has occurred within, the outer evidences will appear. One has to be astonished at the statement of C. C. Morrison: "Any religion which begins in the inner life is sure to end there." [25] On the contrary, if it has no inner source, it is as hypocritical and transitory as it is superficial.

Nonetheless, this was a sensitive point for the Reformers. As Plitt has observed, the Romanists could exhibit their interest in good works by their outward observances and ecclesiastical busyness; the Lutherans, unwilling to display such religiosity, seemed to neglect good works.[26] And when Pietists attempted to correct this impression, they ended in a Puritanic legalism. Lutheranism is still being charged with being "quietistic"—a kind of religious isolationism, unwilling to exert any influence in the terrific struggles occurring in the social and economic order of our day. Some hard and clear thinking is needed at this point.

---

[24] *MSL* XVII, 195. Cf. *Bek.*, 59, n. 2.

[25] Quoted in F. E. Johnson, *The Church and Society* (New York: Abingdon Press, 1935), p. 40.

[26] *Op. cit.*, II, 185.

Chapter V

ARTICLES VII-XIII OF THE
AUGSBURG CONFESSION

In the first six articles of the Augsburg Confession Melanchthon drew with rapid, clear-cut lines the basic elements of evangelical doctrine. God and the incarnate Christ are the dominant figures. In sharpest contrast is mankind, full of sin and misery. Flowing out from God is the grace released by Christ's atonement, and coming through the means of grace.

The articles which follow fill in more of the detail. A statement needs to be made concerning the church and the validity of the means of grace. Each of the sacraments must be defined, and its use indicated. These matters occupy the attention of the next group of articles of the Confession.

ARTICLE VII. OF THE CHURCH

On the doctrine of the church, Eck had no quotation from Luther. But Martin Bucer, the evangelical preacher at Strassburg, was quoted as saying, "Only the predestinated are in the church, but the wicked or reprobate are not of the church" (170). The Romanists were accustomed to give the visible church a high place in their thinking. To their minds the sentence of Bucer was destructive of the church in its historical and empirical existence. The Lutheran emphasis on inward faith rather than outward observance might also appear to be anti-ecclesiastical. Therefore the Confession makes this statement concerning the church.

The article begins with a sentence concerning the perpetuity of the church. If Emperor Charles had been led to believe that the Lutherans wanted to destroy the church, and that this desire was at the bottom of their opposition to indulgences, monasteries, and papal rule, this opening sentence should have reassured him on this matter.

Lutherans knew that the church would always endure, because Christ had said so, and because he would see to it. The church, with its marks of holiness and unity, as confessed in the Creed, is no mere association of well-intentioned men, but it has a divine Builder and Preserver. The German version, which speaks of "one holy Christian Church," says that it must always exist.

The German version follows the Schwabach Articles which declare "that there is no doubt that there is and remains on earth one holy Christian Church until the end of the world, as Christ said in Matthew 28:20, 'Lo, I am with you alway, even unto the end of the world.'" However, the Confession sees the perpetuity of the church carried beyond time and into eternity. With such a conception of the church it would obviously be silly to accuse the Lutherans either of hostility to the church or of schism.

The article next presents a definition of the church. It is the congregation of saints (*congregatio sanctorum*). As will be noted later in the Large Catechism, Luther thought that in the Creed the term "church" is interpreted by the phrase, "communion of saints" (*communio sanctorum*). For the purposes of the Confession, however, the word "congregation" gives a more objective impression than the term "communion" or fellowship.

In this emphasis Melanchthon was presenting a contrast to the purely spiritual conception of the church as held by the Anabaptists. The German version uses the term *Versammlung*—assembly or congregation—which is an improvement over the sentence in the Schwabach Articles: "This church is nothing else than the believers in Christ who hold, believe and teach the above-mentioned articles and items, and for that are persecuted and martyred in the world."

Luther in his Confession of 1528 had said, "I believe that there is on earth one holy Christian Church, that is the congregation and number or assembly of all Christians in all the world, Christ's own bride and his spiritual body, of which he also is the only head, and

79

the bishops or pastors are not heads nor lords nor bridegrooms of the same, but are servants, friends, and, as the word 'bishop' indicates, overseers, administrators or supervisors. And this same Christendom is not simply under the Roman Church or the pope, but in all the world, just as the prophet proclaimed that Christ's gospel should come into all the world, Psalms 2 and 18; thus corporeally Christendom is scattered under the pope, the Turks, the Persians, the Tartars and everywhere, but spiritually it is assembled in one gospel and we believe under one head which is Jesus Christ." [1]

Besides this earthly, empirical aspect of the church there is also the spiritual aspect, viz., that it is composed of saints. That does not mean that saints are sinless, holy men. Luther once said, "God has nothing to do with holy men. A holy man is a fiction." [2] The saints are simply the justified. The only holiness they have is, and grows out of, the righteousness of faith.

As is readily seen this definition of the church gets its direction from the doctrine of justification through faith. Elert has said that here is the first time in history that a definition of the church is given. It is a quite different conception than was held in the Roman Church where the emphasis was on the organization under a papal hierarchy. Evangelical doctrine was bound to teach that the church consists of those who cling to Christ, rather than those who are caught in the net of the pope.

The church, thus evangelically defined, has recognizable marks, i.e., it exists in this world wherever "the Gospel is rightly taught and the sacraments rightly administered." Since the church exists only where there is justifying faith, and since such faith arises only through the means of grace, the use of those means necessarily identifies the church. For the preaching of the gospel there must be an assembly; and if the assembly is a church it must have the preaching of the gospel.

This article speaks of the gospel, and not of the law. That does not mean that Lutherans are antinomian—against the law. That false inference was later drawn, and had to be condemned in other confes-

---

[1] W.A., XXVI, 506.
[2] W.A., XL, Part 2, 347. Quoted in Nygren, op. cit., II, 468.

sional writings, as we shall see. But the central emphasis here is upon justifying faith, and in connection therewith the article quite properly mentions only the gospel.

The word "rightly" occurs twice in the article. It does not appear in the copy sent to Nürnberg on May 31. When it was deemed necessary to qualify or identify the kind of preaching and of sacraments used, a precedent was found in the Schwabach Articles. They declared that the church exists "where the Gospel is preached and the sacraments are rightly used."

Melanchthon was bound to recognize that in the Roman Church the preaching distorted the gospel, and the sacraments had improper use. The cup was withheld from the laity, and the mass had become a sacrifice. But the Reformation had recovered the true meaning of the gospel. Therefore, as the German version of the Confession says, the church exists where "the Gospel is purely preached and the holy sacraments are administered in accordance with the Gospel." The true church, therefore, is the church of justifying faith, the work of the Holy Ghost through the means of grace.

"The Gospel rightly preached and the sacraments rightly administered are the marks or *evidences* by which a believer can positively determine the existence of the church in any given community," writes P. H. Buehring.[3] This is the thought expressed in the German text of the Apology on this article. The evidences become clearer and stronger in proportion as the preaching and the administration of the sacraments conform to the gospel. Anywhere they cease to be evangelical—vehicles of justifying faith—the church has vanished.

The unity of the church is next described. At Augsburg it was necessary for the Lutherans to avoid the charge of schism. Once more the evangelical doctrine of justification gave direction to the statement. The unity of the church is found in agreement concerning the doctrine of justifying faith and the means of its bestowal. As the German version reads, "It is enough for the true unity of the Christian Church that the Gospel be preached in accordance with pure doctrine and the sacraments be administered in keeping with God's Word."

There is liberty, however, in the matter of rites and ceremonies of human origin. Uniformity, however desirable for other reasons, is

---

[3] Unpublished lecture notes.

not a necessity for unity. A lack of uniformity does not disrupt fellowship. This idea was one which from the beginning they planned to present at Augsburg. For it had found expression in the Torgau Articles, where it was said that "The unity of the Christian Church does not consist in external human ordinances; therefore, if we already hold orders dissimilar from each other, we are not on that account members cut off from the church."

The matter of rites and usages is discussed in Article XV. It is sufficient to observe that at this point the mention of rites and ceremonies is somewhat incidental and negative. Rites and ceremonies are not unimportant, but they are nowhere near the center of that which is vital in the church. For at the very heart of the church is God in Christ justifying and sanctifying us who receive his grace through faith.

The unity of the church amid the diversity of churches and sects is a problem engaging many minds. Lutherans, if they are true to their heritage, cannot help but be interested in unity and harmony. The Formula of Concord breathes that spirit. This article points the direction to be taken. It is certainly not one of doctrinal indifference, as many advocates of union urge. On the other hand we must frankly face the question how much of the field of doctrinal theology is included in the phrase "agreement in the doctrine of the Gospel." The will to unity in the church must not be ambushed by sectarian pettiness or betrayed by religious isolationism.

ARTICLE VIII. WHAT THE CHURCH IS

The real theme of this article is the validity of the means of grace. The further statement about the church is somewhat incidental, as is also the sentence concerning the ministry of evil men. The main point still is the bestowal of justifying faith through the divinely established means.

To the Romanists the Lutheran movement seemed to be destructive of much to which they were accustomed in the church. The emphasis on faith seemed to remove all ecclesiastical authority and everything substantial in the sacraments. Thus Eck quoted Luther: "They lie who say that the Mass of a wicked priest is useful *ex opere operato"* (272). What validity is there in the sacraments, if Luther is correct?

The article begins by repeating the definition of the church given in the preceding article. In the copy of the Confession sent to Nürnberg, May 31, these two articles constituted but one article. For that reason the conception of the church as the congregation of saints is continued. In this instance, however, the saints are further identified as true believers, recognizing the fact that theirs is a righteousness of faith.

By mentioning preaching and the sacraments, rites and ceremonies, Melanchthon was seeking to emphasize the fact that Lutherans thought of the church as an institution encountered in human experience. It is more than an idea existing in theologians' minds. But in this article he notes another aspect of its existence on earth, viz., the presence of hypocrites among the saints. Neither among the laity nor among the clergy is everyone thoroughly holy who participates in church activities. The church on earth is a mixed body.

Such a condition is serious enough so far as the laity is concerned. But when the pastors are involved, questions immediately arise as to the value of the sacraments they administer. In the course of church history there have been Christian groups which considered the sacraments valid only when administered by holy men—holy according to the definition of the group.

This article therefore states the Lutheran position. The efficacy of the means of grace is independent of the character of the administrator. If valid sacraments depended upon human sinlessness there would be no communicating of God's grace because all pastors are either Christian sinners or hypocritical saints. The doctrine of original sin which taught that concupiscence remains after baptism did not make an exception of those in the ministry.

After thus clearing the ground of false views, the article declares that the efficacy of the Word and sacraments is assured by their divine source. This is the chief point. Justifying faith arises because of divine action. The means of grace whereby faith is engendered are also part of the divine plan, and function as God's instruments. There is nothing doubtful or uncertain about them for that reason.

However imperfect may be the church on earth, or its ministry, the power of God is operative wherever the gospel of Christ is truly preached and the sacraments are observed in accordance with God's Word. Again the theocentric emphasis is observed. The Christian is encouraged to look away from the human factors involved, and to turn his gaze to God whose Word is sure and whose power is undeniable.

The article repudiates the views of the Donatists, a schismatic group of the fourth century in North Africa. They rejected the ministry of a bishop who had yielded to the pressure of the Roman authorities in the Diocletian persecution. The others, indicated by the words "such like," were likely the Anabaptists. Luther in his Confession of 1528 names the Donatists and Anabaptists as those who taught that the validity of the means of grace was affected by the character of the minister. Bornkamm thinks that Melanchthon took the thought from Luther's Confession.[4]

There is a certain sense in which the Romanists were included. They based the validity of the sacraments (except baptism and marriage) on the power received by a priest at his ordination when he was given the *character indelebilis*—the ineffaceable, specifically priestly nature. Sacraments administered by a priest therefore always had intrinsic worth when performed with proper intention.

The Lutheran view was different. The validity of the sacraments depends upon neither the moral nor the priestly character of the administrator. Their value is entirely in God's promise, his Word, the grace he bestows. Just as a paper dollar has the value of a dollar simply because of the promise of a government, and for no other reason, so the sacraments have worth because God has pledged his Word.

There is, of course, nothing in this article to imply that Lutherans are indifferent to the character of their ministers. Beyond all question, it is expected that they be men of fruitful faith. Incalculable injury is done Christian work when pastors fall from grace. Attention still needs to be given to ministerial ethics. Yet we must remember always that God's church and grace cannot fail. "The Word they still shall let remain."

---

[4] *Bek.*, 61, n. 1.

ARTICLE IX. OF BAPTISM

The preceding article made reference to the sacraments. The Confession continues by making a statement concerning each of the sacraments acknowledged by Lutherans. There was need for doing so, since Eck in his Theses had gathered quotations on each of the sacraments used by the Romanists.

Eck attributed to Luther and Melanchthon this statement: "Baptism neither justifies nor profits anyone, but it is only faith in the word of promise, to which baptism is added, that accomplishes this" (216). And soon thereafter he added the Anabaptist statement that "Infants are not to be baptized; but when those baptized have attained the use of reason, they are to be rebaptized" (227).

But it simply was not true that Lutherans disparaged the efficacy of baptism, or the propriety of its administration to infants. The Confession is satisfied to reply with a brief statement marked by moderation and restraint. It makes no effort to go beyond Scripture, and wisely avoids speculation on difficult questions.

In this article there is no attempt to define a sacrament, nor to argue the sacramental character of baptism, as the Marburg Articles had done. Nor is there a statement as to the authority and nature of baptism, as is the case in the Schwabach Articles. In the Augsburg Confession the nature of the sacraments is treated in Article XIII.

The attempt of Eck to classify Lutherans with Anabaptists induced Melanchthon at first to include in the article only an approval of infant baptism and a condemnation of the Anabaptists. In the final draft there is found the additional statement concerning the necessity and benefit of baptism.

The first point, therefore, is the necessity of baptism. The German version says that it is necessary, but the Latin adds the words "for salvation." In our Lord's teaching, faith and baptism have connected to them the assurance of salvation. This is what the Confession accepts, without attempting to explain how this connection can exist.

Among Lutherans it is customary to distinguish between what is absolutely necessary, and that which is ordinarily necessary. Baptism involves the necessity of the latter kind. It is not so absolutely necessary that a soul would be lost in case baptism is not obtainable. Nevertheless, the exceptions are in the sphere of God's mercy, and must not be imposed upon.

The necessity which the article recognizes rests upon the divine command, and is bound by it. For reasons that are only imperfectly understood, baptism was appointed by our Lord as a means of grace. The lack of an adequate theory on our part is no basis for rejecting a sacrament divinely instituted. We suffer serious loss when we reject Christ's word. "It is not the lack but the contempt of baptism that damns," is the famous phrase attributed to Augustine.[5]

Besides the necessity, the benefit of baptism is also declared in the article. Thereby "is offered the grace of God" and baptized children "are received into His grace." The Schwabach Articles described baptism as "a holy, living, efficacious thing," recalling Paul's words in Titus 3:5, "a washing of regeneration and a renewing of the Holy Ghost." And the Marburg Articles termed baptism "a sign and work of God."

It is evident that there are two aspects of the benefit of baptism here indicated. The proffered grace is a living, vital thing. It is a gift which transforms, regenerates, and produces the new birth. It so reworks the nature which one inherits from his parents that the result is a "new creature." As observed in Article II, those who reject the grace available in baptism suffer the damnation inevitable to all continuing in original sin.

The other aspect is a new relationship to God. To be "received into his grace" is to have a new standing in his sight. Sins are forgiven and mercy is granted. The covenant made in holy baptism is a continuing benefit throughout life. He who has been baptized has the perpetual assurance that God has accepted him into his family. His baptism has given him new credentials and a new kingdom of heaven passport.

The third point made by the article is the propriety of the baptism of children. The doctrine and practice of the Christian Church is inclusive so far as baptism is concerned. It is not a sacrament for males or for adults only. Nor is it to be so excessively individualized that no notice is taken of its social aspects. Baptism is a sacrament

---

[5] Cf. *De baptismo*, IV, 25. *NPNF* IV, 462.

of the church, and therefore involves fellowship and the divine society from which children are by no means to be excluded.

Moreover, it is affirmed that children thus offered in baptism by believing sponsors actually receive the benefit of the sacrament. The main point, as the Marburg Articles indicate, is that baptism "is not a mere empty sign or symbol among Christians, but a sign and work of God." The validity of baptism resides in the divine Word and the promise. Children, born with original sin, are in no less need of baptism than are adults.

The article concludes with a condemnation of the Anabaptist rejection of infant baptism. At the root of the Anabaptist view was the idea that baptism is essentially a human action, indicating the believer's submission to God. Since children were considered incapable of such action, and since the Bible does not specifically command the baptizing of children, the usage was rejected by the Anabaptists. Their views have been perpetuated by their historical successors—the Mennonites—and by the Baptists who are their indirect heirs.

This article makes it clear that Lutherans could not justly be charged with heresy at this point. It sets forth an ecumenical viewpoint concerning baptism. The fact is that the common ground with the Romanists on this doctrine was quite large. There were large areas of agreement concerning the mode, the benefits, the candidates, and the administrants of the sacrament. The article therefore was directed against the Anabaptists, though there may also be a reflection of disagreement with Zwingli.

Since this article follows that on justification by faith, it scarcely needs to be said that faith is presumed, even if it is not mentioned. Article XIII makes that clear. However, the difficulties involved in relating faith to the baptism of children are not mentioned. Such difficulties usually grow out of the assumption that baptism is primarily a human action. The marvel of God's work is overlooked.

ARTICLE X. OF THE LORD'S SUPPER

The Theses which Eck collected concerning the Lord's Supper were mostly quotations from Zwingli and others who taught a purely symbolical interpretation of the Eucharist. Melanchthon was quoted as denouncing transubstantiation, and Luther was cited as rejecting the adoration of the consecrated host and the Corpus Christi procession. Lutheran rejection of usages connected with the Eucharist were mentioned also.

This article in the Confession passes by all incidental matters and concerns itself simply with the central point in the doctrine. The statement is brief and concise in contrast to the extended treatment in the other symbolical writings. This doctrine has been the subject of much discussion and considerable controversy especially between Lutherans and the Reformed whether represented by Zwingli or by Calvin. The relation of this doctrine to that of Christ is treated in the Formula of Concord.

The one point made by this article is that the Body and Blood of Christ are actually present in the sacrament. There is no doubt but that when Christ is present, he is here according to his divine nature, for he is the divine Son of God. But it was not always clear that the union of his two natures was such that where Christ is, there both natures, the human as well as the divine, are actually present. Therefore the article, desiring to avoid a defective doctrine, affirms the presence of "the Body and Blood of Christ."

In view of the doctrines being taught by others in the Reformation movement, it must be noted that the article affirms the reality of Christ's bodily presence in the Eucharist. As the Schwabach Articles said of the sacrament, "It is not only bread and wine." It is more than a reminder of Christ or a rite which exercises spiritual influences. It is a divinely established sacrament in which Christ presents his Body and Blood in some real though indefinable way. There has long been in the church the devout and reverent conviction that the Eucharist was the sublime moment of Christ's communication of his broken Body and his shed Blood.

Moreover, the sacrament is for use. The reality of Christ's bodily presence is not a miracle transpiring on the altar for the adoration of the faithful. As a sacrament it is complete only when received and consumed by the individual communicant. The details of sacramental use are described in the Formula of Concord. This article of the Confession is satisfied to observe that the real presence is communicated to the recipient. Those who receive the sacrament receive the Body and Blood of Christ. For the article speaks of "those who eat."

Other Lutheran writings must be consulted to find an explanation of the real presence. This article simply states the fact. The catechisms speak of the real presence "in" and "under" the elements. At other places only the preposition "in" or "with" is used. But in the last analysis the real presence is inexplicable. It is not an impanation—the inclusion of the Body of Christ locally in the bread. Nor is it consubstantiation, as has been alleged of Lutherans, meaning that Body and bread are mixed to constitute a third substance. It is a sacramental union, as unique as it is incomprehensible.

The article does not explicitly reject transubstantiation; hence the Romanists read their interpretation into it. They would seem to be encouraged in this by the wording of the German text which says "that the true Body and Blood of Christ is truly present in the Lord's Supper under the form of bread and wine." But the language of the Schwabach and the Marburg Articles was such as to exclude transubstantiation. And both Luther and Melanchthon can be quoted as rejecting this "sophistical subtlety." This article is interested in affirming the fact of the real presence, rather than in combating a false theory of it. It stands opposed to those who denied the real presence, rather than to those who misinterpreted it. "Those that teach otherwise" were, therefore, Zwingli and others who taught a purely symbolical interpretation of the Lord's Supper. The Confession rejects the rationalistic doctrine of Zwingli, without accepting the superstitious teaching of Rome.

The article must be seen, therefore, in its historical setting. It is of itself not a complete or adequate statement of Lutheran teaching on the Lord's Supper. It was designed to show that Lutherans did not depart from doctrine widely held in the ancient church to the effect that the Body and Blood of Christ are sacramentally conveyed to the communicant. If the article refrains from attacking transubstantiation, it is necessary only to remember the conditions of the diet, and Melanchthon's effort to avoid trouble.

On the other hand, there was the desire of the Lutherans to escape from being identified with the Zwinglians, whose views were well known. In fact, about two weeks after the public reading of the Augsburg Confession, the printed *Reckoning of the Faith of Ulric Zwingli to the Roman Emperor Charles* reached Augsburg. In it Zwingli said, "I believe that in the Holy Eucharist—i.e., the supper of thanksgiving—the true body of Christ is present by the contemplation of faith. . . . But that the body of Christ in essence and really . . . is present . . . we not only deny, but firmly maintain is an error opposed to God's Word." [6]

The question of both kinds in the sacrament is not mentioned in this article, though discussed in the comparable Marburg Article. Instead, in the Confession, it is reserved for separate treatment in Article XXII among the articles on abuses. Other abuses are listed in Article XXIV where the question of the sacrifice of the mass is discussed also.

This is the article which suffered alteration in the *Variata*. In that edition were omitted the words "truly present" and the phrase disapproving others. The changed article reads, "Concerning the Supper of the Lord they teach that with bread and wine are truly administered the Body and Blood of Christ to those eating in the Supper of the Lord." By these changes Melanchthon presented a statement which those of Calvinistic tendencies could approve, and which therefore aroused the suspicion of both Romanists and Lutherans.

ARTICLE XI. OF CONFESSION

At the beginning of his Four Hundred Four Theses, Eck had placed for the emperor's attention the Forty-one Propositions of the Bull of Leo X against Luther. In the eighth of these Luther is quoted as saying, "Presume in no way to confess venial, or even mortal sins, because it is impossible to know all mortal sins; hence in the primitive church only manifest mortal sins were confessed."

The Romanists were sensitive on this subject. The question about the power and efficacy of indulgences raised in the Ninety-five Theses quite naturally led to an examination of the whole Roman sacrament of penance. In the Romanist doctrine penance consists of contrition, confession, absolution, and satisfaction. The entire sacrament is intended for those in mortal sin who therefore are excluded from

---

[6] *Book of Concord* (Jacobs), II, 200; from Niemeyer, *Collectio Confessionum.*

communion. This relation between confession and the Eucharist quite naturally suggests the same connection in the Augsburg Confession.

There is also the suggestion that confession is a third sacrament. There is such a statement in the Apology, and the matter will be discussed there. But the Reformers were so intent upon the gospel doctrine of God's grace freely given to men that absolution pronounced in connection with confession seemed to be a special instance of that grace.

This article first asserts that private absolution should be retained in Lutheran congregations. It would seem that the Romanist accusations at Augsburg made such an assertion necessary. Neither the Schwabach nor the Marburg Articles made such a statement. They gave their attention instead to the insistence that confession must not be compulsory. But to have discarded it entirely would have been considered a heresy by the Romanists; therefore the statement was made.

However, Lutheran interest was not so much in the acknowledging of sins as in the declaring of God's grace. The Roman usage had directed attention in a legalistic way to sins and offenses against regulations; gospel doctrine focused attention upon the mercy of God to be accepted by faith. Therefore the article declares that it is absolution which is to be retained. The Schwabach Articles spoke of absolution as "God's Word and judgment." The Marburg Articles went further and interpreted confession as "the seeking of counsel from one's pastor or neighbor." In this sense, absolution is not merely a pastoral function, but is any Christian announcement of God's forgiveness for Christ's sake.

Since the article has espoused the retention of private absolution in Lutheran usage, it was quite natural that it should reduce the importance of confessing all sins. Such complete enumeration of sins is not necessary. The naming of specific sins must be left to the option of the individual. Freedom in this matter is implied in this article, though stated explicitly elsewhere.

The article sought to clinch the point by declaring that such enumeration is not even possible. Christians cannot fairly be required to do what is impossible for them. The injustice of compulsory naming of all sins was deeply resented in evangelical circles. But more important than the injustice was the distortion of basic emphasis. The papists directed the Christian's thought to the laws of the church, to his own sins, and therefore to himself. The Evangelicals turned the gaze of the Christian to Christ and the cross. It was for this reason that Luther once gave the startling advice to go to communion sometime without making confession.

The brief statement in this article makes no mention of the advantages of private absolution. They are indicated in the Marburg Articles by the word "consolation" and in the Schwabach Articles by the declaration that "the conscience is freed from sorrow, and pacified." Luther knew all too well from personal experience that the Romanist practice did not bring peace of conscience, but left the penitent in doubt. Article XXV of the Confession treats more fully of this subject.

Nor is there any mention of those rejected by Lutherans. They doubtless were the papists, but it was not advisable to say so at Augsburg. In the Roman Catholic Church auricular confession had received doctrinal support in the teachings of Peter Lombard in the twelfth century. It was made mandatory by the Fourth Lateran Council in the thirteenth century. It had been connected with many abuses in the centuries following. It took a doctrinal reconstruction directed by evangelical insights to demolish the tyrannical system entirely.

ARTICLE XII. OF REPENTANCE

If the Augsburg Confession had been written in the interest of systematic theology the discussion of repentance might have preceded that of the sacraments, just as law precedes gospel. But here systematic interests are incidental to confessional demands. Lutheran doctrine gave special attention to salvation; it is interpreted in terms of justification by faith; and faith is aroused through the church by means of the Word and the sacraments.

Absolution is a special application of the Word of God. But since in the Roman Catholic Church absolution had been distorted into a pseudo sacrament of penance, and with it had developed a mistaken doctrine of repentance, the Confession adds an article on that subject. Nothing of the kind occurs in the Marburg or Schwabach Articles

But at Augsburg Eck had stirred up the fire with his Theses. In the fifth thesis he quoted Luther as saying, "There is no foundation in Holy Scripture or in the ancient Christian teachers for the doctrine that there are three parts of penitence, viz., contrition, confession, and satisfaction." Luther had denied that our Lord's word, "Repent ye!" meant to do penance according to the Romanist doctrine (42). Moreover, Luther and Melanchthon were credited with saying that "It is false and dangerous to think that penance is 'the second raft after shipwreck' " (261).

The article first of all sounds an ecumenical note for the ear of the emperor. It agrees with the Catholic Church that Christians who sin grievously may receive forgiveness when they repent. As noted in connection with the phrase, "the forgiveness of sins," in the Apostles' Creed, there had been a struggle at one time in Rome over the question of a "second forgiveness." Against the rigorist party the church had decided that those sinning mortally after baptism might under proper conditions receive pardon. The article therefore insists that the church ought to impart absolution to penitents.

With this favorable opening, the article proceeds to define repentance as understood evangelically. There are two aspects, and close by is a third.

The first aspect is contrition. It is a profound sense of sin. The distress of it is so keen that the article pictures it sharply as "terrors smiting the conscience." The law has done its work of conveying a "knowledge of sin." The papists also talked of contrition, and sometimes meant by it a thorough sorrow for sin. But in practice it had been denatured into a mild regret for having violated church rules. It was concerned with sins, rather than about sin.

In the strictest and narrowest sense, repentance is contrition, a conscientious distress over sin. But in a broader sense, the second aspect must be included, viz., faith. Evangelical doctrine must give prominence to the gospel. The turning away from sin must be matched by a turning to Christ. The terrors of conscience must be relieved by the consolation of God's grace. Absolution is the announcement that for Christ's sake sins are forgiven.

It is faith, therefore, which is the chief feature of the repentant life. This was something the Romanist doctrine entirely omitted. It had a defective conception of contrition and had no place for faith at all. Instead, having begun with a legalistic definition of contrition, it added legalistic details of confession and satisfaction. It never got out of the groove of the law. Evangelical doctrine, however, escaped from this confinement by grasping the gospel principle of faith.

For those who want to see the picture in its totality, the article adds the good works growing out of faith. In its widest sense, therefore, repentance includes works also. The article is merely repeating in this connection what had already been stated in Article VI. The vital connection between faith and the new obedience shows itself once more. Repentance is thus defined, not in terms of what the penitent leaves behind, but in terms of what he can expect now and in the future.

There are three points of view to which the doctrine of this article is antithetical. First is that of the perfectionists. Such were the Anabaptists who believed that the gift of the Holy Ghost could not be lost. The German version of the article does not name the Anabaptists but is content to speak of those who taught that a Christian can arrive at the stage where he is able to keep from sinning. It is likely that Denk and Schwenkfeld were in mind. There was a certain kind of perfectionism even in the monastic orders of the papacy. A further rejection of perfectionism will be found in the Smalcald Articles, Part III, Article III, and in the Formula of Concord, Chapter IV.

The second rejected viewpoint is that of the strict disciplinarians who allow no restoration to those fallen after baptism. It grows out of a legal conception of Christianity. It sees church discipline as a judicial and penal rather than a reforming thing. And it draws a false distinction between mortal and venial sins. It was the doctrine, as the article states, of the Novatians, a severe, schismatic group of the third century at Rome.

Tucked in at the end was the third rejected viewpoint, whose advocates were not named, but who certainly were the Romanists themselves. In their thinking, remission of sins was secured by works of merit. It was earned by pilgrimages, fasts, and so forth. But all this substituted human actions for the work of Christ. It had no place for faith, in spite of the fact that faith is the only means for receiving remission.

ARTICLE XIII. OF THE USE OF THE SACRAMENTS

To the articles discussing the means of grace Melanchthon added one more. There had been nothing of the kind in the Marburg Articles. The Schwabach Articles merely named baptism and the Eucharist as sacraments by which faith and the Holy Ghost are given. But on the doctrine of the Eucharist Eck had mingled these from Zwingli and Luther. Aroused to vehemence by the Romanist adoration of the host, Zwingli had said, "I do not know whether it was a greater abomination to worship the golden calf in Dan, or that bread" (240). And against the papists Luther had said, "They lie who say that the mass of a wicked priest is useful *ex opere operato*" (272).

Luther agreed with Zwingli in denouncing the adoration of the host, but he disagreed with him significantly in other respects on the doctrine of the sacraments. The symbolic interpretation given by Zwingli was well known at Augsburg. A statement therefore was necessary in the Confession.

The article at the outset indicates the incompleteness of the Zwinglian view. It cannot be denied that the sacraments are "marks of profession among men," but they are more. They are the characteristic rites of Christians in contrast to non-Christians, but they are more than ceremonies. They are actions performed by Christian persons as an evidence of their church affiliation, but that is not all there is to them. To stop there is to fail to realize that the sacraments contain more than reason and sense perceive.

Added to Zwingli's fragmentary doctrine is the fact that God is active in the sacraments. Their chief significance is that they are "signs and testimonies of the will of God toward us." Though they are a part of human worship, being administered by men and received by men, they are nevertheless a divine agency; for they were "instituted to awaken and confirm faith in those who use them." Through them God is functioning in human lives. What man does in the use of the sacraments pales into insignificance in comparison with the great benefit which God bestows.

In this article Melanchthon was not forgetting the evangelical principles underlying his theology. The gospel is always the good news of God's gift—and the sacraments are gifts. Moreover, the only way that the gift can be received is by faith. This is true also of the sacraments. Just as only those will accept and use a dollar bill who believe the promise of the government printed thereon, so the benefits of the sacraments accrue only to those who trust the promises of God.

The place of faith must not be so overemphasized that it becomes central and the gift of God is pushed into the background. The reality of God's grace must be kept well in focus. The objectivity of the sacraments as divinely established channels of mercy needs to be kept in the foreground. Faith does not make the sacraments, nor establish their validity; it simply receives them.

This much of the article was presented at Augsburg, and was accepted with qualifications by the Romanists. But when the Confession was published, the *editio princeps* contained an additional sentence. It made bold to condemn those who taught that the sacraments convey their benefits *ex opere operato*—"by the outward act," making faith unnecessary. Quite clearly the Romanists were indicated. For in Romanist doctrine a sacrament was an *opus operatum*—a work which produced results by power inherent in it, like medicine acting on the body. It functioned of itself.

But such a doctrine was both superstitious and unevangelical. It crowded out faith. It was vigorously opposed by the Lutherans, as will be seen in Melanchthon's discussion in the Apology. It was thoroughly in keeping with the legalism of the papists, and therefore appropriately condemned in this article.

Chapter VI

ARTICLES XIV-XXI OF THE
AUGSBURG CONFESSION

The dominant theme in the Augsburg Confession is that of Christ and his salvation. This soteriological interest has resulted in a larger number of articles dealing with the saving faith than is the case in the ecumenical creeds. Articles IV to XIII treat of faith and how it is either aroused or strengthened.

In the articles which follow, the Confession defines the implications of justifying faith for church order, public worship, life in society, and the end of the world. These are the topics of Articles XIV to XVII. The last four doctrinal articles, XVIII to XXI, are supplementary to others occurring earlier in the Confession.

ARTICLE XIV. OF ECCLESIASTICAL ORDER

This is the briefest article in the Confession. In Latin it consists of but seventeen words. Neither the Marburg nor the Schwabach Articles have any statement of this kind. But because Lutherans refused to consider ordination a sacrament, Eck wanted the emperor to believe that they rejected ordination itself. He quoted Luther as saying, "The Church of Christ ignores the sacrament of ordination" (268). And he attributed to both Luther and Zwingli the statement that "As many of us as have been baptized are all equally priests; and any layman can consecrate churches, confirm children," etc. (269).

The purpose of the article quite evidently is to advocate good order in the church. The radical elements in the Reformation movement by their disorder had brought discredit upon themselves and suspicion upon others. As might be expected, the emperor would have special interest in this matter. Disorders in the church were also public disorders, and came within his jurisdiction. The violence of some Anabaptists was well known, and Eck wanted Charles to believe that Lutherans were of the same lawless kind.

Orderliness in church administration was a genuine interest of the Lutherans. As stated in the Apology and the Smalcald Articles, they were even willing to accept the rule of bishops under certain conditions. Nothing was to be gained by unregulated public worship and mob rule.

The article therefore declares that all those who teach the Word and administer the sacraments in the worship of the church must be "regularly called." The call (*vocatio*), as a divine summons to a task, was not limited to the ministry in the church, as was noted in connection with Article V. The fact of the call was for Luther a consolation in the midst of temptation. He once said, "The *vocatio* causes the devil much pain." [1] For it is a divine authorization, producing good order, whereas the devil loves self-assertive pride and disorder.

The regularity of the call consists in proper church usage. The call of God is recognized in the church by ordination. The ministry of a man is legitimate when his summons to a task and his ability to perform it are certified by the ceremony of ordination. He has by no means set himself up in the office. He has not forced his leadership upon a congregation. He is a minister not only in the church, but also of the church.

Neither Article V in its Latin form nor this article states specifically the agency of God in providing a ministry, but the inference is not to be denied, and the German form of Article V does say so. Contrary to the Romanist point of view which centered attention on human works and therefore considered ordination a work of merit, the evangelical viewpoint was theocentric.: It was God who established the ministry and authorized its perpetuation by the church.

Lutherans, in the course of their history in America, have had at times a controversial interest in the question of the outward call to the ministry. The former Buffalo Synod under Grabau advocated a

---

[1] W.A., *Tischreden*, I, 90. Quoted in *Bek.*, p. 66, n. 3.

teaching that virtually made the ministry self-perpetuating. Other synods have had other views, but agree in general that the authority to perpetuate the ministry resides in the church, rather than in the clergy alone. This topic receives further treatment in the Tractatus appended to the Smalcald Articles.

A complete discussion of the ministry goes beyond the theme of this article, and must be left to dogmatics. It will suffice here to observe that the intent of the article was to espouse good order in the ministerial office. By inference it rejects the views of those who remove the work of the ministry from church control and who leave to each individual the decision as to whether or not God has called him. For such persons ordination loses its importance.

ARTICLE XV. OF RITES AND USAGES

The public worship of the church requires not only a ministry but also common usages. In the course of history rites and ceremonies are continued which have proven their worth or which have been enforced in the church. To discard any of them may have the appearance of radicalism.

It was true that in the Reformation in Switzerland Zwingli had discarded much traditional church usage. Eck could justly quote him as saying, "Nothing is to be received except what is expressly taught in Holy Scripture" (377). Zwingli and others had declared that "Unctions, tonsures, ceremonial vestments, benedictions of water, salt, palms, candles, herbs, consecrations of churches, altars, vases, men, and so forth, are human inventions" (322). To Melanchthon was attributed the statement that "Church ceremonies always obscure liberty and the force of the Gospel; hence it is profitable to disregard them" (321). To Luther, Zwingli, and others was ascribed the view that "We are, therefore, under no obligation to celebrate the festivals of the saints, to fast in Lent and on other days, to abstain from flesh on six festival days, or to obey other human precepts" (363).

This article in its Latin form speaks of rites and usages implying their human origin; the German version makes it explicit. The question at issue, therefore, has nothing to do with divinely instituted rites, but simply with those which had arisen by human design during the history of the church. It is a question of good order in the public worship of the church just as the previous article dealt with good order in the ministry.

With this in mind the article first proposes a positive principle. Under conditions which safeguard the gospel, customary rites and usages should be ("ought to be") observed. Nothing but disorder is to be gained by sweeping out of the church all that Christian experience and devotion have developed. The attitude of "primitivism" which would strip the church of everything not found in the New Testament would keep the church perpetually in an infantile state. Instead of this, Lutherans gladly recognized as devotionally profitable much that was historic and customary. This article sets up a principle of conservatism in declaring that such usages ought to be retained in the church.

But not everything in the pre-Reformation church was to be retained. The article proposes some principles to guide in the selection of what is to be retained and what is to be discarded. First of all, it must be quite clear that usages which involve Christians in sin are to be removed at once. Some of these are discussed later in the Confession. For example, Lutherans could not believe that they could pray to the saints and the Virgin Mary without violating the commandment to worship God only. A little later this same Article XV names some other aspects of papist practice which disqualify rites and ceremonies.

In the second place, the principle of good order must guide the selection. There are no conceivable circumstances in which disorder is advisable. That Christians may unite in common worship at common times, it is important that specific days and hours be appointed. The events of the life of our Lord are worthy of commemoration by special days of celebration. "Holydays, festivals, and the like," by contributing to the tranquillity and unanimity of the church, are most certainly desirable. Much is gained by preserving the ecclesiastical calendar.

But there are two cautions to be observed. The first of these warns against making rites a condition of salvation. They are not to be required or demanded. In the light of the gospel, justification comes only by faith. Ceremonial observances in no way provide us with merit before God. Therefore they cannot be made mandatory in the church.

Stated in a positive way, this principle is one of freedom. Rites and ceremonies are adiaphora. They may be left to the free choice of the people. It was this principle of liberty which was the central theme of the comparable articles in the Marburg and Schwabach Articles.

The second caution is related to the first and logically ought to come first. It declares that rites and ceremonies are not meritorious. They earn neither God's favor, his gifts, nor his pardon. The doctrine of the gospel is quite the opposite of such Romanist doctrine. Whatever value there may be in vows, fasts, holy days, and such things, they can never be justly considered works of merit in God's sight.

At the time of the Reformation the Roman Catholic Church was overburdened with a multitude of holy days. In weariness of it all Luther once said, "Would to God that in Christendom there were no festivals other than Sunday."[2] But the "Instruction of Visitors" of 1528 authorized the retention of the festivals of the Annunciation, Purification, Visitation, John the Baptist, Michael, the Apostles, Magdalene, Christmas, Circumcision, Epiphany, Easter, Ascension, and Pentecost. All this was in keeping with the Lutheran conservatism and appreciation of what was historic.

The obligation to preserve from the past what is evangelically useful, as taught in this article, accounts for the liturgical character of Lutheran worship. It is for this reason that Lutheran and Roman Catholic worship have much in common. In fact, Lutherans had no desire for schism, but for a reform in the church of which they considered themselves a part.

But though Lutherans and Roman Catholics use many ceremonies that are virtually identical in both churches, the purpose and spirit of each is quite distinct. In Romanism everything is discolored with ideas of merit and obligation. Among Lutherans there is instead the freedom of the gospel and its assurance of God's grace.

ARTICLE XVI. OF CIVIL AFFAIRS

If there was one article which would be expected to interest Charles V especially, this would be it. The memory of the Peasants'

[2] W.A., VI, 243. Quoted in *Bek.*, p. 42, n. 7.

War and other civil disorders was certain to arouse an attitude prejudiced against those who would question the established order.

Eck was alert to this possibility. To arouse the emperor's indignation he gathered a considerable list of extreme statements. Only a few can be repeated here. He quoted Luther thus: "We Christians are free, exempt from all the laws of men, liberated through baptism" (334). "The emperor and the princes deal in manifest falsehoods and publish contradictory commandments" (337). "Ever since the beginning of the world, a wise prince has been a most rare bird; for generally they are either the greatest fools or the very worst rascals" (346).

Besides these generalities, there were specific items of accusation. Concerning an oath in court, Melanchthon is quoted: "We must not swear for temporal things; for he who requires an oath of another, or himself swears, must be of a malicious and trifling mind not regarding the truth" (385). Eck followed this with an Anabaptist statement: "It is not allowable for a Christian for any cause to take an oath" (386). Luther said, "All are heathen who contend in court for property or reputation" (387). "If anything be taken from us we ought not to demand it back in court or by war" (388).

As a parting shot in Thesis 403 Eck quoted Luther as saying: "It is proper and in accord with God's Word to excite seditions and tumults; hence there is no better proof that my doctrine is of God than that it excites discords, seditions, and tumults." In the paragraphs following the Theses, Eck accused Luther's doctrines of "disturbing the public peace."

This article of the Confession promptly declares that evangelical doctrine sustains rather than disrupts the social order. Chief attention is given to the participation of the Christian in the affairs and benefits of government. As a document presented to the emperor, this was to be expected. Tied in with legal matters was the holding of property —an economic matter. Besides government, the family is also a part of the social order, and the article gives its warm approval to marriage also.

With regard to the governmental sphere of society, the article expresses faith in the divine approval of civil order. It refrains from saying that Charles ruled by divine right. Luther and those associated with him had been compelled by the events of their day to think this matter over very carefully. Among Luther's writings, his "Of Civil Authority," [3] his discussion "Whether Soldiers Too Can Be Saved," [4] and his publications related to the Peasants' War are well known. It is to be expected that the political theory underlying the Lutheran literature was medieval rather than modern.

The source of authority in government, therefore, is from above. The article declares that "lawful civil ordinances are good works of God." The Schwabach Articles had the statement that "we should honor worldly magistrates and rulers, and be obedient to them, as an estate ordained by God." In connection with Article V attention was called to Luther's Confession of 1528 in which he said that civil authority is one of the three "holy orders and true institutions established by God." [5]

Since civil authority has this divine sanction, it is entirely appropriate that Christians participate in its functions. The regulations of government must be administered by those in public office. Those accused of offenses against the laws must be given a fair hearing, and, if guilty, be compelled to suffer the penalty, even execution. The courts are one form of public redress available to those who suffer injury. The other form of public redress is a just war, in which there is the obligation to serve as soldiers. Moreover, civil government offers certain safeguards to the individual. It protects his dealings by legal contracts, his wealth by legal title, and his veracity by legal oath.

It might seem that marriage is also a provision of civil government, since it is governed by laws. But since the article a little further on mentions the state and the family, there is good reason for thinking of marriage as another estate in an individual's life in society. To use the two categories of state and family is in keeping with Luther's Confession of 1528.[6] Since marriage is a "holy estate ordained of God" it deserves "to be held in honor by all." It is within the sphere of a Christian's right. Indeed, the church has the duty of preserving the state and the family as "ordinances of God."

---

[3] W.A., XI, 245 ff. Phila. ed., III, 228 ff.
[4] W.A., XIX, 623 ff. Phila. ed., V, 32 ff.
[5] W.A., XXVI, 504.
[6] W A., XXVI, 504.

The article condemns the Anabaptists on the one side, and the papists on the other, though the latter are not identified by name. Both extremes had this in common, that they thought a man could not be a true Christian while continuing in the ordinary affairs of life. Both Anabaptists and monks felt that they could be genuinely holy only if they turned their backs on civil government and marriage. Both considered public office and the sex life of marriage as somewhat tainted, perhaps even a thing of the devil.

However, they are guilty of two mistakes. In the first place, they despise as something evil that which God has established. What God has made must be good. In the second place, they misunderstand the gospel. They think that righteousness consists in human deeds rather than "in the fear of God and in faith." This is a much more serious mistake, and in making this error the Anabaptists show themselves to be legalists. That is, they show themselves to be trusting in works, just as the papists do.

When the gospel is rightly understood it does not take us out of the social order but enables us to live the life of faith in it. Marriage is blessed and the home sanctified. Civil order is preserved and the public good is protected. There is only one ground for civil disobedience, and that is found when governmental laws command what is sinful. Then a conscience bound to God must obey him rather than the state.

In recent years this article has been the topic of much discussion. The relation of a Christian to his government, especially if it is totalitarian, has been a subject that has caused much deep and anguished thought. Christian thought on the problem of war, particularly modern total war, has also been disquieting.

The statements made in this article concerning the functions of government are in keeping with the views of Luther expressed in his writing, "Of Civil Authority." [7] He there indicated the limits of the authority of the state. It has jurisdiction over the external aspects of life affecting body and property. It has no jurisdiction over soul and conscience. But within its sphere it should be obeyed, as taught in Romans 13:1, 2 and I Peter 2:13, 14.

---

[7] W.A., XI, 245 ff. Phila. ed., III, 228 ff.

It has been charged that such obedience plays directly into the hands of dictators. The article seems to presume a benevolent monarch, but Luther was correct in saying that such a ruler is rare. Unquestioning obedience seems to be a thoroughly reactionary and foolish thing. If it is said that the article authorizes obedience only for "lawful ordinances," "just punishments," "just wars," and "save only when commanded to sin," the qualifications may be shown to be inadequate. For every government asserts that its acts and policies are lawful and just. The individual Christian rarely is in a position to have all the facts. And when his nation is at war, his judgment is biased. The brutal fact is that the Christian citizen must conform to laws which provide at best only a rough justice. He must support wars which are simply the lesser of two evils.

Even the phrase "just wars" in this article does not glorify or bless war. The Apology calls war a calamity. In the discussion of the fifth petition of the Lord's Prayer in the Large Catechism, Luther calls war and bloodshed a calamity. And he adds that it is the devil who "causes so much confusion, murder, sedition, and war."

However, the whole question which this article faces is not one that is primarily political. Instead, it is essentially religious. Lutherans were defending themselves against heresy rather than treason. They were professing what "our churches teach." They were answering the question, "Is the perfection of the gospel to be found in forsaking civil offices?"

The answer they gave was that Christian faith will exhibit itself in good works, and that among these good works is participation in civic affairs, including even the bitter necessity of engaging in war. Christians must support good order in the state, for they are not anarchists. They have both an interest in and a duty to peaceful conditions. It is a mistake to think that the presence of sin in society excuses us from our duty.

ARTICLE XVII. OF CHRIST'S RETURN FOR JUDGMENT

A common characteristic of sects is their abnormal interest in eschatology. Usually they have distorted and erroneous interpretations of the second coming of Christ. Fanaticism of this sort appeared in the Reformation age, and the Romanists blamed it on the Lutheran movement. Though Eck cited no quotation from Lutherans on the doctrine of the last things, he did quote John Denk as saying, "Wicked spirits will hereafter be saved together with the damned" (394).

This article, therefore, professes simply the ecumenical faith concerning the second coming. At the end of the world, the judicial Christ will appear. There will be a resurrection of the dead. The godly will receive eternal life, the ungodly eternal punishment. All this in the article was part of the ancient creeds. It is also the viewpoint of the Schwabach Articles.

The influence of evangelical doctrine is seen in the terms used to state this doctrine. The criterion of judgment is that of faith. Those who receive eternal life are identified in the Latin version as "the godly and elect." But the German version speaks of them as "the believers (or faithful—*Glaubigen*) and elect." Both versions agree in calling those condemned the "ungodly." But the Schwabach Articles referred to them as "unbelievers." That they are "elect" recalls the fact that the source of their salvation and their faith is God. It is in no sense the product of their own activity.

In view of Ecks quotation from Denk, the article condemns the universalist doctrine of the Anabaptists. In the manuscript showing the form which the Confession had at the end of May, 1530, when a copy was sent to Nürnberg, the followers of Origen were included with the Anabaptists in the category of universalists. The consensus of Christian doctrine has been that the Scriptures teach an eternity of punishment as well as of bliss.

The article condemns also those who advocate chiliastic views identified as "Jewish." As Plitt has observed, the Anabaptists thought of themselves as the true kingdom of God, but suffering oppression.[8] The more militant of them were convinced that it was their duty to take up arms and overthrow the oppressors. Others looked for God to do it. They believed that the Jews were still God's chosen people who would soon be converted. Then God would re-establish the kingdom at Jerusalem. Both Luther and Melanchthon heard rumors that some Anabaptists were making preparations for going to Palestine as soon as the expected Messiah or *Führer* appeared.

Such a gross and materialistic interpretation of the kingdom of

---

[8] *Op. cit.*, II, 420 f.

God could not be tolerated. The Confession was so worded as to clear the Lutherans of such a fanatical opinion. Their understanding of the gospel was sufficiently clear that they would not confuse the kingdom of God with temporal power. There was no sense in which the ultimate victory of Christ would be a kind of Zionism. The righteousness of faith is not to triumph by force of arms.

This article declares that in Lutheran congregations the ancient faith of the church concerning the last things was taught. The statement which Luther made in his Confession of 1528 is almost identical with that made in this article.[9] It shows an unwillingness to speculate about what is not in the experience of the church, or about which there has been no clear revelation. Whatever else there is to say about the doctrine of last things may be left to dogmatics. The history of Lutheran doctrine on this theme lies beyond the purpose of this article.

ARTICLE XVIII. OF FREE WILL

Apparently it had been intended at first that the doctrinal articles of the Confession would be complete with Article XVII. Neither the Marburg nor Schwabach Articles go beyond that. But in the course of the preparation of the Confession it seemed to be necessary to supplement the articles already written with four additional doctrinal ones.

It may be that Article XVIII was prepared in answer to Eck's Thesis 332, ascribed to Luther and others. The thesis reads: "It is under the tutelage of Satan that the term 'free will' has entered, and that, with the purpose of seducing men from the way of right; for it is a mere figment, since the will contributes nothing towards its own willing, and that it has any activity in good works is erroneous."

It must be observed at the outset that the article places limits to its problem. The possession of free will by man may be investigated either in his state before the fall, or after the fall and before regeneration, or after regeneration. There may be a study of human nature as created, or as born, or as reborn. This article is concerned only with the second state. It inquires about free will in unregenerate mankind, born according to nature and possessing original sin. The

---

[9] *W.A.*, XXVI, 509.

state of innocence before the fall, and the state of grace after regeneration, are excluded from consideration.

Within these limits mankind has a certain liberty of action in external and civil affairs, as distinguished from spiritual matters. In the world in which he lives, a man can choose to obey or disobey the laws. He can make choices in national loyalties, in business, and in the management of his own affairs; and his choices can be good. He may even choose to go to church and hear the Word.

He can attack problems and arrive at solutions by the use of logic. He can determine upon a wise course of procedure by purely rational methods. He is not an instinct-driven animal, but has capacities for reflection that distinguish him from the brutes. The fall may have brutalized him, but it did not make him a brute. However, it must be acknowledged that his choices are often illegal, selfish, or evil.

The article recognizes in the spiritual sphere of man's life the entire absence of ability to choose the good. Unregenerate human nature has no power to perform the righteousness of God. Without the agency of the Holy Spirit, man by nature has no free will whereby he can choose to love and fear God and put his choice into action. There is only the bondage of the will to choose evil and that continually.

As scriptural evidence for this doctrine the article quotes I Corinthians 2:14, "But the natural man receiveth not the things of the Spirit of God; for they are foolishness unto him; neither can he know them, because they are spiritually discerned." It is more than a case of spiritual ignorance; it is a case of spiritual inability.

Free will in spiritual matters, in the sense of being able to possess the righteousness of faith, arises only by the activity of the Holy Spirit. When he works in a man's life through the means of grace, there results in that man the capacity to choose and direct his life in the way of God. This is exactly what the Confession has been saying in Articles IV and V.

In addition to the scriptural quotation, the article presents one from patristic sources. Melanchthon used a writing attributed to Augustine, but which is now known to have been written by a pseudo-Augustine.[10] The quotation merely repeats the theme of

---

[10] *Hypomnesticon contra Pelagianos et Coelestinianos,* MSL XLIV, 1623. Cited in *Bek.,* p. 71, n. 2.

this article in acknowledging a certain freedom in external affairs and a bondage in spiritual matters.

In the *editio princeps* Melanchthon added a section rejecting certain other doctrines. Since Pelagianism stood condemned as a heresy in the history of the church, the Lutherans could present an acceptable position before the emperor by joining in the condemnation. But their attitude was more than a posture. The Pelagian doctrine that human nature, by powers inherent at birth, has free will to love God is utterly at variance with evangelical doctrine. Gospel teaching of faith alone and grace alone left no place for the righteousness of human works performed by the unregenerate. Lutherans were doing more than joining in the common clamor against Pelagius; they condemned his doctrine with a vehemence born of earnest conviction.

The "others" mentioned in the article were certainly the Romanists, though they did not recognize themselves. They officially condemned Pelagius, but their condemnation was a mere front, concealing the fact that they had absorbed much of his doctrine. They had largely reduced the Christian religion to a performance of external rites and usages which even unregenerate mankind could do. They even assumed that such human nature was able to do something in the way of "the substance of the act"—the disposition to love God. But their Semi-Pelagianism was offensive to gospel doctrine as the Lutherans professed it.

This article makes no attempt at solving the philosophical problem of the freedom of the will. Zwingli and Calvin both looked at the doctrines of God and of man with somewhat philosophical eyes. There are still sufficient problems of this sort to engage the philosophical activities of thinking minds. This article, however, is interested in the religious implications. It gives a definition of free will in a theological sense. Remembering that fact will save confusion and pointless discussion.

ARTICLE XIX. OF THE CAUSE OF SIN

There was a further aspect of this denial of free will in spiritual matters. If man has no free will, who is responsible for the rise of sin? Eck's Thesis Eighty-six was a quotation from Melanchthon: "The opinion is certain that all things are done by God, both good and evil, not only permissively but properly, as the adultery of David, etc. Accordingly the betrayal of Judas no less than the call of Paul is His proper work," (and Eck added) "i.e., God wills sins." These were phrases which Eck had gathered from Melanchthon's *Annotations on Romans*.[11] The problem arises in connection with Romans 1:24.

Thomas Münzer wrote to Luther in 1524: "You make yourself plainly an arch-devil by proving from Isaiah that God is the cause of sin. That's what you have succeeded in doing with your fantastic speculation following your Augustine. Certainly a blasphemous doctrine of free will, treating man with contempt." [12]

This article distinguishes between the fact of human life and its moral quality, between its existence and its evil. God is certainly the Creator of life. Humanity exists because of his creative act. His Providence is the basis for its continued existence. Without his power and support it would perish.

But the rational beings—the men and angels he created—had in their original state the possibility of choosing either evil or good. Sin arose when they chose evil. The immoral quality of their life is the result of the action of their will. It is not something for which God is responsible. John 8:44 is quoted in support of the statement that the devil is the source of his own sin.

The doctrine Melanchthon wrote into this article is an about-face from his former position. Both he and Luther had expressed themselves in terms that appear to be a divine determinism. In the course of time Melanchthon modified his teaching at some points. Neither Luther nor Melanchthon was ultimately willing to declare that God was the author of sin. And the interpretation which Luther gave of God hardening Pharoah's heart stops short of saying that sin arose in the universe through the will of God.

Lutheran doctrine as set forth in the Confession was unwilling to probe into matters about which there has been no revelation. There are many speculative questions in religion for which the Scriptures give no answer. Concerning them we must be content to be unin-

---

[11] Cf. *Bek.*, 72, n. 1.
[12] Plitt, *op. cit.*, II, 424; quoted in Neve, *op. cit.*, p. 297 f.

formed. But the Confession is quite definitely convinced that there are some things specifically revealed. It is to them we must give our attention. Among them is the basic truth of the love of God, his *agape*. Since God is boundless, unceasing Love, it is inconceivable that he should be the author of sin. It is evident, therefore, that the Confession had grasped the essential theme of the gospel so clearly that it could not be misled at this point.

ARTICLE XX. OF FAITH AND GOOD WORKS

This is much the longest of the doctrinal articles of the Confession. It is supplementary to Articles IV and VI. It departs from the brevity characteristic of the other articles and launches out into discussion.

The necessity for the article lay in the fact that the Romanists were quite vigorous in their charges that Lutherans were opposed to good works. Eck quoted Luther: "Faith alone is necessary; all other things are most free, neither commanded nor prohibited" (194). "Love does not justify, but faith which is preferred to love (Melanchthon). Moreover it justifies with respect to no works, whether good or bad" (195). Without naming the author, Eck lists this statement: "God cares not for our works; or if they be anything before him, nevertheless all are equal in merit" (203).

The first sentence of the article acknowledges that it was written to answer a false accusation. Melanchthon found material for its construction in the Torgau Articles, but he thoroughly reworked it. The German text of the *editio princeps* varies considerably in phraseology from that of the *Book of Concord*. In it the article consists of two parts under the captions, "Where and What Faith Is" and "That One Should and Must Do Good Works, and How One Can Do Them, and How They Please God." Melanchthon thus indicated the outline of the article.

It is not true, the article declares, that Lutherans reject good works. The fact is that they teach and encourage in daily life the good works which God requires. Evidence may be found in catechetical and other writings. This article reaffirms what had been said in Articles VI and XVI.

By contrast the good works of the papists appear to be "childish and needless." The list of things given in the article, recalling those mentioned in Article XV, reveals at once the fact that they are purely of human origin. These are not works which hallow and brighten the common tasks of life. Instead they take one away from his normal duties and create false and arbitrary standards of life. It is foolish to think that God is more pleased with a pilgrimage to a distant shrine than he is with attending faithfully to one's duties at home.

The evangelical doctrine of faith has been so warmly preached that the papists have taken notice. Their former preaching of works has been amended so that it now speaks of justification by faith *and* works. This is some improvement. It is more consoling than was their former doctrine.

Concerning faith, a doctrine too long obscured among the papists, several things are to be observed. To begin with, faith is the only way by which we obtain justification. Works are entirely excluded. They "cannot reconcile God or merit forgiveness of sins, grace, and justification." Faith is trust in Christ alone for salvation. It exalts Christ, whereas the papist doctrine of works despises his grace and merit.

The evidence for this doctrine is to be found in many places in Scripture, for example, in Ephesians 2:8. Nor is this simply a Lutheran interpretation of Scripture. The Latin version of the article declares that there are many possible quotations from Augustine. The German version cites his book, *De spiritu et litera*.[13] The Latin text adds a quotation from the writing *De vocatione gentium* ascribed to Ambrose, but now recognized as pseudo-Ambrose.[14] Without a doubt, Lutherans were not alone in their understanding of the gospel.

The consequences of this doctrine are apparent. Faith is the source of consolation for the Christian. His mind is at rest; he has "peace with God" as stated in Romans 5:1. The terrified conscience finds relief. But it is not so with the papist doctrine. Plagued by the uncertainty of works, people go here and there—on pilgrimages, to monasteries—in futile search for peace. They devise new rites and invent new practices but they fail to find consolation.

The problem in part is in understanding correctly the nature of faith. The papists have thought of it as a cognitive thing, a knowledge of history. According to evangelical doctrine, however, it is

---

[13] *MSL* XLIV, 221. Cf. *Bek.*, p. 74, n. 1.
[14] *MSL* LI 670. Cf. *Bek.*, p. 74, n. 2.

trust—the confidence that for Christ's sake we have God's mercy.

In another respect the problem is that of the proper conception of God. Evangelical doctrine thinks of him as Father—a God of boundless love. The devils and the papists regard him as an austere judge, "and expect no good from Him." He must somehow be appeased by human works and services. But the gospel reveals him as crossing the barrier to men, as giving his Son as a sacrifice, as pouring out his love freely. It is faith which receives his grace and justification.

Such is the doctrine of faith which occupies the major part of this article. When that is firmly established, the doctrine of works may be more briefly stated. In quick succession the article states that works are necessary, that they are in keeping with the will of God, and that they arise out of believing hearts renewed by the Holy Spirit. Good works are the evidence of the regenerate life, not the cause of it. They are the result of God's grace, not the price of it. They are the response of a revitalized spirit to his love, not a down payment for it. Never meritorious, nor arising from unregenerate natural powers, they are the splendid fruits of faith.

In the concluding paragraph the article summarizes its argument. Lutheran doctrine does not forbid good works but instead shows how they are possible. Without faith, human nature produces only the works of the flesh. With the faith begotten by the Holy Spirit it can fear and love God.

The wholesomeness and practicality of this article are obvious. Realized in Christian practice, it should relieve the church of the charge of "quietism." It portrays a Christian, accepted into God's favor, and vigorously at work performing his proper duties in the midst of life. There is strength and consecrated manhood and muscle in it. But, as Leonhard Fendt has observed, it does not substitute ethics for dogmatics, human culture for the righteousness of faith.[15] God is still at the center of things. Our faith is not in the progress of civilization, but in the Christ who gave himself for us.

ARTICLE XXI. OF THE INVOCATION OF SAINTS

This was a matter which the Lutherans from the first intended to discuss at Augsburg. In the Torgau Articles they had written: "Touch-

---

[15] *Op. cit.*, p. 89.

ing the saints, it is taught that the example of their faith is useful to us; also that their good works are serviceable to us for instruction, to do the like, each one according to his calling.

"But to pray the saints for anything, and through their merit to procure anything, is an honor that belongs alone to God and our Lord Christ. Therefore the saints are not to be invoked as intercessors; for Christ has commanded us to adhere to him as the one intercessor and mediator. As Paul says: 'To us Christ is Mediator'; and Christ says: 'Come unto me, all ye that labor and are heavy laden.' To the illustration, that a good advocate at court is useful, it is easy to answer that such an advocate would do injury, if the prince had given an order that the petition was to be presented by the person himself."

Eck had no trouble finding quotations rejecting the worship of saints. From Luther he took the statement "that those worshiping the saints for temporal advantages are little better than those who for money make a covenant with the devil" (112). The quotation from Melanchthon reads, "Prayers to the saints for avoiding any temporal evil are to be shunned, since they cannot aid us" (113). Again from Luther, "Only through Christ do we have access to God; accordingly confidence in the saints falls" (114). There were other quotations of a similar sort.

It was after the middle of June that Melanchthon added this article to the other doctrinal articles of the Confession. The reasons can only be surmised. It would seem that the positive testimony concerning the meditation of Christ determined its inclusion here.

Luther was deeply interested in a statement on this matter. His letter to Jonas on July 21 criticized the lack of a vigorous attack on the worship of saints.[16] It has been supposed that he somehow overlooked this article in the copy of the Confession he had. He had written in his Confession of 1528, "The invocation of saints has been attacked by others before me. And I am satisfied and believe that Christ alone is to be invoked as our Mediator. So says Scripture; and it is certain that there is nothing in the Scriptures concerning the invocation of saints, which therefore must be uncertain and not to be believed." [17]

---

[16] W.A., *Briefe*, V, 496.
[17] W.A., XXVI, 508.

First of all this article acknowledges the value of Christian biography. The historical appreciation of the saints is approved. They may be remembered as examples of faith and life. The German text, with a little more fullness, says that our memory of the saints strengthens our faith as we see how they received faith and how they were helped through faith. There is a stimulus also to conduct, as we follow the example of saints whose position in life resembles ours. The emperor may take a saintly king as his model. Here was a courteous gesture, applauding the plan of the emperor to defend his domain against Turkish invasion.

But the article specifically rejects the invocation of saints. The veneration of saints, and even of their images, and the offering of petitions to them had become a widely extended abuse in Catholicism. The article rejects the practice incisively by saying that such invocation is without scriptural ground. That is enough to make it highly questionable.

The decisive blow to the practice is the fact that Christ is our only Mediator. Rites of human origin may be tolerated if they do not obscure or conflict with the gospel. But this practice intrudes a host of saints into the place of Christ. The Scriptures, however, give Christ all the honor. The Latin text quotes I John 2:1, "If any man sin, we have an Advocate with the Father," etc. The German text adds I Timothy 2:5, "For there is one God, and one Mediator between God and men, the man Christ Jesus." And recalling thoughts of the Saviour, the High Priest, the Mercy-seat, and the Advocate (as found in Hebrews 8), it points to Romans 8:34, "It is Christ that died, yea rather, that is risen again, who is even at the right hand of God, who also maketh intercession for us."

Here is Scripture testimony that cannot be denied. A theology of justification by faith, that is centered in Christ, cannot tolerate practices that becloud his work. Here was conviction that would not waver. The saints must keep their place. The article refrains from attacking the many abuses and follies connected with the practice. It discreetly refrains even from mentioning the Virgin Mary. But its positive conviction was clear; its testimony is unambiguous. It is sufficient to affirm that Christ, our only Mediator, has promised to hear our prayers.

The doctrinal articles are followed by a concluding paragraph. It declares that these articles represent virtually the "sum of our doctrine." It is in accord with Scripture and the Church Catholic, and even the Roman Church as it was in history. Therefore Lutherans are not heretics. The existing disagreements concern illegal abuses. Lutheran correction of them should be tolerated, for uniformity is not a canonical requirement. The fact is that Lutheran congregations observe the ancient rites. However, their ceremonies have been cleansed of notorious abuses.

It is true, of course, that this concluding paragraph is typical of Melanchthon's overenthusiasm. His hope for a peaceful solution of the religious issues gave a rose-colored appearance to the situation. The Catholic Church had never been as thoroughly evangelical as was here presumed, and the Evangelical Church would never be sufficiently Catholic to suit the papists. Toleration was no basis for unity in the church. It could provide at best only a fragile peace. The doctrine of the gospel was too powerful to be kept in an unequal yoke with Romanism. The history after Augsburg demonstrates that fact.

Chapter VII

AUGSBURG CONFESSION ARTICLES ON ABUSES

When in the course of the centuries the doctrine of the Roman
Catholic Church underwent change, the common people were unaware
of it. Few of the theologians recognized the alterations in the teaching of the church. But when the changes were in matters of practice,
so that the rules of the church produced irritating injustices, there was
widespead knowledge and complaint about it.

The worldliness and wealth of the Roman Catholic Church offended
spiritually minded men like the strict Franciscans and the Waldenses.
The greed of the papal hierarchy with its unceasing demands for
money aroused political resistance in France and elsewhere. Wycliffe
found much popular support for his attack on the covetousness of the
Romanists, and Savonarola aroused a city by his denunciation of papist
corruption. The Lutheran Reformation moved forward on a strong
ground swell of resentment against injustices in the system prevailing
under the pope.

The common man, who may have understood little of doctrine,
knew well enough the injustices and oppression he had to endure.
The learned man who had read Erasmus understood the follies of the
church under the papacy. The tyranny had become unbearable, and
the Lutherans prepared to go to Augsburg with some modest requests
for relief. Their statement of grievances was the Torgau Articles.
Reworked and rearranged, they furnished much of the material for
the articles on abuses—Articles XXII to XXVIII.

The paragraph in the Confession which introduces these articles
repeats the claim expressed in the conclusion of the doctrinal articles
to the effect that Lutherans have not departed from the faith of "the

117

Church Catholic." It acknowledges that changes have been made in some usages where there have been abuses.

It is charged that the abuses corrected are of recent origin, that their acceptance in the practice of the church was a mistake, and that they are contrary to church law. These articles were prepared to give these arguments in detail. Moreover, since the Lutheran position has been misrepresented, a defense of it is here made. Here are the true facts. Let the emperor decide the matter, not from rumor, but from reliable testimony. Dignified and reverent worship is of great importance, and abuses which do damage to it should by all means be corrected.

ARTICLE XXII. OF BOTH KINDS IN THE LORD'S SUPPER

There was no question about the Lutheran desire for reform in the Lord's Supper. The Torgau Articles had declared that "This custom of receiving only one form of the sacrament is also one that cannot be observed without sin. For Christ commanded: 'Drink ye all of this.' So too it is known that the church for a long time administered both forms to the laity, as may be found in Cyprian, and in the canons. But how it was changed, and who forbade both forms to be administered, is not known."

Some of the Hussites had put up a vigorous fight for both kinds in the Lord's Supper though they suffered condemnation for it. Eck was quite eager to accuse the Lutherans of Hussite heresy. Concerning communion in both kinds he had four theses, the first of which is from Luther: "To deny both kinds to the laity is godless and tyrannical, and bishops sin who give one kind alone" (251).

However the Lutherans stood their ground. They were accustomed to use both bread and wine in the Lord's Supper as administered to the laity. The article first defends the Lutheran practice from Scripture. The words of institution as reported by Matthew show that the cup was given to the disciples and that they were bidden to drink from it. The Roman Church had come to call this "priestly communion," insisting that the disciples were not laymen. Without arguing that point, the article cites I Corinthians which reports that the laity of that congregation received both the bread and the wine.

The Romanists defended their position by a doctrine of "concomitance." Alexander of Hales had originated the phrase, and with its development by Thomas Aquinas it became a part of scholastic theology, finding acceptance at the Council of Trent.[1] It teaches that the living Christ—body and blood, humanity and divinity together—is present in the Eucharist. Therefore the "whole Christ" is present in either of the elements, and only one needs to be administered. Lutherans were willing to grant the possibility of the premise, but definitely denied the conclusion. Luther wrote in Part III, Article VI of the Smalcald Articles, "For although it may perhaps be true that there is as much under one as under both, yet the one form is not the entire ordinance and institution established and commanded by Christ."

The scriptural practice was observed in the church for centuries and then for some reason was changed. The article does not indicate when the change was made. Apparently it was in the twelfth century that withholding the cup from the laity became common practice. The article refers to Cardinal Nicholas of Cusa, a prominent member of the Roman hierarchy in the fifteenth century. In his Third Letter to the Bohemians, he stated that withholding the cup from the laity goes back to the Fourth Lateran Council, 1215.[2]

There is further defense of the Lutheran position from the practice of the ancient church. Cyprian is cited. In his Epistle 57 he asked, "How do we make people fit for the cup of martyrdom, if we do not first admit them to drink the cup of the Lord in the Church by the right of administering the Communion?"[3] The article gives the quotation from Jerome found in his Commentary on Zephaniah.[4] The substance of the command of Gelasius I, a fifth-century pope, is stated;[5] the full text of the quotation is given in the *Variata*.[6] It reads: "We have ascertained that certain men, only a portion of the holy body having been received, abstain from the cup of the holy blood; since

---

[1] Sess. XIII, Canon 3.
[2] *Opera* (Paris: 1514), II, f. Bb iij. Cited in *Bek.*, 86, n. 1.
[3] *CSEL* III, 2, 652. Cited in *Bek.*, 85, n. 2.
[4] *MSL* XXV; Opp. Hier. 6, 1375A. Cited in *Bek.*, 85, n. 3.
[5] *Decr. Grat.* P. III De consecr. dist. 2 c. 12. Cited in *Bek.*, 85, n. 4.
[6] *C.R.*, XXVII, 381. *Book of Concord* (Jacobs), II, 160.

these are taught to be bound by some superstition or other, without doubt let them either receive the whole sacrament or be kept back from the whole sacrament, because a division of one and the same mystery cannot occur without great sacrilege."

The conclusion to be drawn from this scriptural and patristic evidence is that the withholding of the cup from the laity is illegal. Charles might not understand the theology of the matter, but he ought to understand its legal status. Since the Romanist practice is contrary both to the Bible and the law of the church, it ought at least be permitted to Lutherans to do what is legal and scriptural. In fact, to do anything else violates their consciences.

Added to the end of the article is a statement on the Corpus Christi procession. The day after Charles had reached Augsburg such a procession was held. The Lutherans were commanded to participate, but steadfastly refused. At that time the Saxons prepared a statement giving the reasons for their refusal. The sentence of this article is likely related to that statement. At least it was added to the article after that event.

The Lutheran position in this matter does not mean that Lutherans will accept nothing except that which has specific scriptural authorization. Such a radical position had been held by reformatory groups before and during the Reformation. Instead, it means that Lutherans will not tolerate modifications that change essentially the practices instituted by Christ. What is consistent therewith may be added, but the basic structure is not to be altered. Nor will any usages be tolerated which are attached to the perversion of Christ's institutions. The reasons for rejecting communion in one kind only also apply to the procession. The Reformation eliminates both.

ARTICLE XXIII. OF THE MARRIAGE OF PRIESTS

The Lutheran protest against enforced celibacy, as stated in the Torgau Articles, was as follows:

These are the ordinances which cannot be observed without sin. First they forbid the priests marriage. This is contrary to God. For Paul writes: "It is better to marry than to burn." This is God's command, and can be abolished by no man. So also it is known that the church thus held for a long time; and that the councils ordered that marriage should not be forbidden the

priests. Likewise that to the observance of this prohibition, the priesthood
in Germany has been with difficulty coerced by violence, and a bishop of
Mentz was almost killed when he published the papal prohibition. What
good results therefrom is easily seen, and there is ground for apprehension
that if marriage continue forbidden, still'worse will happen; for the longer
the world lasts, the weaker it is.

Here were Lutheran convictions that Eck did not need to mis-
represent. The marriage of priests was of course a topic of great
interest to the papists. Eck had gathered five theses on celibacy. Typical of them is the first, attributed to Luther: "Ordination does not
hinder marriage or break the contract, but celibacy has been introduced by the devil" (295).

The article begins by stating the situation. Unchastity among the
priests was a ground of common complaint. A comment by Pope Pius II
as reported by Platina—a fifteenth-century director of the Vatican
Library and author of *Lives of the Popes*—is quoted to show that even
a pope thought it was better for priests to be married.[7] Lutheran
pastors, desiring to be free of scandal, have become married, as were
both Luther and Melanchthon.

There is scriptural justification for this also. Paul approved marriage
for prudential reasons, namely, to avoid the sins of unchastity (I Cor.
7:2, 9). More than this, the powers of procreation and the institution
of marriage come from the Creator. Exceptions to the married state
constitute special cases—a God-given power of continence. All do not
have this power, as our Lord said (Matt. 19:11). Therefore, even
though they are pastors, they ought to be married. And they are fully
justified therein. There is an implied suggestion in this article that
there are advantages for pastors in being unmarried; Melanchthon
makes this explicit in the Apology.

There is ancient precedent for the marriage of priests. There is
Paul's direction to Timothy (I Tim. 3:2). Further evidence that priests
were married is seen in the efforts of Pope Gregory VII to enforce
celibacy, and of a riot that occurred at a synod in 1075 when Arch-
bishop Siegfried of Mainz attempted to put into effect the pope's rule.

The next argument, based on the conditions of that time, sounds
strange in modern ears. Human nature is growing weaker, says the

---

[7] *De vitis ac gestis pontificum*, 302. Cited in *Bek.*, p. 87, n. 2.

article, and less able to obey rigorist rules. There is no longer the former strength to resist sexual desire. Hence a concession must be made to human nature if there are to be pastors in the church.

The perversion of the papist position is apparent. The ancient practice of the church permitted the marriage of priests; enforced celibacy has produced great scandal; God honors marriage; even heathen communities honor it. Yet when a priest marries, the papal authorities attack him with the greatest cruelties. The papist practice is obviously a "doctrine of devils" (I Tim. 4:3).

Celibacy was connected with monastic vows, which are discussed in Article XXVII. This article anticipates that discussion by observing that God's laws cannot be annulled by human laws or by vows. Cyprian is quoted as permitting marriage to women who had taken a vow. And church law makes exceptions for those who took vows as minors.

This article attacks celibacy as an evidence of tyranny in the papal system. It is both unreasonable and unjust to enforce celibacy in the church. There was ample reason for deep resentment against this abuse. But Lutherans also had sound evangelical background for their position. As noted in connection with Article XVI, Lutherans had the conviction that the righteousness of faith was productive of good works within normal social relations, one of which is marriage. Celibacy is not a meritorious work either for the laity or the clergy. The home may be more of a place of holiness than a monastery. Faith in Christ must be kept in focus; the works of the law then find their proper place.

ARTICLE XXIV. OF THE MASS

Throughout Christian history it has been recognized that the Lord's Supper is a sublime moment in public worship. The Reformation was not disposed to change that fact. But in the Roman Catholic mass the Table of the Lord, which should be kept most holy, had been profaned by several serious abuses.

Lutherans were much disturbed about the matter. The statement they prepared in the Torgau Articles is too long to be quoted in full. Briefly stated, its argument is this: the papists have made the mass a work of merit and have commercialized it; it is a memorial and not a meritorious offering; grace is a gift received through faith, but the papists omit faith; the cup of the New Testament is God's work, not man's; greedy and unbelieving priests say mass; Lutheran pastors teach their people to use the sacrament reverently and intelligently, not with Zwinglian doctrine, but with the doctrine of the real presence; this is the true, historic, Christian communion devoid of mercenary aspects.

If Eck wanted quotations from Luther, there were plenty to be found in the *Babylonian Captivity* and elsewhere. Eck gathered ten theses on the mass. The first is from Luther: "The Gospel does not allow the mass as a sacrifice, because to retain the use of masses under the name of sacrifices is to deny Christ" (270). "The mass has been changed into a sacrifice of Satan, and that, too, by a common error; but this is the very worst idolatry and infidelity, and is worse than heathen" (274).

This article sets itself to make clear what the Lutherans accept and what they reject. In the *Variata* Melanchthon developed his argument under six points, more than doubling the size of the article. In the *editio princeps* the article describes Lutheran usage in connection with the sacrament, and protests against two abuses. The word "mass" is used in the sense of "holy communion."

To begin with, the article shows the conservative practice among Lutherans. It is untrue that they have discarded the mass. Instead it is retained and with it the usual ceremonies, except that hymns in German are inserted for the edification of the uneducated. The Torgau Articles included a statement on German singing. There is congregational participation in the sacrament. The people are examined and instructed before being admitted to the sacrament; thereby devotion is nourished.

But in the pre-Reformation church there has been a great abuse: the mass was "bought and sold"! Such is the statement in the German text. "Good men," such as Tauler, Gerson, and Biel, complained about it. This is surely using the sacrament unworthily, recalling Paul's words in I Corinthians 11:27. The private masses were those for hire; therefore Lutherans have abandoned them. Yet the bishops have known and permitted this abuse. As a result, there are now great disturbances.

Since "the Lord will not hold him guiltless that taketh his name in vain," the same must be true of his sacrament.

The second abuse is that the mass has been made into a sacrifice. It was presumed to atone for sins, mortal as well as venial, those of the dead as well as of the living. Yet Christ is our only sacrifice, as indicated in Hebrews 10:10-14. And we are justified for Christ's sake through faith. In fact, the mass was designed to remind us of Christ's sacrifice. This "remembering" is more than mere recollection; it is also trust.

Lutherans use the mass as a sacrament, publicly, and on holy days. Daily and private masses are abolished. Public use was the ancient practice as substantiated by Chrysostom, the eighteenth Nicene Canon, and Paul's words in I Corinthians 11:33. Lutheran usage, thus based on Scripture and the fathers, cannot be justly disapproved. It has a precedent in ancient Alexandria where there was no Eucharist on weekdays, according to Cassiodorus' *Tripartite History*—a work much used in the middle ages.

This article is a relatively brief statement of Lutheran convictions. A much longer treatment will be found in the Apology. Luther expresses himself on it with characteristic vigor in the Smalcald Articles. In the *Variata* Melanchthon attacked the idea of the mass as a sacrifice with the following arguments: (1) forgiveness of sin comes only by faith; (2) Christ is our only sacrifice; (3) in the words of institution of the Lord's Supper there is no command to offer it as a sacrifice; (4) rites without faith are dead works; (5) God's grace is not based on human merit; (6) by Christ's institution it is only a sacrament.

The declaration of Article X limited itself to the doctrine of the Lord's Supper. This article looks more at the practice, yet with doctrine always in view. The disposition of Lutherans is to relate practice to doctrine. Liturgical usages are guided by theological principles.

In this instance, the doctrine of the real presence in the sacrament administered to communicants made the commercialization of it appear little short of blasphemous. The sacrament is not the exclusive possession of the clergy who may sell it for their own profit. It is the possession of the whole church to be used faithfully.

The doctrine of the real presence also indicated most clearly that the Lord's Supper is a sacrament, not a sacrifice. It is something God gives to the communicants, not something they offer him. Pure doctrine is therefore the guide for purifying practice; mercenary and sacrificial masses are abolished.

ARTICLE XXV. OF CONFESSION

The Torgau Articles contained a statement of approximately the same size as this article. The Torgau statement said nothing of satisfactions but indicated why in Lutheran practice there were no prescribed times or methods of confession. This article of the Confession omitted the statement on prescribed times, substituting a longer attack on compulsory enumeration of sins. The Roman Catholic rule requiring annual confession and an enumeration of sins was a burden and an abuse against which the Lutherans were determined to protest at Augsburg.

The effect of Eck's Theses was to increase this determination. One of his theses has been noted in connection with Article XI. Five others on this topic are listed. Luther and others were accused of saying: "That secret sins pertain to sacramental confession can be proved in no way of reason or from the Scriptures; I suspect that this was an invention either of the avaricious or the curious" (256). There was no mistake about it; the Reformation had made a heavy attack on the Romanist penitential system.

This article grants that there is a place for confession in the church; therefore it is retained among Lutherans. It is an appropriate preparation for partaking of the sacrament. Luther so directed in his *Formula missae*,[8] as did Melanchthon in his *Instruction of Visitors*.[9] It is connected with catechetical instruction so that the people understand the evangelical meaning of absolution. They are taught to believe God's Word. Their attention is turned from their sins and toward Christ. Luther's Small and Large Cathechisms instruct persons how to make confession.

In the Romanist system there was a scheme of satisfactions which were works to be performed by the penitent whereby he secured merit with God. The righteousness of faith, which the papists neglected, is

---

[8] W.A., XII, 215.
[9] C.R., XXVI, 72.

taught instead of satisfactions. Instead of neglecting confession, therefore, the Lutherans are using it in its full, positive, gospel meaning.

The enumeration of sins in confession is attacked on three grounds. First is its impossibility of fulfillment. No one can ever know all his own sins. Psalm 19:13 and Jeremiah 17:9 are quoted in support of this position. Second is the result of this requirement upon the individual. Because of his conscious inability to meet the requirement, he is left in a state of anxiety and distress. Third, the ancient church did not require it. This article quotes Chrysostom as a competent witness. And the Gloss (commentary or explanation) of the canon law of the church as assembled in the *Decretum Gratiani* admitted that Romanist confession is only by human right.

In view of all this the Lutherans have reformed the usage of confession, giving emphasis to the consolation of absolution.

This article, which describes an evangelical use of confession, cracks open the system of the papists at an important point. Under the pope, penance was a device for keeping the people in subjection, as well as for raising revenue. To the authorities at Rome it was unthinkable that there should be liberty for Christians. The clergy ruled in the church. It was for the people to obey.

The Reformation, however, repudiated such tyranny. There was to be as much liberty as is consistent with fellowship in the church. The rites and usages of the church were to be for the benefit of the people, not their subjection. And the church consists of laity and clergy, not one without the other. Christian laity therefore could be trusted to make use of the church's ministry and to seek absolution. The law of confession was abolished; the gospel of absolution was revived.

Luther, in his Confession of 1528, said:

I have a high opinion of private confession, because therein, privately and to each one separately, is spoken God's Word and absolution for the forgiveness of sins, and as often as he desires he may thereby have such forgiveness, as well as comfort, advice and report. I think that it is a truly necessary thing for souls, so much so that it may not be forced on anyone by laws and commands, but may be free to each according to his need, to be made use of when and where he will, just as it is free to secure advice and comfort, report or teaching when and where the need or the will impels. And

I believe that one is not compelled to enumerate or report all sins, but those most pressing, or which one is willing to name. All these things I have written in the *Little Prayer Book*.[10]

ARTICLE XXVI. OF THE DISTINCTION OF MEATS

This article discusses the papist doctrine that traditional usages of human origin merit grace. The distinction of meats is only an incidental phase of it. The Torgau Articles contained a treatment of about the same length as this article, but under the title, "Of the Doctrines and Ordinances of Men." In it there is less space devoted to traditional usages as works of merit and more attention given to liberty and diversity in such usages. The Romanists charged that such diversity disrupted the unity of the church and that Lutherans therefore were schismatics. The Torgau statement insisted on the one hand that some Romanist usages were sinful because they were contrary to the gospel, and on the other hand that diversity in rites does not split the unity of the church.

There was a suspicion of rebellion against church authorities in the position which the Lutherans were prepared to take at Augsburg. The emperor might be expected to take an unfavorable view of anything rebellious, and Eck was alert to make the most of the fact. Therefore, after giving a long list of theses that reflected Reformation criticisms of secular authorities, he followed them with attacks on ecclesiastical power and church rules. From Luther and others: "We are therefore under no obligation to celebrate the festivals of the saints, to fast in Lent and on other days, to abstain from flesh on six festival days, or to obey other human precepts" (363).

At Augsburg Melanchthon shifted the ground of attack. The Confession had come to have as its backbone the doctrine of justification for Christ's sake through faith. The papist doctrine based justification on the merits of works. This, therefore, was to be the place of battle. The article opens with a survey of the position of the enemy: the general public believed that traditional usages of human origin are works which merit God's grace.

Evangelical objections are three: first, it obscures "the doctrine of grace and of the righteousness of faith"; second, it obscures the com-

---

[10] *W.A.,* XXVI, 507.

mandments of God; and third, it leaves consciences in despair. Christ is worth infinitely more than fasting on Friday. The law of God is vastly higher than a liturgical rubric. That which consoles is much to be preferred to that which distresses.

What had happened in the church was that writers on the *Summa* of Thomas Aquinas, as well as other theologians, were so absorbed in the minutiae and intricacies of regulations imposed on the people that they had no time to study the Scriptures. Gerson, chancellor of the University of Paris, and others had protested against this trend, and a quotation from a letter of Augustine to Januarius declared that human traditions are matters of indifference.[11]

Therefore it was not rebellion, but the impulse of the gospel, that moved Lutheran teachers to criticize traditional usages and to declare the doctrine of grace. For such human works cannot be meritorious.

The evangelical position is supported by many quotations from Scripture. Our Lord defended the disciples who neglected Hebrew traditions (Matt. 15:3, 9). Paul rejected the idea that the kingdom of God consists of matters of meat and drink (Rom. 14:17), of holydays and sabbaths (Col. 2:16), or of ordinances of touch and taste (Col. 2:20). Peter rejected burdensome rites of Hebrew origin (Acts 15:10). Paul goes so far as to call "the prohibition of meats a doctrine of devils" (I Tim. 4:1, 3).

Lutherans were accused of being opposed to bodily discipline and fasting. They were put in the same heretical category with Jovinian, a fourth-century ascetic who wrote against celibacy and other monastic usages, and therefore was condemned by the papacy. Instead, evangelical teaching encouraged bodily self-discipline as a means of overcoming slothfulness and temptations to sin. It finds authority for doing so in the words both of our Lord and of Paul.

There are also other traditional usages continued in evangelical congregations for the sake of good order, such as the regular lessons of Scripture, and the festivals. But they are clearly understood to be no basis of merit and to be optional. Evidences of such liberty in the ancient church are found in the various dates of Easter, as well as

---

[11] Ep. 54, 2.2. *MSL* XXXIII, 200. Cited in *Bek.*, p. 103, n. 3.

in a quotation from Irenaeus, from Pope Gregory I, and the *Tripartite History* of Cassiodorus.[12]

This article takes a somewhat more negative attitude toward rites and usages than does Article XV. In that article it is asserted that certain traditional usages ought to be observed; encouragement is given for their continuance. But in this article there is simply the statement that some usages are continued, while the main theme is the attack on the compulsion and alleged merit of such usages among papists.

Nevertheless, this article is far from being purely negative. If it tears apart the papist practice, its purpose is to construct truly evangelical practice. It does much more than protest against the excessive and mistaken regulations of the papal system. It has in view the strengthening of Christian faith in the free forgiveness of sins for Christ's sake. The usages of the church must aid and express faith, rather than become a substitute for it. With this faith there is also the fruit of it in daily life. It honors the father and mother in the family and the ruler in the state, rather than despising them as the monks did. It affirms "the dignity of civil affairs" of the normal, everyday sort, rather than the artificial sanctimoniousness of abnormal monastic life. There is a piety of a healthy, natural kind which grows spontaneously out of a life nourished by the gospel. It is this for which the article contends.

ARTICLE XXVII. OF MONASTIC VOWS

The doctrine of works of merit so permeated Roman Catholic teaching that, no matter where the teaching is examined, there the doctrine of merit is encountered. Similarly in papist practice, the belief in meritorious works offered resistance to evangelical faith in almost every aspect of church life. Monastic vows were simply another obnoxious example.

In the Torgau Articles there is a section "Of Vows," with the subtitle, "Of Monastic Life." It begins:

This subject of monastic life does not concern My Lord, for his Electoral Grace has ordered the monks neither to go out of nor to go into monasteries,

---

[12] For sources, cf. *Bek.*, p. 107, nn. 3, 4, 5.

but it is proper to ask of them themselves the reason why this has happened. It is a private matter, and does not pertain to the church at large. Nevertheless the reasons are recounted why My Lord has not again founded monasteries, and why his Electoral Grace has tolerated the persons who have abandoned them.

Three reasons were given. First, monastic life is falsely thought to be a way of meriting God's grace. Second, vows of celibacy are contrary to God's command. Third, the monastic life is by compulsion connected with godless services such as the mass for the dead. These reasons are supported by appropriate quotations.

It sometimes happened in the Reformation era that civil authorities were moved by greed to seize the rich holdings of monastic institutions. Eck had reason to be on his guard against the cupidity of the princes. He was careful, therefore, to deal with monastic vows as one of the aspects of church practice and doctrine co-ordinate with the sacraments.

His theses numbered 300 to 320 deal with the question of vows. Some of the most striking are these: "To become a monk is to apostatize from the faith, to deny Christ, and to become a Jew; their vows, accordingly, are worthless" (305). "I discourage all from entering any religious order, unless he know that the works of the members of these orders however arduous and holy, in God's eyes are no better than the works of farmers laboring in the fields" (312). "No saint became a saint through monasticism" (314). These are quoted from Luther.

At Augsburg Melanchthon reworked and enlarged the Torgau statement so that the finished article had increased in length fourfold. It opens with a brief review of the history of monastic institutions. Founded originally as free associations, they had been corrupted by vows until they had become virtual prisons. Vows, even those taken by minors or women, were made irrevocable, however unbearable was the discipline. The most famous case was that of Gottschalk, a monk of Orbais. Because he had taken his vow as a child, a synod at Mainz in 829 voted to release him, but his abbot compelled him to remain. This is the monk who later began the famous controversy concerning predestination.[13]

---

[13] Cf. *NSH* V, 35 f.

Worse than this is the Romanist teaching that vows are equal to baptism, and that they merit grace. Such teaching was common among the scholastics. After Luther had taken his vow as a monk he was congratulated that he was now as pure as a child after baptism. In fact, the Romanists considered the monastic life something better than baptism and the normal life of Christian laymen. Formerly the monasteries were schools of theology and institutions for training pastors, but they had become ways of earning grace. Papists considered monastic life to be the state of perfection.

Quite in contrast, the Lutherans taught, first, that marriage is permitted to all by the will of God, and that God's command is superior to the authority of vows. Moreover, vows are not irrevocable as some canonical laws declare, for the popes have released some persons from vows, a notable case being that of King Ramiro II of Aragon who was a monk when he succeeded to the throne.

In the second place, Lutherans taught that a vow should be free, and not coerced, especially on minors. Some canon laws declare invalid such vows as are taken before the age of fifteen, or eighteen in other instances. Yet many vows are taken at an earlier age.

Thirdly, the Lutherans believed that vows should not annul existing marriages, even as Augustine had said.

There are other arguments in addition to these three. It is affirmed that it is wicked to make human deeds become a way to merit grace. Second, when the monks so teach, they deny Christ and ascribe to their own works what belongs to Christ. They even presume to have a surplus of merits to share with others, for they think their life is that of Christian perfection, instead of that of the righteousness of faith.

In the third place, vows obscure the true service of God in faith and love. They merely exalt celibacy, begging, and "vile apparel." They induce people to think that normal life and everyday duties are tainted with sin. But God's commands to us are to live faithfully, performing our normal duties. Man-made rules should not replace them.

Since the Romanists' arguments for the monastic life are false and wicked, monastic vows are null and void.

This article points out how perverted and abnormal is the monastic way of life. It is a distortion not only of natural human relations, but even more of the ideal of Christian life. It was a frustrated tower of

Babel attempting to reach God. The memory of papist compulsions was a bad dream from which the Lutherans were glad to awaken. Aroused from the fantasies of monasticism they could face the clear actualities of living in God's sight. Christ, rather than the head of the monastic order, leads on!

Leonhard Fendt writes:

There is a great distinction here: the Catholic Church has monasteries, the Reformation Church has none. But the difference must not mean that where there are no monasteries the matter has been made easy. Instead, where there are no monasteries there is esteemed the ultimate yearning of monks and nuns for all without distinction—the yearning: Thy grace and Thy Kingdom, O Lord! And this yearning awaits fulfillment, not by the way of human power, but through God's miracle in Christ. "With might of ours can naught be done." [14]

ARTICLE XXVIII. OF THE POWER OF THE BISHOPS

The Torgau Articles have no declaration directly related to this article. The statement therein "Of the Jurisdiction and Sovereignty of Bishops" defends the management of the church by civil rulers in Lutheran areas. The bishops lost the support of the people; therefore the elector had to assume the responsibility. The bishops had failed to reprove false doctrine. They had tried to punish married priests, but the elector could not in good conscience assist in the punishments. By their unjust decisions in matrimonial cases the bishops have forfeited their authority. Such is the Torgau statement, which nonetheless furnishes an interesting background for this article.

Found with the Torgau Articles in the Weimar archives was another document, now designated as "C." It contains a discussion "Of the Power of the Keys" which seems to be a preliminary form of this article. It begins with a statement of the papal claim to rule both the church and the state. It asserts that the power of the keys obtains only in spiritual matters and must be distinguished from civil affairs. In fact, the church officers should function in the church and refrain from civil rule. If the pope exercises civil authority, he gets it from the emperor, not from God. He has no right to establish usages contrary to the gospel; if he enforces them, he is to be resisted, and

---

[14] *Op. cit.*, p. 121.

obedience given to God. For he has authority from the keys only to preach the gospel and administer the sacraments—something any pastor has the power to do.

There are many things which the Church of Rome could tolerate, but lack of submission to her authority is not one of them. It is surprising, as one remembers the controversies between Thomists and Scotists, to observe the amount of theological divergence permissible in Romanism. But a denial of the power of the hierarchy immediately arouses the papists to action.

Eck had to think of the emperor's attitude in this matter. He knew quite well the history of the contest between the popes and the emperors for supremacy. There was still vivid in his mind the treatment Charles gave to Pope Clement VII who had been antagonistic to him. Charles knew both how to keep the pope in his place and how to make submission to him.

Eck was aware that his cause would fare better if he kept the issue out of the political field and confined it to religious matters. James I of England at a later date, recognizing that the end of episcopacy would imperil his crown, answered the Millenary Petition with the famous words, "No bishop, no king!" Charles V might also be expected to see that if Lutherans repudiated the authority of bishops in church matters, they might think of rejecting other authority.

One can imagine how Eck would call the emperor's attention to this quotation from Luther: "It is only a matter that should be laughed at, if a great sedition should arise against bishops and their rule; because those exposing their fortunes and bodies to such an emergency are sons of God, true Christians; and in a short time matters will come to such a pass that there will be no bishop, no prince under the sun, no cathedral church, no monastery" (376). "No pope or bishop has the right of imposing a single syllable upon any man" (366). And from Melanchthon, "It is not allowable for a bishop to do aught except to teach the Word of God. Preaching the gospel is so peculiarly the prerogative of a bishop that it is not proper to substitute another for him, to teach in his place. If, therefore, he do not teach, he is not a bishop" (356).

Melanchthon evidently worked with much care over this article, which is much enlarged over earlier forms and is the longest of the articles on abuses. It begins with a statement of the problem, of which there are two phases. On the one hand, the power of the church and that of the sword have been confused, with damage to peace and to conscience. The claims of Gregory VII and Boniface VIII to supremacy over the state will be remembered. On the other hand, the bishops have assumed the power to establish new usages in the church.

The power of the bishops is next defined. They have the power of the keys (the original title of this article), which according to Scripture is "to preach the gospel, to remit and retain sins, and to administer sacraments." It concerns eternal things only, as Paul says in Romans 1:16. "It does not interfere with civil government; no more than the art of singing interferes with civil government." The government of the state, however, deals only with the external things of life—justice and peace.

Church and state should be separate, each keeping within its own sphere. Each in its sphere should be honored as a blessing from God. If, in any instance, bishops have the sword, they received it not from God, but from kings.

The real duties of bishops as church officers are "to forgive sins, to discern doctrine, to reject doctrines contrary to the gospel, and to exclude from the communion of the church wicked men whose wickedness is known, and this without human force, simply by the Word." If bishops teach heresy they must be resisted; as our Lord said, "Beware of false prophets" (Matt. 7:15). Church law and Augustine are quoted to the same effect. If bishops have other functions, as in judging matrimonial cases, they have them by human law. If they are unjust judges, the princes must step in.

Having expressed the Lutheran position on the secular and spiritual power of bishops, the article next turns to the second phase, viz., the enforcement of new usages by the bishops. This is the larger part of the article.

The papists defend their doctrine, that bishops have the power to alter usages, from John 16:12, 13 (the Holy Spirit "will show you things to come"), from Acts 15:29 (the advice of the Apostles to "abstain from meats offered to idols," etc.), and from the change from Sabbath to Lord's Day. Eck had used such arguments in his writings.

The evangelical answer is that bishops must not alter the gospel. Even the cannon law of the church says so. Yet to make traditions into works of merit is against the gospel and Christ. Nevertheless the papists have increased holy days, ceremonies, and so forth.

It is an abuse when they declare it sinful to neglect rules about meat, canonical hours, and so forth. Eck had quoted Luther as saying, "I believe that they sin more who read the hours coldly than they who omit them; for they are hypocrites" (280). Where did bishops get this power, which both Peter and Paul denied? Paul rejected such laws: "Let no man judge you in meat or drink, or in respect of an holyday," etc. (Col. 2:16); and our Lord spoke against them (Matt. 15:14). If the bishops have power to enforce traditions, why does the Scripture prohibit them? It is clearly illegal for bishops to enforce such rules. Christian liberty must be preserved, and the gospel of free grace preached.

On the other hand, there is a proper function of bishops. "This we answer" to Eck's Theses. It is that they should rule for the sake of good order. Their regulations for orderliness, and not for merit, are permissible, as, for example, were Paul's church rules for the Corinthians. There must be peace and charity in the church, but not rules to earn salvation. Such orderly regulations are the observance of the Lord's Day, Easter, Pentecost, and so forth.

The change from Sabbath to the Lord's Day was not made by church authority, but by the gospel and apostolic authority for the sake of good order, and as an evidence of Christian liberty from Hebrew law. Luther discusses this in his Large Catechism with reference to the Third Commandment.

Fundamentally the Romanists have a wrong basis for church usages. Much papist discussion assumes that Christian worship must be ceremonial legalism like Levitical worship. It fails utterly to understand the righteousness of faith.

Externally in the church the usages change. The apostolic command to abstain from blood was a temporary rule. It is quite proper that traditional usages should change. Yet at the heart of the church should be the gospel which must be kept clearly in mind and which does not change. It is reprehensible, therefore, that bishops enforce usages offensive to consciences, as when they command celibacy and when they refuse ordination to men of evangelical faith.

It is the Lutheran request that outmoded and erroneous ordinances be repealed. It is perfectly legal to do so, and the unity of the church will not be endangered by the change in traditional usages. If no relief is granted, then God rather than men will be obeyed. There is no desire to overthrow episcopal government; but let the bishops permit gospel preaching and a change in usages offensive to conscience. If they refuse, the responsibility for schism rests with them.

This article makes clear what should be obvious to any student of the Lutheran Church, namely, that Lutherans value pure doctrine above church polity. Bishops may be useful and desirable, but when they interfere with gospel doctrine, episcopacy must go. The essential fact of faith in Christ must be pre-eminent over all other matters in church life. Melanchthon has more to say on this subject in the Apology and in the Tractatus appended to the Smalcald Articles. But the heart of the Lutheran position has been given here.

The conclusion of this section of the Confession states that these are the chief matters in controversy, though there are many other abuses, notably indulgences. The Confession is interested in the solution of the problems, not in personal reproaches. The positions taken have been biblical and ecumenical. These articles are presented to the emperor in accordance with the imperial edict. Further testimony will be presented if desired.

Then follow the signatures, beginning with Elector John "the Steadfast." There cannot be absolute certainty about all the original signatures. Some sources add Count Albrecht of Mansfeld to the list.

Chapter VIII

THE ORIGIN OF THE APOLOGY

There had been many anxieties connected with securing the public presentation and reading of the Confession before the emperor. That it had been presented and read was a satisfying triumph for the Lutherans, but it was not the end of their anxiety. There remained the question as to what Charles would do with their declaration.

The terms of the emperor's summons to the diet seemed to imply that the Romanists also would present a confession. But they persistently refused to be considered a mere "party" in the church, declaring that they were "satisfied with and remained in the Christian faith, the holy Gospel of the Christian Church and His Majesty's Edict" of Worms. The purpose of their action was to give the Lutheran party the appearance of a sect.

There were several possible courses of action open to the emperor. One of these was to reject the Lutheran requests entirely. Some of his papist advisers urged this upon him. They were insistent that the Lutherans should be compelled to adhere to the Edict of Worms.

The fact was that the Confession aroused the papists to a high pitch of fanaticism. Melanchthon wrote that "sophists and monks are daily streaming into the city in order to influence the hatred of the emperor against us." [1] In a letter to Luther, Jonas said, "Faber is goaded on by furies and Eck is not a whit more sensible. Both insist in every manner imaginable that the affair ought to be managed by force and must not be heard." [2] The emperor's father-confessor de-

---

[1] C.R., II, 141. Quoted in *Conc. Trig.*, Hist. Intro., p. 31.
[2] C.R., II, 154. Quoted in *ibid.*

clared concerning the Lutherans that "the true rhubarb to cure them is force."

The possibility that Charles might approve the arguments of the Lutherans was too remote to be considered. Yet it was a fact that he had treated the Elector of Saxony with some consideration, and had granted some of the requests of the Lutherans, such as permission to read the Confession. The quite moderate tone of the Confession may not have been without its effect on him, as it was on others. Moreover, it discredited, to some degree at least, the accusations of Eck and his Four Hundred Four Theses.

Diplomacy suggested that Charles secure the advice of learned and impartial men and make a decision based on their judgment. As a matter of fact, the Catholic estates held a conference the day after the reading of the Confession. On the following day they offered Charles their advice that the best course of action was to appoint a committee to prepare a reply to the Confession. The committee should approve what was orthodox in the Confession and should refute the rest from Scripture. The reply to the Confession should then be read publicly.

On July 5 Charles announced his decision. A committee would prepare a reply to the Confession. Lutherans should submit to his judgment. If they refused, they would be required to obey the Edict of Worms, and the whole religious matter would be referred to a council.

Of course Eck was a prominent member of the committee, which was selected by the papal legate and appointed by the emperor. It consisted of about twenty theologians, some of whom were bitterly hostile to the Lutherans, but who are described by the Confutation as "learned, mature, approved and honorable men of different nations."

On July 12 the committee presented to Charles a document of 351 pages which was the result of their labor. But he rejected it as much too long and too polemical. Several other drafts met the same fate. It was not until the committee came with their fifth document that their statement was accepted, and that somewhat grudgingly. It was read in German on August 3 in the episcopal palace in the room where the Confession had been read.

This document, known as the "Confutation," was read in the emperor's name as his own answer to the Confession. A copy was denied the Lutherans unless they would agree to three conditions: that they would not publish it; that they would not reply to it; and that they would accept its conclusions. The Confutation closed with a threat implied in the statement that Charles, as "a defender and advocate of the Catholic and Christian Church . . . must care for such matters as the nature of the charge committed to him and his integrity of conscience require."

The Lutherans were unwilling to risk the danger of accepting the document under these "most perilous conditions," as Melanchthon called them in the preface of the Apology. If any irresponsible person would have published the Confutation, they would be held responsible. Some of the papists were capable of such a trick.

Though the Confutation was not published until 1573, having by that time undergone some editorial corrections, the Lutherans knew its contents fairly well at Augsburg. At least one of their number had taken notes during the public reading of the Confutation. During the discussions with the Romanists which followed, more of the details of the Confutation were reviewed and became familiar to the Lutherans. After they left Augsburg a complete copy of the text came into their hands, apparently from Nürnberg. Melanchthon says in his preface, "I have recently seen the Confutation."

Meanwhile, by the direction of Charles, conferences were held between the representatives of the Romanists and of the Lutherans. Seven men from each side discussed the articles during the days of August 13-21. The purpose was to find a solution of the differences between them. But as the days went by, it became increasingly clear that no unity was possible. The differences were basic and irreconcilable. There could be no hope of a peaceful settlement of the religious question without a complete surrender by one side or the other.

Concerning the negotiations Luther wrote to Melanchthon:

In sum, it does not please me at all that unity of doctrine is to be discussed, since this is utterly impossible, unless the pope would abolish his entire popery. It would have sufficed if we had presented to them the reasons for our faith and desired peace. But how can we hope that we shall win them over to accept the truth? We have come to hear whether they approve our doctrine or not, permitting them to remain what they are, only inquiring whether they acknowledge our doctrine to be correct or condemn it. If they condemn it, what does it avail to discuss the question of unity any longer with avowed enemies? If they acknowledge it to be right, what necessity is there of retaining old abuses?[3]

When it became obvious that the Romanists would not yield anything, the evangelical estates decided on a reply to the Confutation. On August 29 they authorized Dr. Brück and others to prepare a defense of the Confession. Melanchthon, who had the chief responsibility for the task, worked energetically at it and had a hurried Latin draft ready by September 20. He had the assistance and advice of others whom he did not identify by name.

Two days later Dr. Brück presented the document to the emperor. Charles directed the Count Palatine to accept it, but Ferdinand, his brother, whispered something into his ear, and he declined to receive the document. He declared that the Lutherans had been successfully answered in the Confutation. The papists had had their way. Luther later called the Romanist conduct "leaky, leprous and filthy." He added that "they lie like reprobates when they boast that our Confession has been refuted."[4]

The next day the Saxons started for home. The diet adjourned some weeks later, the emperor demanding the submission of the Lutherans by the fifteenth of the following April. The consequences of refusal were not named but sternly intimated.

After the diet, while on his way home, Melanchthon began a thorough revision of the document prepared at Augsburg. The defense, i.e., the Apology, of the Confession was carefully elaborated, strengthened, and enriched. All winter long he worked at the task as rapidly as he could, though he had expected to have it in print much sooner. Finally, late in April or early in May of 1531, it was published in Latin with the Confession in the editio princeps. A German version (for it was more than a translation) was prepared by Justus Jonas with Melanchthon's aid and published later in the year. The Book of Concord includes these texts, though other editions of them with editorial emendations had appeared later.

---

[3] W.A., Briefe, V, 578. Quoted in Conc. Trig., Hist. Intro., p. 29.
[4] W.A., XXX, Part 3, 336. Quoted in op. cit., p. 41.

The published work was received by Lutherans with great joy. It raised their enthusiasm and strengthened their convictions. But the Romanists viewed it with dismay. A copy was sent by Albrecht of Mainz to the emperor to show him how the Romanist cause was suffering and how important it was to publish the Confutation.

One's first impression of the Apology is of its size and scholarship. It is almost seven times as long as the Confession. By itself it would form a fair-sized book. A mere cursory examination reveals the extensive treatment of some of the parts and a further reading shows that the treatment has been thorough. It is a serious and substantial piece of theological writing.

The scholarship becomes even more apparent when attention is given to the references made to authorities. The references are both scriptural and patristic. The biblical quotations reveal a thorough mastery of the Scriptures. Melanchthon showed the ability to quote not only extensively but also with keen discrimination. He demonstrated that the Reformers were thoroughly acquainted with the Word of God. Furthermore, they knew how to use it. They understood its nature and the basic import of its message.

No less impressive is the array of citations from the writings of the church fathers. In proving that Lutherans were both apostolic and ecumenical in their doctrines, the Apology was able to vindicate their position from authors approved in the church. The literature of previous centuries of the church had been studied carefully. The teachings of the scholastics, as they deviated from positions held in earlier centuries, were well known, and the Apology could evaluate them impressively. Melanchthon's citations are not without their errors, but he exhausted such resources as were available to him in his search for historical fact.

The scholarship of the Apology means, of course, that the document was intended for those theologically trained, rather than for general reading by laymen. It is a carefully prepared document designed to meet the somewhat technical attacks made by the Confutation; hence its attention to theological detail. Its proficiency in this respect strengthened the confidence of scholars in the solid worth of Reformation doctrine, as Schaff has observed. They could be sure that the Reformation was not a fanatical insurrection of an ignorant rabble. It could command the best intellectual talents of the day.

Moreover, the Apology demonstrated that the Confession could be defended successfully. Scholarship may be used to bolster up a losing cause, but in this instance it was in the service of a victorious movement. The Apology makes evident to any fair-minded person that the Confutation had failed to upset the Confession. By comparison, the Confutation appears amateurish and lacking in theological skill. Against the weak and inept arguments of the Romanists the Apology set forth the strength of gospel doctrine.

But the Apology is something more than a triumphant vindication of the Confession; it is also an exposition of it by its author. At that time, Dr. Brück spoke of the Apology as "a defense and an interpretation of the Confession." Matters stated concisely in the Confession are here treated more fully. The Confession contains the end product of thinking on such doctrines as, for example, that of the church. The Apology exhibits the evidence and the method whereby the end product was attained. It demonstrates that the framework of evangelical doctrine is ample to support the structure. If the Confession were a house of cards, a puff of criticism would make it collapse; instead, it is solidly built.

Apparently Luther also had felt the need of an exposition of the Confession and thought of writing one. What he thought of Melanchthon's Apology can only be inferred since no statement of his in evaluation of the Apology is known.

The Apology as an adequate defense of the Confession is successful therefore also in defending an evangelical interpretation of Christianity. It exhibits a profound as well as a scholarly understanding of the gospel. Melanchthon, as he himself says in a letter of January 1, worked hardest on the doctrine of justification by faith. His treatment of this doctrine constitutes virtually a third of the entire Apology. He interpreted all other doctrines in its light. The Apology, therefore, is a classic on justification and related doctrines.

Looking back from our time to the sixteenth century, we see the Apology as an outstanding example of the theological writing of the Reformation age. Those who would sample the literary style and the patterns of thinking of that day would do well to read the Apology.

Melanchthon wrote in the preface, "It has always been my custom in these controversies to retain, so far as I was at all able, the form of the ordinarily received doctrine, in order that at some time concord could be reached the more readily."

Yet in the Apology the battle lines between Roman Catholic and evangelical doctrines are drawn with fine precision. However much our patterns of thinking may have changed, the distinctions made by the Apology still stand. It is therefore unmistakably clear that Romanist doctrine always includes human righteousness in the ground of justification. It was so in the sixteenth century, and the situation has not changed.

The gospel doctrine of Christ alone and faith alone, which the Confutation attacked, had to be stated in the clearest theological terms possible. In his writing Melanchthon discussed justification not only in its forensic aspect, but also in its relation to sanctification. There was the need of showing both how men are *accounted* holy and how they *become* holy. Moreover, the doctrine thus stated evangelically could not be harmonized with that taught under the papacy.

The purpose of the Apology to defend the Confession, and with it the gospel doctrine, against a specific opponent was accompanied by a vigorous mood. For the Apology is a piece of polemical writing. It is markedly aggressive in contrast to the calmness of the Confession. Melanchthon declared, "I have entirely laid aside the mildness which I formerly exercised toward the opponents." [5] In the Apology he attacked, sometimes with sarcasm and vehemence, the unscriptural positions of the Romanists.

In general, however, the mood of the Apology is earnest rather than biting. Jacobs remarked:

Regarded as a whole, its spirit is so mild and conciliatory, its style so clear and chaste, its language so animated and eloquent, its entire mode of reasoning so manifestly the sincere expression of a mind that has been long and deeply absorbed in the contemplation of divine things, that its careful study cannot fail to afford rich edification.[6]

---

[5] *C.R.*, II, 494. Quoted in *Conc. Trig.*, Hist. Intro., p. 45.
[6] *Book of Concord*, II, 41.

Above these other aspects is the fact that the Apology is a confessional writing. Though authorized by the Lutheran nobility, it was published as a private writing, as Melanchthon says in the preface, and it bears his name as author. Yet a year later it was approved at a conference of evangelical estates at Schweinfurth. It was acknowledged in the Wittenberg Concord of 1536. At Smalcald in 1537 it was approved by the clergy assembled there and was named in the *Recess* signed by the princes, thus being given a place beside the Augsburg Confession. It was cited as authoritative at the conference at Worms in 1540. It was recognized as official in the Religious Peace Treaty of Augsburg in 1555. Church orders and *corpora doctrinae* of various areas named it. Therefore it was only to be expected that it would be included in the *Book of Concord*.

There is more to its confessional significance than its official authorization. Even though it is manifestly a theological treatise, it is clearly an earnest statement of doctrinal conviction also. It is a declaration in scholarly form of doctrines most earnestly believed. The very fact of its scholarship adds to its importance as a witness to the gospel as Lutherans understand it. Therefore its insights are scholarly, not superficial; its conclusions are weighty, rather than weak; its convictions are solidly grounded, instead of being impulsive and vacillating. It expresses in phrases familiar in academic circles the faith preached in the parishes and lodged in devout hearts. In short, it has symbolical significance because it confesses the gospel of Jesus Christ as Lutherans believe it.

Chapter IX

OUTLINE OF THE APOLOGY (ARTICLES I-VI)

The preface of the Apology, as printed, is addressed to the reader. Reminding him that after the presentation of the Augsburg Confession the Romanists tried to answer it in their Confutation, Melanchthon writes that the Lutherans were denied a copy of the Confutation except under conditions too dangerous to accept.

In the negotiations which followed the presentation of the Confutation, peace was possible only if the Lutherans would "approve certain manifest abuses and errors, and . . . assent to the Confutation." Since this was impossible, the princes ordered the writing of an Apology or defense of the Confession. After it was written the emperor refused to accept it.

The Apology was designed to show how unscriptural is the Confutation. Melanchthon acknowledges his authorship of the Apology. The method of treatment in it is made necessary by the opponents' deceitfulness. However unpleasant the discord or however great the danger may be, the chief doctrines of the Lutherans must be defended. Other good men also support them. May Christ judge the issue and bring concord.

Article I, "Of God," is treated in a brief paragraph which begins, "The first article of our Confession our adversaries approve."

Concerning Article II, "Of Original Sin," the Confutation had both praise and criticism. It approved the statement that original sin is truly sin. But it found fault with two things: that original sin is defined as "without the fear of God, without trust in God" (they said that is actual sin); and that concupiscence remains after baptism—something not mentioned in the Confession but found in Luther's writings. The

145

Apology concerns itself with these two items which the opponents have distorted.

First is the matter of definition. Lutherans teach that original sin is a lack of power to do good deeds and is an evil inclination. This is the ancient definition. It is opposed to the view that original sin is only a defect or a condition, not a disease. Jacobs identified this view as Zwinglian.[1] Yet in the Marburg Articles Luther and Zwingli agreed that "original sin is innate and inherited from Adam, and is such a sin as to condemn all men." Zwingli preferred to reserve the term "sin" for transgressions of the law. He called original sin a disease or a condition. The Apology stresses both the positive and the negative phases of original sin, in contrast to the scholastics who quite overlooked the human inability to fear and love God.

According to this ancient definition righteousness included obedience to both tables of the law. The first table commands us to fear and love God. Lack of righteousness is therefore properly defined as the absence of such fear and love of God. Augustine taught that when good is removed, evil replaces it. The scholastics can be quoted to the same effect. What the Lutherans profess is a truly scriptural and ecumenical position.

Second, the opponents criticize Luther for saying that concupiscence remains after baptism. But Augustine so taught. And Paul wrote the same in Romans 7:7, 23. The opponents say that the remaining concupiscence is not sin but that it is only a burden. However, concupiscence is not an indifferent matter; what offends God can never be indifferent. The scholastics' arguments about it are mere quibblings.

Luther taught that the guilt of concupiscence remaining after baptism is removed by Christ's merits. Yet the Christian must always struggle against concupiscence. For this struggle he needs divine grace continually.

The Lutheran teaching is that original sin is a slavery from which Christ delivers. In spite of the misrepresentations of the adversaries, this doctrine is orthodox.

In this article Melanchthon saw quite clearly that the difficulty with the opponents was their Pelagianism. When original sin is

---

[1] *Op. cit.,* II, 370.

defined in the light of Christ and free grace, the result is that found in the Confession. Part of the problem lay also in the idea of concupiscence. The Romanists were accustomed to the term *fomes*— a dry tinder always ready to burst into flame. By it they meant an inclination which is essentially fleshly, physical. The evangelical position, as stated in Melanchthon's *Loci*, is "that the word 'flesh' means all man's powers and faculties." [2]

Article III, "Of Christ," is restated in a brief paragraph. No discussion was needed since it was approved in the Confutation.

Article IV, and with it Articles V, VI, and XX, met stiff opposition because they contain the doctrine of justification by faith. The Confutation in discussing Article IV approved the condemnation of the Pelagians, but at once attempted an argument for the merit of divinely assisted works—a Semi-Pelagian position. In dealing with Article V the Confutation agreed that the Holy Ghost is given through the Word and sacraments but denied that it was by faith alone. With reference to Article VI, the Confutation approved the statement that faith must produce works but insisted that justification is by works, not by faith. The same is true of the treatment of Article XX.

Melanchthon therefore began his discussion in the Apology with a statement of the issue: the Confutation opposed the doctrine of "Christ alone" and "faith alone" in justification, whereas the Lutherans taught it. After stating the problem, Melanchthon rehearsed the Romish arguments against justification by faith, and then, in giving the arguments for it, stated what faith is, how it arises and justifies, and that it rests in Christ alone. The outline thus used reminds one of the scholastic method used by Aquinas consisting of the problem (*quaestio*), the arguments against (*quod non*), the arguments for (*quod sic*), and the author's answer (*responsio*).

First, therefore, are the arguments of the adversaries. Presuming that law and gospel ought to be distinguished, they choose only the law—a natural, rational thing accepted by the scholastics. They attribute justification to the works of the law. If works save, what place has Christ? They answer that for Christ's sake we are given an inclination to goodness which is meritorious. "Thus they bury Christ."

---

[2] *C.R.*, XXI, 104. Tr. in Hill, *op. cit.*, p. 92.

They argue for a distinction between *meritum congrui* (merit ascribed to works done before justification) and *meritum condigni* (the merit of works performed after the infusion of grace). In this distinction not only do they confuse sincere consciences but they also stress a righteousness of reason and of the law, which, however, leads to despair.

The righteousness of reason is of use in civil affairs. There is some value in the first use of the law, viz., to restrain those who would do wrong. But to think of it as a basis for the remission of sin is to be Pelagian. Such a position involves four errors: that we can merit pardon; that we are justified by works; that we can by nature love God; and that we can be sinless. Against such Pelagianism Augustine argued at great length.[3]

In their thinking of the law, the adversaries neglect the first table of duties. Yet man by nature, knowing God's wrath against sin, cannot love God. All men are guilty of sin and cannot merit pardon by keeping the law. But justification is by free promise. Faith, which is trust in Christ, obtains pardon and justification; by faith comes regeneration and the Holy Ghost. The adversaries, however, teach only the merit of works.

The second section describes the nature of justifying faith. It is not only knowledge (*notitia*) but also assent (*assensus*) and (the German version adds) trust—*fiducia*. It is more than knowledge; for it knows that Christ died and arose. But more than that it believes that he secured for us the forgiveness of sin of which the Creed speaks.

Analyzed in another way, faith implies three things: a promise, a gift, and Christ's payment for the gift. It accepts God's proffered mercy—something which even the Old Testament reveals.

The third section, which declares that faith comes through the means of grace, is related to Article V of the Confession. When law and gospel are preached, there is aroused terror, followed by consolation. The faith which receives the consolation both justifies and quickens.

The adversaries think that grace is bestowed by the sacraments by their inherent power or function (*ex opere operato*). Their doc-

---

[3] *De natura et gratia*, 40, 47. MSL XLIV, 270. Cited in *Bek.*, p. 165, n. 2.

trine of regeneration is very inadequate. But Paul clearly teaches that justification occurs only through the Word which is apprehended by faith. Since Christ is our Mediator, we must trust him in that capacity and be reconciled to God. There is no other way.

It is not that faith produces works, which in turn merit justification. Instead, faith accepts Christ's merits. The believer for Christ's sake is accounted righteous. "Because 'to be justified' means that, out of unjust men, just men be made, or born again, it means also that they should be pronounced or accounted just. For Scripture speaks in both ways."

The adversaries are offended by the word "alone." Let them then delete from Paul's writings the words "freely," "not of works," "it is the gift," and so forth. For "confidence in the merit of love or of works is excluded in justification."

In the fourth section the Apology sums up the doctrine that remission of sins is obtained by faith in Christ alone. "To attain the remission of sins is to be justified." All remission of sins is by Christ the Mediator. He is apprehended only by faith. Therefore faith alone obtains the remission of sins. In contrast, the adversaries teach us to trust in our merits.

The Apostles Paul and Peter speak of Christ as our only Mediator, and of faith as our only way of access. There is really no other way for men tainted with sin. The Apostles therefore teach that faith justifies. For example, "in the Epistle to the Romans, Paul expressly discusses this topic, and declares that, when we believe that God for Christ's sake is reconciled to us, we are justified freely by faith."

Augustine taught "that man is not justified by the precepts of a good life, but by faith in Jesus Christ." [4] The doctrine thus taught is not incidental, but is central with Paul in his Epistle to the Romans. It is found also in John's Gospel, in Acts, Habakkuk, and Isaiah. In fact, "Scripture is full of such testimonies."

Among the church fathers, Ambrose may be quoted to the same effect,[5] and also Augustine in his writing *Of the Spirit and the Letter*.[6]

---

[4] *De spiritu et litera*, 13, 22. *MSL* XLIV, 214 f. Cited in *Bek.*, p. 179, n. 1.

[5] Ep. 73. *MSL* XVI, 1307 f. Cited in *Bek.*, p. 181, n. 2.

[6] 29, 51. *MSL* XLIV, 232. Cited in *Bek.*, p. 182, n. 2.

In contrast, the adversaries, accustomed to scholastic distinctions, explain the "faith" in these passages as *fides formata*—a faith fruitful in love which justifies. But that would be to trust in our work of love, not in Christ. "We also say that love ought to follow faith. . . . Nor indeed is this faith idle knowledge, neither can it coexist with mortal sin, but it is a work of the Holy Ghost, whereby we are freed from death, and terrified minds are encouraged and quickened."

Melanchthon concluded with a summary—his *responsio*—saying "that by faith alone, we obtain the remission of sins for Christ's sake, and that by faith alone we are justified, i.e., from unrighteous men made righteous, or regenerated. . . . In this alone the office of Christ is recognized. . . . In the church it is necessary that there should be doctrine from which the pious may receive the sure hope of salvation." The adversaries, however, utterly reject this doctrine.

Thus far Melanchthon has been concerned about giving a clear and precise understanding of justification in an evangelical sense. He next turned to a detailed consideration of the positions of his opponents. He first analyzed their doctrine of love and the fulfilling of the law, scrutinizing it from the standpoint of the gospel. Then he replied to each of their arguments in detail. This is a long discussion, being about one fourth of the entire Apology. In Jacobs' *Book of Concord* it is "Chapter III"; in the *Concordia Triglotta* it is designated as "Article III."

In discussing "Love and the Fulfilling of the Law," the Apology sets forth its thesis on the basis of which the Romish arguments are to be answered. The thesis is that faith and regeneration precede love and obeying the law.

The Scriptures truly may be quoted, as the adversaries had done, to show that Christians should fully obey God's law. But "these things cannot occur until we have been justified by faith, and, regenerated, we receive the Holy Ghost." Anyone can partially obey the laws of the second table of duties, but only the twice-born can obey the first table. The adversaries do not understand this. "The Law cannot be truly kept unless the Holy Ghost be received." Only then can we have a clear understanding of the law, discovering that we are far from obeying it perfectly.

"The adversaries falsely charge against us that our theologians do not teach good works, whereas they not only require these but also show how they can be done." In fact, "we teach not only how the law can be observed, but also how God is pleased if anything be done." Faith is united with repentance—a deserting of evil deeds— and with the new life which gives itself to good deeds.

But "from these effects of faith the adversaries select one, viz., love, and teach that love justifies. . . . They proclaim that they fulfill the law, although this glory belongs properly to Christ." The fact is, however, that "in this life we cannot satisfy the law, because carnal nature does not cease to bring forth wicked dispositions."

The question may be asked, "If love is a spiritual gift, why does it not justify?" The answer has four parts. The first says that Christ's merits, not our own, save us through faith. Any other view dishonors Christ. No virtue of ours, whatever it may be, is meritorious for salvation. To the woman who anointed his feet (Luke 7:47) Jesus said, "Thy faith hath saved thee," even though he acknowledged that "she loved much." Thus, if remission of sins depends on meritorious virtues, only the virtuous can have it; and they do not need it.

The second part of the answer says that our obedience to the law is far from perfect, and hence cannot be acceptable for merit.

In the third place, remission of sin is always a gift. Christ continues to be the Mediator of the regenerate also, for they continue to commit sin and their new obedience is not sufficient to merit eternal life. All remission of sin is a gift received by faith.

The final part of the answer is that our new obedience, such as it is, becomes acceptable to God because of faith. "All Scripture, all the church cries out that the law cannot be satisfied." Look about at the wickedness of this world, at the sins even among the saints. Augusine[7] and Jerome[8] say the same thing. If Christ's merits do not save us we are lost. However, for Christ's sake through faith the believer's sins are not imputed to him. The only conclusion that can be drawn is that we are not justified by love, but only for the sake of Christ through faith.

---

[7] *Retractationes*, I, 19, 3. *MSL* XXXII, 615. Cited in *Bek.*, p. 195, n. 1.

[8] *Dial. adv. Pelagianos*, I, 5. *MSL* XXIII, 500 f. Cited in *Bek.*, p. 195, n. 2.

The Apology next presents a rebuttal of the arguments of the adversaries. They urgently insist upon good works; but at the same time they omit faith. They quite overlook the fact that the good works commanded in Scripture are the fruits of faith. Moreover, if, as the adversaries say, good works justify, then the promises of God are valueless. The truth is that because of human infirmity good works are never perfect; but God accepts them for Christ's sake and uses them for holy purposes.

The adversaries declare that each good work has its proportionate reward. This is freely acknowledged to be true. But the remission of sins is not included, for it is a gift provided abundantly, without proportion, to all. Good works are an exercise of faith, strengthening it, as in the case of Abraham.

In former times unbelievers imitated the good works of believers, presuming that such deeds are meritorious. In this way the idea of the merit of good works became prevalent. Hence this godless opinion is as ancient as it is false. Moreover, it is the view of our adversaries. Lutheran teaching is "that by faith for Christ's sake we are accounted righteous before God."

The Apology next takes up the Scripture passages cited by the adversaries. The first is I Corinthians 13:2, "Though I have all faith," etc., "and have not charity, I am nothing." But this simply says that love is a necessary fruit of justifying faith. It does not say that love justifies.

Second, they quote I Corinthians 13:13, "The greatest of these is charity." Even though love is the greatest virtue since it keeps the great commandment, yet no works of the law justify, not even love (which in us is always quite imperfect).

Their third quotation was Colossians 3:14, "Charity which is the bond of perfectness." But if this means that love justifies, what need is there of Christ? Instead, Paul is here talking of love as a basis of Christian unity. Incidentally, see how unloving are the adversaries in their brutal persecution of the Evangelicals!

A fourth quotation is I Peter 4:8, "Charity shall cover the multitude of sins." But here they repeat the same mistaken interpretation and overlook what Peter said about faith. This quotation Peter took from Proverbs 10:12. Its meaning is the same as that of the third quotation. Hatred divides, but love unites, forgives, and pacifies brethren. It does not justify.

They seem to have a decisive quotation in James 2:24, "Ye see then how by works a man is justified, and not by faith only." But their minds are so filled with ideas of meritorious works that they misread the passage. For James speaks of faith, and they omit that. In preceding verses James said that love follows faith, and that it is a mark of the regenerate life, a virtue of those justified for Christ's sake. He did not say that works justify, or that Christ is only partly our Propitiator, leaving us to do the rest of the work of redemption.

Other passages cited are Luke 6:37, "Forgive and ye shall be forgiven"; Isaiah 58:7, 9, "Is it not to deal thy bread to the hungry? . . . Then shalt thou call, and the Lord shall answer." Daniel 4:27, "Break off thy sins . . . by showing mercy to the poor." Matthew 5:3, 7, "Blessed are the poor in spirit; for theirs is the kingdom of heaven. Blessed are the merciful; for they shall obtain mercy." But they give the same false interpretation to these also.

It must always be remembered that the unregenerate cannot keep the law and that "without faith it is impossible to please God" (Heb. 11:6). It is not enough to preach the works of the law; the promises of the gospel are needed also. Repentance, regeneration, and faith are presupposed in the exhortation to good works in the many passages in Isaiah, Luke, Daniel, Ezekiel, Matthew, and elsewhere.

All these passages teach that works, however much they are praised, are not done without Christ. In this sense we must understand Matthew 19:17, "If thou wilt enter into life, keep the commandments." This rule applies also to similar verses of Scripture.

The Bible also teaches that repentance (which implies a new way of life) and remission of sins must be related to faith. "Yet Christ often connects the promise of the remission of sins to good works, not because he means that good works are a propitiation, for they follow reconciliation; but for two reasons. One is because good fruits ought necessarily to follow. Therefore he admonishes that, if good fruits do not follow, the repentance is hypocritical and feigned. The other reason is because we have need of external signs of so great a promise, because a conscience full of fear has need of manifold consolation."

Even the apocryphal passage of Tobit 4:11, "Alms free from every sin, and from death," is to be understood in the same way. In all this the adversaries often pick mutilated phrases from the context. They did it in quoting Luke 11:41, "Give alms of such things as ye have; and behold all things are clean unto you." In this passage they ignore the fact that Christ was stressing purity of the heart. They continually point to the law and thereby leave tender consciences in despair. They teach contrary to Romans 4:5, which says that "faith is counted for righteousness."

It may be confidently affirmed, therefore, that the passages they cite are not opposed to Lutheran doctrine, but are co-ordinate therewith.

Having examined the Scripture passages quoted by the Confutation, the Apology next contrasts the Roman doctrine of justification with that of the gospel. The Romanists teach two modes of justification. The first is by meritorious works *de congruo* or *de condigno*, which is a doctrine based on reason. The second is by an infused habit or inclination, which is meritorious. But neither leaves any place for Christ, or regeneration, or faith. Neither is scriptural in the sense of the "righteousness of faith" (Romans 4:13). Love is truly the fulfilling of the law, something, however, which unregenerate human nature cannot do. It is surprising that the adversaries fail to see the clear teaching of Scripture or to notice that their doctrine omits Christ and leads to despair.

They have raised several objections to the doctrine of justification by faith. If they say that the devils believe, the reply is that the faith of devils is only knowledge; it is not trust in Christ.

If they say that righteousness is of the will, while faith is of the intellect, so that the two cannot be united, the reply is that the two are actually united, because the will commands the intellect. Moreover, there is really no problem here, because justification is forensic—a declaring the believer righteous for Christ's sake; it is not based on human conduct or merits. In this doctrine evangelical faith honors God and his promises.

If they say that faith is confused with hope (which looks forward to things promised), the answer is that these two cannot be separated except in thought.

All such objections are answered by the doctrine that it is by faith that we are justified, reconciled, and regenerated.

Underlying the Roman positions is their doctrine of *meritum condigni,* though the term does not appear in the Confutation. The Apology examines the doctrine and makes four criticisms of it. It substitutes good works and love for Christ and faith. It leaves consciences in doubt. It cannot clearly identify works that are meritorious from those that are not. It is opposed to the doctrine of salvation by grace as taught by the Fathers, especially Augustine[9] and Cyprian,[10] and by Scripture in many passages which declare both the futility of works to earn salvation and the certainty of salvation through God's mercy.

The adversaries have tried to find weaknesses in the evangelical doctrine. They have said that good works would not be needed if it is true that they do not merit salvation. But Lutheran teaching is that the purpose of our justification is to enable us to do good works.

They have said that eternal life is called a reward, and therefore is merited. But their inference is unjustified; for if they will read further they will see eternal life called a gift. "Reward" in Scripture must be understood as due because of promise, not because of merits. Thus Paul says, "There is laid up for me a crown of righteousness, which the Lord, the righteous judge shall give me" (II Tim. 4:8). In matters other than justification, good works are indeed rewarding in their consequences. But the adversaries always connect rewards with justification and so misinterpret Scripture.

When they quote such passages as Romans 2:6, "Who will render to every man according to his works," they entirely neglect faith as the foundation of good works. They must be reminded again that "without faith it is impossible to please God" (Heb. 11:6). The chief fault of the adversaries is that "they abolish the righteousness of faith, and exclude Christ as Mediator."

It is no small matter therefore when the scholastics utterly ignore justifying faith. Faith is not mere knowledge, as they think, but is confidence in the work of Christ. This is seen in our prayers which

---

[9] *De gratia et lib. arb.,* 9, 21. *MSL* XLIV, 893. Cited in *Bek.,* p. 222, n. 1.

[10] *De orat. dom.,* 22. *MSL* IV, 552B. Cited in *Bek.,* p. 222, n. 3.

ask that blessings be given "for Christ's sake." Regardless of what the scholastics say, this evangelical doctrine is in accord with Scripture, the church fathers, and the ecumenical church which confesses Christ as Propitiator.

In fact, in spite of the pronouncements of popes and theologians, there is still some faith within the Roman Church. The influence of high ecclesiastics should not be allowed to lead us away from the true doctrine. Even though the papists cruelly persecute and oppress, the true church will continue to teach the pure gospel of justification by faith in the merits of Christ. "Hence the judgments of our adversaries will not disturb us, since they defend human opinions contrary to the gospel, contrary to the authority of the holy fathers, who have written in the church, and contrary to the testimonies of godly minds."

This extended treatment is impressive in its earnestness. There is no wavering from the main point. The petty questions and speculations of the scholastics are shown to be insignificant in the light of the central evangelical principle. Having grasped what is basic in the doctrine of justification, the Apology clings to it in repeated, almost repetitious, declarations. The repeated arguments, like hammer blows, are needed to clinch the point. Though the reiterated positions may at first seem tedious, yet with continued study they are seen to be necessary and important. No matter which way the Romish argument turns to find a way of escape, it is met at every point by the evangelical doctrine.

The Apology in this section shows also the soundness of its exegesis. The faults in the Roman system were that it took preconceived notions into its interpretation of Scripture, and that it took verses out of their context to use as proof-texts. Either of these would have been sufficient to produce erroneous results. In clear contrast the Apology indicates the thorough, scholarly methods of the Lutheran theologians in their study of the Bible. It finds in the Word of God the basic doctrine of salvation, not merely in a verse or two but sustained throughout its message. With this insight Melanchthon is able to avoid the mistakes of the Romanists.

There is ample evidence also of the Christocentric quality of the doctrine defended. Any teaching which obscured or eclipsed, even partially, the work of Christ could not be tolerated. The Apology sets forth in clearest terms the doctrine of *solus Christus*—"Christ alone." His work of redemption is so complete that nothing needs to be added. It is an effrontery even to suggest the possibility of such an addition. In the evangelical doctrine of justification, therefore, Christ is the only Mediator; he alone makes full atonement for our sins.

The Apology in discussing justification could not be expected to free itself entirely from scholastic methods and terminology. Yet the approach is so fresh and the treatment so incisive that in comparison the scholastic theology is dry and barren. Here there is no quibbling over minutiae. Instead, the Apology goes to the heart of the matter. It presents a doctrine which is a living faith. It proclaims a teaching which is edifying and consoling, which therefore meets the deepest spiritual needs of the Christian.

Melanchthon was at some pains to show that this doctrine was no novelty in the Christian religion. The Romanists were willing to acknowledge that Lutheran faith concerning God and Christ conformed to that in the church universal. But they could quite truthfully say that the doctrine of meritorious works had been taught in the Roman Church for a thousand years. That was an argument which was impressive to many minds.

To meet it the Apology needed to show not only that the doctrine of justification accepted by Lutherans was taught in Scripture, but also that it was affirmed in the ancient church. In this latter aspect, the work was not so easy, for the ancient church gave its major attention to the doctrines of God and Christ. Melanchthon had to rely heavily on Augustine, though he quoted twice from Ambrose,[11] once from Cyprian,[12] and once from Jerome.[13] Near the end of the section he wrote, "We know that those things which we have said are in harmony with the prophetic and apostolic Scriptures, with the holy Fathers, Ambrose, Augustine and many others, and with the whole Church of Christ, which certainly confesses that Christ is Propitiator and Justifier."

---

[11] Chap. II, sec. 103; Jacobs, *op. cit.*, p. 101. Cf. note 5 above. And Chap. III, sec. 219; Jacobs, p. 150. *Expos. evang. sec. Luc.*, VIII, 32. *MSL* XV, 1774. Cited in *Bek.*, p. 226, n. 1.

[12] Chap. III, sec. 201; Jacobs, p. 147. Cf. note 10 above.

[13] Chap. III, sec. 52; Jacobs, p. 112. Cf. note 8 above.

Chapter X

OUTLINE OF THE APOLOGY
(ARTICLES VII-XXI)

The Apology defended the doctrine of justification by faith at considerable length and with great earnestness because of its central significance. The reflection of this doctrine in other matters is to be seen also. The Apology therefore continues its program of meeting article by article the Confutation's objections to the Augsburg Confession.

Article VII, "Of the Church," next comes up for attention. The adversaries rejected the article because it spoke of the church as the congregation of saints. They insisted that the visible church includes both good and bad. The Confession agrees, having so stated in Article VIII.

Yet in principle the church is "a fellowship of faith and the Holy Ghost in hearts." It is marked by the pure doctrine of the gospel and by the sacraments administered in accordance with it. The church is the Body of Christ. This Paul taught in Ephesians 5:25. It is the faith expressed in the Creed, which speaks of a holy church, the communion of saints.

The necessity for this article is in the fact that the church is endangered both within and without. Lest Christians despair, they need to be reassured concerning the perpetuity of the church with its blessings. Though the external church includes wicked persons, yet it is necessary to teach that the church is the Body of Christ. All must understand that membership involves righteousness of the heart, and not mere outward rites such as the Hebrews observed.

The church is the kingdom of Christ, in contrast to the kingdom of the devil. Until the time when the kingdom of Christ is clearly revealed, the wicked mingle with believers and may even hold office in the church. Christ's parables, for example, that of the wheat and the tares, depict this mixed condition in the church. The godless are not members of the true church, which is an actual reality marked by the Word and the sacraments.

The foundation (knowledge of Christ and faith) is solid and firm, even though some persons, as parts of the building, are weak. Romish errors, however, do not overthrow faith or injure the foundation. For the true church has the Holy Ghost and faith, as Lyra has said.[1]

Romanists want the church defined as the absolute monarchy of the pope, with both swords, i.e., spiritual and civil power. Such a papacy is actually Antichrist. Lutherans, on the other hand, exalt Christ and the means of grace, rather than the pope and works of merit.

Lutherans acknowledge the true church as consisting, in a proper sense, of believers, though unbelievers are mingled with them, among clergy and laity alike. The sacraments are valid in spite of sinful pastors, because God gives the blessing. Lutherans oppose the Donatists and Wycliffites who said that sacraments given by sinful priests are invalid.

With regard to uniformity of rites, the adversaries distinguish between universal and particular rites. But the distinction is meaningless. Unity in the gospel alone is essential. In the past, rites have been so stressed that they came to be considered as meriting justification. It has even happened that excommunications have been pronounced and schisms have occurred over rites and usages. It is well that "for the sake of tranquillity universal rites be observed," such as the Lord's Day, festival days, etc., which have educational value. But they are not necessary for righteousness before God, any more than is the German style of clothing.

The righteousness of faith is the chief consideration, and, for this, human rites are useless, as Paul wrote to the Colossians (2:16, 17)

---

[1] Nicolaus de Lyra, a French Franciscan who died 1340, wrote a commentary of the Bible which Luther used extensively.

and Romans (14:17). Romanists insist on rites said to be apostolic; yet they neglect apostolic doctrine which joined righteousness to faith, not to rites. True, the Apostles observed days and customs, but if they are necessary for justification, why have the bishops made changes in them, e.g., in the date of Easter?

Without citing more history, it is necessary only to see that the adversaries really misunderstand the gospel. They insist on uniformity in human rites, yet they have changed Christ's ordinance—the Lord's Supper!

Concerning Article VIII Melanchthon wrote, "The entire eighth article has been approved." Truly we must "beware of false prophets." But imperfections in the ministry should not cause schisms like that of the Donatists. Nor should ministers who own property be disqualified, as Wycliffe taught.

Article IX, "Of Baptism," was approved by the Confutation. The Anabaptists err in rejecting infant baptism, for children are included in the promise of salvation, which comes through the means of grace. The command to baptize is universal, and therefore includes children. Moreover, God has approved infant baptism by granting the Holy Spirit to those thus baptized.

Article X, "Of the Lord's Supper," also was approved by the Confutation. The doctrine of the real presence is in accord with I Corinthians 10:16 which declares that the bread is the communion of the Lord's body. The Roman and the Greek churches teach a bodily presence, as did also Vulgarius[2] (Theophylact) and Cyril of Alexandria.[3] It is ancient and ecumenical doctrine that Christ is present in the sacrament both spiritually and bodily.

Melanchthon did not at this place contrast the Lutheran with the Roman Catholic teaching. He simply indicated that both recognize the reality of the presence of Christ according to his human as well as his divine nature. For a rejection of the doctrine of transubstantiation, one must turn to the Smalcald Articles and the Formula of Concord.

---

[2] *Comm. in ev. Marc.* 14, 22. *MSG* 123, 649D. Cited in *Bek.*, p. 248, n. 2.

[3] *Joh. lib.* X, 2. *MSG* 74, 341 A/B.D. Cited in *Bek.*, p. 248, n. 3.

Article XI, "Of Confession," was approved by the Confutation. "But they add a correction, . . that annual confession be made, and . . . all sins . . . which can be recalled be recounted." Lutherans, however, regard absolution as the special message of the gospel announcing remission of sins freely for Christ's sake. This is a consoling doctrine.

As to time, wrote Melanchthon, we use the sacrament (absolution and the Lord's Supper) often in a year, rather than on a fixed date each year. The enumeration of sins, though useful, is not required. Such enumeration is not based on Scripture. It brings doubt to conscientious minds. It has led to grievous abuses. It is not necessary for justification. It demands the impossible. Evangelical confession has its values, but confession as used by the Romanists has no place for Christ and faith, being concerned largely with human traditions.

In dealing with Article XII, "Of Repentance," Melanchthon found it necessary to discuss at some length the Romish doctrine. First of all, he stated the problem. The Confutation approved the forgiveness of sins to those fallen from grace after baptism. But it denounced the defining of repentance as contrition and faith, even though that is scriptural. It disapprovingly recalled, as Eck's Theses had done, that Luther rejected the three-part definition by the papists. Melanchthon then addressed the emperor, requesting careful attention to the statement of this important doctrine.

Now for a look at the Roman Catholic doctrine. Before Luther the doctrine was in confusion in the complicated speculations of the scholastics. They distinguished learnedly between contrition and attrition. But their teaching gave no consolation to Christians because it omitted faith. Their finespun theories are full of error and hypocrisy, obscuring the benefits of Christ.

After contrition, the next act in their play is confession. They require an enumeration of all sins, most of them being against mere human traditions. No mention is made of consoling faith.

In their third act are satisfactions, performed either in this life or in purgatory. Often the satisfactions are foolish observances or indulgences substituted for them.

There are eleven errors in their doctrine, all contrary to the Scriptures and the fathers:

1. Good works are meritorious.
2. Attrition merits grace.
3. Merely detesting a crime removes the sin.
4. Contrition, not faith, produces remission of sin.
5. The power of the keys remits sins, not before God, but before the church.
6. The power of the keys commutes eternal punishment into temporal satisfactions.
7. By divine right the enumeration of sins is necessary.
8. Common people believe that satisfactions release from purgatory.
9. The sacrament of penance without grace obtains grace.
10. Indulgences free from purgatory.
11. Where judgment of serious crimes is referred to high officials, both punishment and release from guilt is involved.

Against this background the Lutheran teaching is examined. In evangelical doctrine repentance consists of contrition and faith, followed by good works. Contrition arises when sins are reproved by God's Word. Thus Scripture speaks in many places, e.g., "For mine iniquities are gone over mine head, as a heavy burden they are too heavy for me" (Ps. 38:4). The law accuses and terrifies. How can men have meritorious love toward a God whose wrath they dread?

For this reason faith is added, for when the promises of God are accepted, the heart is consoled. "This faith shows the distinction between the contrition of Judas and Peter." With faith bestowed, man can fear and love God. Filial fear is the believer's dread of sin, but servile fear is the unbeliever's dread of God's wrath.

The power of the keys presents the consolation of the gospel through absolution. It remits sins before God. In a sense, absolution may be called a sacrament of repentance. The Word and the sacraments further strengthen faith and include remission of sins. This is a clear and thoroughly evangelical doctrine of repentance.

In support of this evangelical statement of the doctrine Melanchthon next indicated the scriptural basis. In the invitation in Matthew 11:28, "Come unto me, all ye that labor and are heavy laden, and I will give you rest," the words "labor and are heavy laden" picture the distress of conscience, and the coming to Christ is faith. The same is taught in Mark 1:15, "Repent ye and believe the gospel." This faith is not mere knowledge, but it is trust and may also include the fruits of faith.

Repentance and faith are united in Colossians 2:11, 12, 14, and many other passages. To terrify the conscience is called God's "strange work" in Isaiah 28:21; but God's consoling promises are also available at once. The law is that part of Scripture which reveals and reproves sin. The gospel is that which promises grace. The effects of law and gospel are shown in the lives of such persons as Adam, David, and the sinful woman who anointed Christ's feet.

On this basis Melanchthon argued that faith is necessary. The Romanists teach that remission of sins is received by the sacrament of penance *ex opere operato*, and not by faith. They think of faith as a thing of knowledge. Lutherans teach that faith trusts God's mercy, and that it consoles and justifies. These are the points in the dispute.

Melanchthon vindicated his doctrine by four logical deductions. First, he asked, is absolution a part of repentance? If not, confession brings no relief. On the other hand, if it is, then faith is needed, because absolution is received only by faith.

In the second place, all admit that the purpose of repentance is to receive remission of sin. What receives the remission is a part of penance. Faith alone receives remission, hence faith is part of repentance. This is what Peter taught in Acts 10:43: "Whosoever believeth in him shall receive remission of sins."

The Romanists say they follow the consensus of the church, but the consensus Peter followed was that of "all the prophets" which the papists have no right to change, though they have done so. Though great names like Scotus, Gabriel, and others be cited in great number, Lutherans will not hesitate to oppose them with the consensus of the prophets. Even some of the fathers, such as Bernard,[4] agree with the prophets.

As a third item, the adversaries say that if a contrite person shows a deed of love to God, it merits remission of sin. But love is fulfilling the law. This is to put confidence in works and law rather than in

---

[4] *Sermo in festo b. Mariae virg.*, I, 1. *MSL* 183, 383A. Cited in *Bek.*, p. 266, n. 1.

Christ and the gospel, which then are superfluous. We turn from the law to the gospel; from works to Christ. "Yea, it is a reproach to Christ and a repeal of the gospel to believe that we obtain the remission of sins on account of the law, or otherwise than by faith in Christ." Neither works nor love can be of as much value as Christ.

Hence Paul insists that we are not justified by the law, but by the grace of God received through faith. We know that this is the genuine meaning of Paul's words. Christ said, "I am the vine, ye are the branches." The adversaries would make us branches of the mass instead of Christ.

In the fourth place, how can consciences ever be at peace under the Roman doctrine of works, since the law always accuses us? The fact is that the only peace is in the consolation of the gospel. Moreover, Paul said in Romans 14:23, "Whatsoever is not of faith is sin."

In conclusion Melanchthon remarked that Lutherans dislike controversy and prefer concord. But since the adversaries condemn the truth, Lutherans dare not desert the cause of Christ, and therefore have given an explanation of their doctrine. The fact is that "there are sentences extant in the fathers, not only concerning contrition and works, but also concerning faith. But the adversaries, since they understand neither the nature of repentance, nor the language of the fathers, select passages concerning a part of repentance, viz., concerning works; they pass over the declarations made elsewhere concerning faith, since they do not understand them."

In the Jacobs edition of the *Book of Concord* the discussion of repentance and Article XII is indicated as Chapter V. But remembering that the Roman sacrament of penance consists of three items: contrition, confession, and satisfaction (absolution is sometimes inserted after confession to make four items), it will be observed that the treatment thus far has been confined to contrition. In the next section, indicated as Chapter VI, Melanchthon proceeded to discuss also the topics of confession and satisfaction. Here he examined in greater detail these doctrines, a part of which he had treated briefly in connection with Article XI.

Confession, the second part of penance, next receives attention. It is retained in the church chiefly because of absolution, which is the power of the keys proclaimed to individuals. "Wherefore it would be wicked to remove private absolution from the church." Yet it must not be a kind of judicial examination.

The adversaries quote Proverbs 27:23: "Be thou diligent to know the state of thy flocks." But that has nothing to do with confession. True confession to God is taught in Psalm 32:5, "I said, I will confess my transgressions unto the Lord." It is also in Psalm 51:4, "Against thee, thee only, have I sinned." Confession to our fellow men is taught in James 5:16, "Confess your faults one to another," the purpose being reconciliation. Nowhere in Scripture is it taught that an enumeration of sins is necessary.

Some church writers mention public confession, but these were instances of persons being restored to fellowship after having fallen away from the church. The repentance of such persons was examined to see if it was genuine; and certain things called "satisfactions" were required of the penitent. The custom is obsolete but the name "satisfaction" remains and is applied to acts imposed by the priest upon those making confession.

But they are merely human customs and are not by divine appointment. Nor must they be thought to be meritorious, thereby replacing faith. The adversaries say that satisfactions do not remit guilt, but only punishment during life and in purgatory. "This entire matter is fictitious." The scholastics failed to note the history of the word and its use in church discipline but imagined that satisfactions appease God.

The adversaries quote from Scripture statements such as Matthew 3:8, "Bring forth, therefore, fruits meet for repentance." And they cite passages from the fathers but always they distort the quotation to mean satisfactions. Melanchthon was aroused to indignation: "May God put to confusion these godless sophists who so wickedly distort God's Word to their own most vain dreams!" They argue that since Christ says "Repent," and the Apostles preach repentance, "therefore satisfactions redeem the punishments of purgatory! Who taught these asses such logic?" And they would deceitfully lead people to believe that when we reject satisfactions we are thereby opposed to repentance!

Cardinal Campegius is reminded that the Roman Church endangers her position by such absurdities. In many lands men are suspicious of the papal policy which refuses to give fair consideration to these important doctrines, but which simply answers evangelical teaching with persecutions, thereby arousing intense bitterness.

The point is that the quotations cited by the Romanists have nothing to do with canonical satisfactions. God's Word teaches that repentance involves leaving sin and showing in life the fruits of faith. But these fruits are certainly not meritorious satisfactions.

The adversaries argue that satisfactions are optional in this life, that they can be paid in purgatory and may be remitted by indulgences. But works which are genuinely the fruits of faith are necessary as the normal product of faith; they are expected in this present life and cannot be replaced by indulgences. Therefore the Scripture in the passages quoted by the adversaries is speaking of the fruits of faith rather than of satisfactions. And the power of the keys refers to forgiveness of sins and not to purgatory or canonical satisfactions.

The papists teach that Christ atoned for guilt, but our satisfactions (Melanchthon called them "frigid observances devised by men") redeem from eternal death. "It is incredible with what grief we recite these absurdities of the adversaries, which cannot but cause one who considers them to be enraged against such doctrines of demons." Their teaching obscures the law. They declare that a man can do works of supererogation, i.e., more than the law requires, and therefore can have a surplus of merits. In addition they include in good works things done in obedience to human traditions, such as days of fasting, pilgrimages, etc. Such teaching is "vain and wicked," doubly obscuring the law which no one can keep perfectly.

Furthermore, their teaching obscures repentance and grace. Only Christ has overcome sin and death, and God's grace is received only by faith, not by satisfactions. Papists insist that sins should have some punishment. That is true, but the punishment is a terrified conscience, and besides it is not meritorious. They mistakenly substitute a pilgrimage for terrors of the heart.

Lutherans agree with them that God punishes sin. "Contrition is therefore more truly a punishment than is satisfaction." A guilty conscience is a genuine affliction, which acts of satisfaction cannot relieve. Citing the punishments incurred by Adam and David, the papists assume that each sin has a special punishment by which its guilt is remitted.

But there is no such teaching in Scripture. Instead, all sins are forgiven for Christ's sake. As in the case of Job, afflictions are not always punishments, but have other uses. In reading I Corinthians 11:31, "If we would judge ourselves, we should not be judged by the Lord," the papists think that self-inflicted punishments appease God. "Our adversaries pay the penalty for despising grammar when they understand 'to judge' to be the same as to make a pilgrimage clad in mail." The truth is that only thorough contrition is acceptable to God.

The church fathers understood satisfactions simply as church discipline, and purgatory as a purification of imperfect souls. (Pseudo-) Augustine wrote[5] of satisfactions as being bodily self-discipline to avoid temptation. Gregory made restitution of stolen property a part of repentance.[6] (Pseudo-) Chrysostom[7] combined humility with repentance. Others wrote of public confession of notorious sins. But they did not make such acts necessary conditions for remission of sins.

In conclusion, Melanchthon observed that Lutherans regard satisfactions as not commanded in God's Word but as unjustly imposed by the papists. Lutherans teach that the repentant life produces the good fruits which are commanded by God. They reject satisfactions as works meriting the remission of sins. Indulgences, which formerly released individuals from church discipline, but now are thought to release from purgatory, are also rejected. The power of the keys refers to the remission of sins in absolution. Thus the evangelical doctrine exalts faith and consoles consciences, whereas the doctrine of the adversaries is purely a human invention.

When Melanchthon's discussion is examined in its entirety, it will be noticed that he left no part of the evangelical doctrine undefended. From Scripture, from history, from logic, from personal piety, and from theology he vindicated the Lutheran teaching. And from all these viewpoints the Roman doctrine is shown to be untenable. Worse than that, it is tyranny and a perversion of the gospel. Nothing can

---

[5] *De eccl. dogm.* 24. *MSL* XLIII, 1218. Cf. *Bek.*, p. 288, n. 3.

[6] *Decr. Grat.* II. C. 33. q. 3. Cited in *Bek.*, p. 289, n. 1.

[7] *Ibid.* Cited in *Bek.*, p. 289, n. 2.

be tolerated in the church if it leaves out faith and obscures Christ. The evangelical doctrine, however, is both consoling and true.

Article XIII of the Confession deals with the "Number and Use of the Sacraments." The Confutation had approved the article but insisted that there are seven sacraments. The number, replied Melanchthon, is unimportant so long as the sacraments are of divine origin.

By definition, sacraments are "rites which have the command of God and to which the promise of grace has been added." Therefore the true sacraments are baptism, the Lord's Supper and absolution. "It has been well said by Augustine that a sacrament is a 'visible word.'"

Here, as in dealing with Articles XI and XII in the Apology, Melanchthon speaks of absolution as a sacrament. In the Large Catechism at the beginning of the discussion of baptism, Luther named only two sacraments, and the Lutheran Church follows that classification.

Luther wrote in the *Babylonian Captivity*, "At the outset I must deny that there are seven sacraments, and hold for the present to but three—baptism, penance, and bread. . . . To be sure, if I desire to use the term in its scriptural sense, I should allow but a single sacrament (I Tim. 3:16) with three sacramental signs." [8] But near the end of the document he said, "Hence there are, strictly speaking, but two sacraments in the Church of God—baptism and bread; for only in these two do we find both the divinely instituted sign and the promise of forgiveness of sins." [9]

In this light Melanchthon examined the other rites which the Roman Church called sacraments. Two of them, confirmation and extreme unction, are dismissed at once on the ground that "they do not have God's command."

Another Roman sacrament is holy orders. But the papists connect the priesthood with sacrifice. However, Christ has made the complete sacrifice and no other is necessary. Pastors, in evangelical teaching, are "called to teach the gospel and administer the sacraments." "If

---

[8] W.A., VI, 501. Phila. ed., II, 177.
[9] W.A., VI, 572. Phila. ed., II, 291 f.

ordination be understood as applying to the ministry of the Word, we are not unwilling to call ordination a sacrament. . . . For the church has the command to appoint ministers."

Matrimony has both God's command and promises pertaining to the bodily life. But if it is called a sacrament, it should be distinguished from the others. If everything which has God's command is a sacrament, then the magistracy, and, more particularly, prayer should be included.

With regard to the use of the sacraments, Melanchthon wrote that "we condemn the whole crowd of scholastic doctors who teach that the sacraments confer grace *ex opere operato*." Paul taught that faith alone receives the benefit (Rom. 4:9). The sacraments are signs of promises which must be received by faith. The doctrine of *opus operatum* produces great abuses and is without patristic or scriptural authority.

With regard to Article XIV, "Of Ecclesiastical Orders," the papists approved the statement that pastors should be rightly called; but they insisted on canonical ordination, i.e., by bishops. Lutherans are willing to accept episcopal rule, if it is acknowledged to be only by human right. But some bishops have persecuted evangelical pastors and therefore have been rejected. Bishops are acceptable if they permit evangelical doctrine.

Article XV is given the title, "Of Human Traditions in the Church." The Confutation agreed that rites, which can be observed without sin, are profitable for peace and good order. But it refused to agree that rites of human origin are not meritorious.

Papists are like the Jews when they declare that rites earn remission of sins. These obscure the gospel. For Paul clearly teaches in Ephesians 2:8, "By grace are ye saved through faith; and that not of yourselves: it is the gift of God." If human observances justify before God, then Christ is no longer honored as Mediator. But if we are forgiven for Christ's sake, the idea of meritorious ceremonies is impious.

The rites established by the fathers were for good order, not for merit. There is no way of knowing which human rites are meritorious; otherwise even heathen rites would be approved. "As these services have no testimony of God's Word, conscience must doubt as to whether they please God." A religion of meritorious works is really the kingdom of Antichrist and is no better than that of the Mohammedans.

From an evangelical viewpoint there are at least four principles applicable to liturgical usages. The first principle is that of liberty. It provides that uniformity in rites is not necessary. The fathers did not consider traditions necessary for justification.

Rites were observed from a second principle, viz., that of orderliness for the people, so that they might have a common time for worship. Lutherans also keep the good customs of the past as a matter of utility, not for merit. God is not reconciled to us by vestments. Traditions may have good reason to support them but they easily are mistaken as being works of merit.

It is easy to imitate rites, but not faith. When confidence is placed in rites, many evils follow, the gospel is obscured, and ordinary obligations are neglected. Consciences are disturbed lest something has been omitted. The many books written show the excessive concern with rites. Better than this false wisdom is the gospel of free grace and of liberty from the tyranny of ceremonies. Bishops have no power to make rites necessary for justification. The Apostles wished this liberty from the tyranny of the law to continue.

There is a principle of historicity which regards rites as venerable and good customs, like soldiers' uniforms or academic gowns. They may be changed or even abandoned, as was done by Christ's disciples.

Lutherans continue a moderate use of old traditions as useful to peace and spiritual growth. This is the principle of edification. Many Lutheran people receive the Lord's Supper weekly. They learn to pray. Their children are given catechetical instruction. Their worship is gospel-centered. The sermons addressed to them proclaim repentance, the righteousness of faith, and such matters. Even fasting and bodily discipline have their use, but not as works of merit.

There have been many difficulties with rites, because they were said to be necessary. On the other hand, freedom also has been abused. There must be no uncontrolled liberty, but changes made in customary historic rites must be well justified. Indeed, "such old customs (should) be observed which can be observed without sin or without great inconvenience." Good order and edification are the chief concerns.

Melanchthon, in this discussion, wrote more than a rebuttal of the Romanist doctrine of meritorious rites. He indicated also the evangelical principles for liturgical usages. The principles of liberty and historicity are noted for their values, but they are not accepted without limitations. If unrestricted, the one runs to fanaticism, the other to ceremonialism. But orderliness and edification need no reservations, and Melanchthon wrote of them without qualifications.

Article XVI, "Of Political Order," was acceptable to the writers of the Confutation. Though "the kingdom of Christ is spiritual," it nevertheless "permits us outwardly to use legitimate political ordinances, .. just as it permits us to use medicine or the art of building." "Carlstadt was insane" in reviving the laws of Moses.

The monks also distort the truth by their poverty and celibacy. The gospel does not destroy business or the family, as Julian the Apostate and Celsus taught.[10] But we are under civil laws, just as we are under natural law. Private redress is forbidden. Public redress is a function of government and is not overthrown by the gospel.

Nor is it a virtue to refrain from owning property, as the monks hypocritically teach, and as Wycliffe required of his priests. Contracts are lawful before God as well as before men. This summary of Lutheran doctrine shows to all how Lutherans support civil functions with good conscience, and how they reject as unscriptural the "Satanic communion" of the monks.

Article XVII, "Of Christ's Return to Judgment," "the adversaries receive without exception."

Article XVIII, "Of Free Will," the Confutation accepted, but added some irrelevant ideas. The papists denounced the Pelagians, yet teach the same doctrine. Lutherans teach that the will is free in rational and civil affairs. Good conduct of this kind is called "righteousness of the flesh" in Scripture. Such good conduct is rare enough.

The papists teach that civil good works have merit *de congruo,* even though they lack the fear and love of God. But how "can a corrupt tree bring forth good fruit"? In spiritual matters there is no

---

[10] For sources cf. *Bek.,* p. 308, nn. 2, 3.

free will. Natural man cannot love God, and even saints do it imperfectly.

In brief, Lutherans teach free will in civil affairs, where men can respond to discipline. But in spiritual affairs the work of the Holy Spirit is necessary.

Article XIX, "Of the Cause of Sin," the adversaries receive also.

But Article XX, "Of Good Works," they reject and condemn. They oppose the gospel teaching that sins are forgiven freely for Christ's sake. "The blasphemy of ascribing Christ's honor to our works is not to be endured." It should be condemned by the emperor and the nobility. For this matter has had ample discussion in connection with Article IV.

Isaiah said concerning Christ, "The Lord hath laid on him the iniquities of us all." If the Lutherans had not been consoled and sustained by this pure gospel, they would have been terrified by the decree issued against them in the *Recess* of the diet, November 19. But no danger could make them desert the truth of Scripture.

The adversaries quoted II Peter 1:10, "Give diligence to make your calling sure." But Peter is speaking of works which follow rather than precede the remission of sins. The adversaries make a cause out of what is an effect. They say that our doctrine was condemned a thousand years ago. Yet the opposite is true, for Pelagius, rather than Augustine, was condemned. Lutherans teach that the Holy Ghost begets faith, out of which grow the fruits of the Spirit.

Article XXI, "Of the Invocation of Saints," was also condemned by the papists. Yet all they urged was that saints should be honored and should pray for others. Their quotations from Cyprian and Jerome do not teach the invocation of saints.

Lutherans approve honoring the saints by thanking God for their example, by being encouraged by their success, and by imitating their virtues. But the adversaries want us to pray to the saints. Lutherans grant that angels pray for us and perhaps the saints in heaven pray also, but the Scripture does not say so. The only possible quotation is II Maccabees 15:14.

The adversaries dispute many fine points in this doctrine. But it is not based on Scripture. It is a recent invention of theirs, for it did not exist in the ancient church. They insist on invoking the saints and on applying the merits of saints to others, thereby making saints mediators in place of Christ. But a mediator should have God's approval. There is such approval for Christ, but none for the saints. And a mediator should have made satisfaction for others. This Christ has done, but not the saints.

It is no false interpretation of the adversaries to say that they approve the invocation of saints and trust in their merit; for many authors may be cited. For example, in their form of absolution are these words, "The passion of our Lord Jesus Christ, the merits of the most blessed Virgin Mary and of all the saints be to thee for the remission of sins." The prayer for the dying reads, "Mother of grace, protect us from the enemy, receive us in the hour of death."

If Mary does this, what does Christ do? In common usage she has replaced Christ. Even Hilary taught that the merits of saints cannot be transferred to others. Lutherans cannot accept a doctrine which substitutes the saints for Christ.

Moreover, some have imagined that each saint had a particular blessing to give, e.g., Valentine heals epilepsy. Thus they imitate the worship of pagan deities and even superstitiously reverence images, some of which are cleverly designed to nod assent or refusal. Fabulous stories arose concerning the saints, even of purely fictional persons such as St. Christopher.

Truly, examples of bravery and mercy should encourage us rather than produce superstitious practices. But the papal authorities approve these practices because they yield revenue. They censure us for honoring Christ and for correcting abuses. The Confutation is quite silent about these notorious abuses, about which many before Luther made complaint. If the Confutation had been candid, it would have objected to the abuses also for the good of the church. The emperor, in seeking to promote the prosperity of the church, should support sound doctrine, and cleanse the church of abuses.

Chapter XI

OUTLINE OF THE APOLOGY
(ARTICLES ON ABUSES)

The statement on the invocation of saints had been included in the doctrinal articles of the Confession because of its declaration concerning Christ as the only Mediator. The Apology had given the same emphasis, yet gave considerable attention to the abuses connected with the invocation of saints. Without any pause it takes up the other abuses treated in the Confession.

Article XXII, "Of Both Kinds in the Lord's Supper," took up a matter that had arisen in the few centuries before the Reformation. The clergy had withheld the cup from the laity. The Apology declares that the entire sacrament is for both laity and clergy, as Paul's words imply. Christ's ordinance should not be changed. Communion in both kinds is still the practice in the Eastern churches and formerly was also in the West.

The Confutation brazenly claims that the ancient church used one kind only, but produces no evidence. The Scripture quoted by it either does not refer to the sacrament, or does so in a figure of speech whereby when one part is named the whole is signified. Their reference to lay communion in the ancient church is deceitful since it has nothing to do with one kind only.

If, as the adversaries claim, the use of one kind exalts the clergy over the laity, it is purely a man-made imposition. They quote, as evidence of one kind only, the story of Eli's sons, who were condemned to lose the part of the sacrifice belonging to the priests. Is one kind only, therefore, a punishment? They say the laymen should be content. Such impudent tyranny! They cite the danger of spilling but such arguments do not suffice to change Christ's ordinance. Let the papists beware when they persecute those using the sacrament aright!

Article XXIII, "Of the Marriage of Priests," aroused Melanchthon to an extended and indignant statement. The major part is concerned with "The Reasons for Disapproving Celibacy."

The wicked impudence of those opposing in God's name the marriage of priests! The immorality of the papists is notorious. Yet they ask the emperor to punish clergymen honorably married and of good character. They do not sincerely defend celibacy for few of them are chaste. The law of celibacy is opposed to divine, to natural, and to ecclesiastical laws, and in addition produces superstitions and dangers.

That it is opposed to divine laws is indicated by the fact that God created the two sexes among human beings and provided for their normal union in marriage. The papists' argument that God's plan was to operate only until the earth was populated is a silly effort to nullify the divine order.

That it is opposed to natural law is seen in the fact that marriage, as a natural right of mankind, is immutable, as jurists have declared. Natural right cannot be removed, nor human nature changed, by legislation. Besides, natural right has been established by God.

It is opposed to the law found in the Christian Church because it is contrary to apostolic advice. Paul advised marriage, rather than fornication, for men. The papists object that he did not say "priests." What impertinence! "As though priests are not men!" All who have sexual desire have the right to marriage; in fact, Paul commands it. Christ showed that continence is a special gift possessed by few. God certainly prefers chaste marriage to impure celibacy.

It is opposed to Christian law as formulated in the canons of the church. The ancient church laws neither forbade marriages nor dissolved those of married priests. The popes, by reversing the ancient laws of synods, show the spirit of Antichrist in their contempt of women.

A superstition has arisen in connection with celibacy. The papists insist that, as Hebrew priests were continent during periods of active service, so the Christian priest, who should always pray, should be celibate. Yet the marital relations of Hebrew priests did not disqualify them from prayer.

There are, however, two better answers to this Roman view. The first is that the Scriptures speak of God's blessing on the married life of believers. No such thing is said of celibacy. Nor is celibacy, without faith, a righteousness before God. A clean heart rather than celibacy is the true purity. Celibacy most certainly does not merit justification.

Virginity is not thereby disparaged. It may be argued that "just as one gift surpasses another, as prophecy surpasses eloquence, the science of military affairs surpasses agriculture, and eloquence surpasses architecture, so virginity is a more excellent gift than marriage." Yet for all that, justification is for Christ's sake through faith. Virginity is superior to marriage only in that it is free of domestic duties and the individual can be devoted to worship and the service of others.

The second answer to the Roman position is that the Hebrew ideas of ceremonial impurity have been superseded by New Testament teaching. To be sure, marriage must not interfere with public duties or with prayer. Such continence is merely the part of wisdom. But there is no excuse for the celibacy of idle monks.

Some heretical sects have made the mistake of despising marriage. One such, the Encratites in the second century, taught that holiness consists of abstaining from wine, meat, and marriage. But when men trust in such deeds, they neglect Christ. Continence, however praiseworthy, never merits God's justifying grace. The pretensions of the immoral papists are hypocritical and therefore worse than the Encratites whom they condemn.

The dangers involved in celibacy are real and serious. The law of celibacy puts souls in jeopardy and produces scandals. But the popes give no heed to protests against this regulation. Other papal laws have been changed and so should this be. The vast corruption of the times should be corrected promptly. Let honorable marriage be publicly defended by civil and church authorities.

However, the popes are unrelenting. Lutherans, when they repudiate the law of celibacy, are accused of schism. But they cannot be united with such vicious falsehood and brutal injustice so manifestly displeasing to God.

The second part of Melanchthon's discussion is a reply to "The Arguments of the Adversaries." He observed that the real reason for the law of celibacy is the papal desire for absolute rule, whereas the gospel allows liberty.

The first Romanist claim is that the law of celibacy was revealed by God. They make that absurd claim in the very face of scriptural approval of marriage.

Their second claim is that priests should be pure. Yet the only real purity is in the heart and not in outward observances. Nor is it to be conceded that marriage is impurity.

In the third place, the adversaries claim that "the marriage of priests is the heresy of Jovinian." He was a polemical writer against celibacy who was excommunicated in Rome in 390 for his views. But such a claim is a distortion of the historical fact. It is not true that the church called marriage of priests a heresy. The authors of the Confutation apparently thought that only ignorant men would read it. No wonder they refused to give the Lutherans a copy.

With such groundless arguments the law of celibacy is defended. God indeed will judge them. Let the princes therefore be reassured that they are doing right in giving civil sanction to the marriage of priests.

If Melanchthon gave considerable attention to the Roman law of celibacy—a matter of large importance to the papists—it is not surprising that he wrote at greater length about Article XXIV, "Of the Mass." For here is a topic on which the Romanists were very sensitive. Melanchthon's treatment of the topic is long, being about one third of the entire section of the Apology devoted to the discussion of abuses.

His preliminary statement was designed to clear up certain incidental phases of the topic before entering upon a discussion of the main point. He declared that Lutherans have not discarded the mass (Lord's Supper), but administer it every Lord's Day with the usual ceremonies, propers, and vestments. The adversaries argue for the use of Latin. Lutherans use Latin for the learned and German for the uneducated; for the ceremonies do not confer benefits *ex opere operato*.

Lutherans, like the Greek churches, have no private masses. The Romanists developed private masses as a means of financial profit.

The heap of papist arguments to the effect that the mass is a sacrifice is upset by the entire absence of proof that it confers grace *ex opere operato* or that it benefits others. Let the adversaries stay by the main topic in dispute, viz., the automatic benefit of the mass and the transfer of merit. Lutherans insist that such doctrines contradict the words of Paul, "Being justified by faith." But the papists sell masses to appease God or to benefit those in purgatory. And the Confutation talks much of "sacrifice," a term avoided in the Confession. This matter needs to be clarified.

"What a sacrifice is, and what are the species of sacrifice," is the theme next considered in the Apology. A proper definition and classification is desirable. The Socratic advice to analyze a problem carefully was ignored by the adversaries.

By definition, "A sacrament is a ceremony or work, in which God presents to us that which the promise annexed to the ceremony offers." "A sacrifice, on the contrary, is a ceremony or work which we render God in order to afford him honor."

There are two kinds of sacrifice: propitiatory, i.e., offerings to propitiate God: and eucharistic, i.e., giving thanks to God. This distinction will serve to avoid much confusion.

For Christians, the only propitiatory sacrifice is the death of Christ. "We are sanctified through the offering of the body of Jesus Christ once for all" (Heb. 10:10). All others are sacrifices of praise, i.e., eucharistic. For example, in Hebrews 13:15, "By him therefore let us offer the sacrifice of praise to God continually."

New Testament worship is "in spirit and in truth," which is by faith, not *ex opere operato*. Jeremiah also proclaimed the righteousness of the heart rather than the formalities of ceremonies. The Psalms likewise encourage trust rather than animal sacrifices. "Thou delightest not in burnt offering. The sacrifices of God are a broken spirit" (Ps. 51:16, 17).

If the adversaries quote Malachi 1:11, "In every place incense shall be offered unto my name, and a pure offering," they have no support for their doctrine of merits. Neither is there any support for their papist views in their quotation of Malachi 3:3, "And he shall purify the sons of Levi . . . that they may offer unto the Lord an offering in righteousness." For they pervert the term "sacrifice" and omit the gospel.

They make daily Jewish sacrifices a reason for daily masses. Such reasoning from analogy is precarious. Even granting the value of a daily sacrifice of praise, it is still not an *opus operatum*. It is permissible to give a symbolic interpretation of Jewish sacrifice. The sacrifice of the lamb signifies the death of Christ; the libation is the spread of the sanctifying gospel; the oblation of wheat represents faith, prayer, and thanksgiving. All these aspects are needed in true spiritual worship.

Instead of making the gospel central in worship, the "adversaries retain only the ceremony, and publicly apply this to sacrilegious gain." The Confutation bewails the removal of candles and images from altars but says nothing about repentance and faith.

Among Lutherans the gospel with its consolation is preached, good works and the use of the sacraments are taught. The sacrament of the altar is used not for money but for God's mercy. Word and sacrament are combined in worship and the sacrifice of praise is offered daily. It is pure doctrine and devout use of sacraments that constitute real worship rather than such things as candles and golden vessels.

The adversaries cite Hebrews 5:1, "Every high priest taken from among men is ordained for men in things pertaining to God, that he may offer both gifts and sacrifices for sins." Thus the papists imitate the Levites, ignoring the fact that four verses later it is said that Christ is our high priest. For in the New Testament the only sacrifice is that of Christ. Even the Levitical sacrifices did not merit remission of sins, but typified it. The papists, in following the example of the Levites, place the sacrifice of the mass ahead of Christ.

To summarize, it conflicts with the gospel to teach that the mass justifies *ex opere operato*, or that its merits can be applied to others. The Scripture cited by the opponents fails to support their doctrine. Moreover, their doctrine is recent, rather than apostolic, and it has produced great avarice and abuses.

The Apology next notes briefly "What the Fathers thought concerning Sacrifice." It is true that the church fathers called the mass a sacrifice, but they clearly indicated the significance to be eucharistic rather than propitiatory.

A discussion "Of the use of the Sacrament, and of Sacrifice" follows. Some teach that the Lord's Supper is both a mark of profession and a sign of obedient fellowship. Hence it is something men do. Lutherans teach that sacraments indicate what God does. "Sacraments in the New Testament are *signs of grace*." In a sacrament are two things: the sign and the Word of promise received by faith. The sign, seen by the eyes, stimulates faith. Thus the sacrament consoles consciences. Not only does it revive in the memory the work of Christ, but it also quickens faith to cling to him.

It also becomes to the believer, who receives the benefit, an occasion for gratitude—a sacrifice of thanksgiving. Church fathers, e.g., Ambrose,[1] speak of these two effects, viz., benefit and praise, though the adversaries pervert the sacrament into an *opus operatum*. (Pseudo-) Cyprian (Arnold of Bonneval) said, "Piety, in thanking the Bestower of such abundant blessing, makes a distinction between what has been given and what has been forgiven."[2] Because of such thanksgiving, the term "eucharist" arose in the church.

Here the Apology turns to a discussion "Of the Term Mass." The following outline is of the Latin version of the Apology.

The adversaries say that the Greek word for "mass" is "liturgy" which means sacrifice. On the contrary, it means public administration of the sacrament, though among the Greeks it also meant civil administration, public burdens, etc. Paul used the term to mean a collection. The Greek verb means, "I attend to, I administer public goods."

The adversaries foolishly give the word "mass" a Hebrew derivation. Instead, in early Christian worship the faithful brought to church gifts of bread, wine, and other things, some of which was used for the Lord's Supper, the rest being given to the poor. In this sense "mass" is a contribution or an offering, but not a sacrifice. Phrases in the Greek rite agree better with ideas of a sacrifice of prayer, faith,

---

[1] *Expositio in Psalmum* 118.c.18, 28. *MSL* XV, 1462C. Cited in *Bek.*, p. 371, n. 1.

[2] *De coena Domini et prima institutione. MSL* 189, 1647 c. Cited in *Bek.*, p. 371, n. 2.

and thanksgiving, than with the *opus operatum*. Some think that "mass" is related to "remission" so that *Ite, missa est* in the conclusion of the mass means, "Depart, ye have forgiveness." But even that does not prove the papist doctrine.

The German version of this section is shorter and sharper. As translated in the *Concordia Triglotta*, it begins, "Here you can see what rude asses our adversaries are. They say that the term *missa* is derived from the term *misbeach*, which signifies an altar; hence we are to conclude that the mass is a sacrifice; for sacrifices are offered on an altar. Again, the word *liturgia*, by which the Greeks call the mass, is also to denote a sacrifice. This claim we shall briefly answer. All the world sees that from such reasons this heathenish and antichristian error does not fellow necessarily, that the mass benefits *ex opere operato sine bono motu utentis*. Therefore they are asses, because in such a highly important matter they bring forward such silly things. Nor do the asses know any grammar. For *missa* and *liturgia* do not mean sacrifice." Etc.[3]

In the last section the Apology treats "Of the Mass for the Dead." There is no scriptural basis for masses for the dead, however much money they may yield. The sacrament is for the living. It dishonors God and the gospel to make the mass a work of merit. The remission of sins cannot be received except by faith. Yet the papists have sacrilegiously turned the sacrament into pretended benefit for the dead to papal financial profit.

Since there is no scriptural justification for the doctrine, the practice must be deemed worthless. Neither does the Greek rite make the mass a satisfaction for punishment in purgatory.

Prayer for the dead is not prohibited among Lutherans, but use of the Lord's Supper as an *opus operatum* is condemned, even though approved by Gregory and others of later times. The adversaries try to identify Lutherans with Aerius, a fourth-century presbyter of Sebaste in Pontus, who, they say, denied that the mass is a sacrifice. The fact is that his opposition was to prayers for the dead.

They call him a heretic, but the real heresy is in the doctrine of the papists. They follow the common, worldly view that "services

---

[3] P. 413.

and sacrifices are propitious." This papist paganism will long endure. But those who believe the gospel must condemn rites which obscure Christ and faith.

This discussion, which Melanchthon considers brief, emphasizes the Lutheran esteem of the sacrament and Lutheran rejection of what profanes it.

The Apology contains no separate treatment at this place of Article XXV, but has discussed confession in connection with Article XI. Nor is there here a defense of Article XXVI, for Melanchthon covered the matter in the Apology in expounding Article XV.

Article XXVII, "Of Monastic Vows," also aroused Melanchthon to vigorous speech. He began with an anecdote. In Eisenach, a monk named John Hilten was in prison "because he had protested against certain notorious abuses." As an old man, he was interested in the prophecies of Daniel and the Apocalypse. He predicted the overthrow of the power of the monks.

His prophecy has not yet been fulfilled. The hypocrisy, avarice, and cruelty of the monks have not yet ended. Formerly the monasteries were schools. Now they have become wealthy institutions full of idlers. Moreover, they persecute and kill good men who oppose them.

It is not their abuses, however, but the underlying doctrine that is here to be discussed. The questions at issue may be grouped thus: 1. Are vows meritorious as satisfactions for sins? 2. Are they necessary for holiness, or are they optional? 3. Are they lawful? 4. Are they truly religous? 5. Are they canonical? The answers to these questions are those Luther wrote in "Concerning Monastic Vows."

The Lutheran answer to the first question is "No." Since it is certain in the gospel that our sins are forgiven for Christ's sake, monastic vows cannot merit that forgiveness, and therefore vows cannot rightfully be demanded of anyone. If God's law given through Moses does not justify, how much less can monastic laws benefit.

The monks boast of poverty, obedience, and chastity. Yet monasteries are rich; monks violate the law with impunity; and their chastity is a stench!

The point is that "he who, indeed, in addition to Christ's propitiation, opposes his own merits to God's wrath, and on account of his own merits endeavors to obtain the remission of sins, whether he present the works of the Mosaic law, or of the Decalogue, or of the rule of Benedict, or of the rule of Augustine, or of other rules, *annuls the promise of Christ, has cast away Christ, and has fallen from grace.* This is the belief of Paul."

The adversaries call this a wicked opinion. However, theirs is the blasphemy; for they believe with Thomas Aquinas that "the monastic profession is equal to baptism."

The Lutheran answer to the second question is that vows are optional. If not impure, monastic vows are adiaphora—matters of in-difference. They may be beneficial under proper conditions.

But the adversaries impudently claim that vows are superior to other Christian works. "It is an unheard-of, pharisaic, yea an actually diabolical pride for a sordid [lousy] barefoot monk or any similar godless hypocrite to say, yea preach and teach, that he has observed and fulfilled the holy high commandment so perfectly, and, according to the demands and will of God, has done so many good works, that merit even superabounds to him."

Monastic works are not urged by the gospel but are human tradi-tions. Human perfection does not lie in that direction, yet the papists claim that eternal life is thereby merited. On the other hand, even Bernard said that eternal life is the gift of God.

Though the monks say that the monastic life is the way to per-fection, it is no more so than that of a farmer or a mechanic who fears God. There is a story that the hermit Anthony was directed in a dream to observe that a pious shoemaker was as righteous as any monk.

The monks, however, think that their way of life is so superior that they have surplus merits to sell. The Confutation quoted Mat-thew 19:29, "Everyone that hath forsaken houses," etc. But Christ forbids deserting one's family, except to escape tyranny and to be faithful to Christ. No monastic vows are involved.

The Confutation cites also Matthew 19:21, "If thou wilt be perfect, go and sell that thou hast, and give to the poor . . . and come and follow me." But this passage teaches charity and justice rather than abandoning property. Those poor in spirit and free of greed have

God's favor. Abandoning property is not a way to earn heaven. The true Christian way is following Christ in faith.

Concerning the third question, the answer is that vows of celibacy are unnatural, since they are contrary to man's native endowments and therefore opposed to natural law.

To the fourth question the reply is made that vows are ungodly. They cannot be binding when they require godless ceremonies which put human works which are commercialized in place of Christ. The educational value of monastic life could be acknowledged if it were not made meritorious and compulsory.

Lutherans, in answer to the fifth question, declare that vows are uncanonical. It is a fact that church law annuls vows made by the immature or by those coerced. Hence vows are not so irrevocable as the papists teach.

They cite the case of the Nazarites. But this is not a parallel instance, for Nazarite vows were not for the purpose of earning remission of sins. Nor were the Rechabites a precedent, for they were really poor and they also were married, whereas monasteries are both wealthy and unchaste. The papists misinterpret Scripture when they cite certain verses and explain them contrary to the chief teaching of Christ and of Paul. They misconstrue I Timothy 5:11 concerning widows, in spite of Paul's clear teaching on faith. And if the papists insist on I Timothy 5:9, then no one younger than sixty can become a nun. Yet the fact is that this verse has no relation to monastic vows.

These are the reasons and answers given by Lutherans to the papists. Good men need to know that the monastic life is contrary to the gospel. The central fact is that "God only approves services instituted by his Word, which services avail when used in faith."

Article XXVIII, "Of Ecclesiastical Power," concludes the Confession. The Apology declares that the papists seek to preserve their ecclesiastical power, even though the people suffer. Their priesthood is corrupt, their rule is tyrannical, and they are indifferent to the anguish of the common people.

They teach that bishops have the power to make the conditions for gaining eternal life. On the contrary, remission of sins is God's free gift. Hence the claims of the bishops are false.

The Augsburg Confession has named the duties of bishops, but these duties are neglected by the Romanist bishops. The power of a bishop is never above the law but under it. God's command gives them the task of the ministry and of the keys, but not the right to form new rules equal to the gospel. For Christians have liberty in man-made ceremonies. Human traditions, valuable for good order, are yet not meritorious or substitutes for the teachings of Christ.

Hebrews 13:17, "Obey them that have the rule over you," which the adversaries quote, applies only in so far as the rule is accordant with the gospel. The same is true of Matthew 23:3, "Whatsoever they bid you observe, that observe," because always we must obey God rather than men.

They accuse our doctrine of producing public disorders. But these disturbances are more than offset by the good produced by gospel doctrine. And no excesses of fanatics can cause us to abandon the gospel. Moreover, the papists themselves have not been free of scandals. The German version adds that it was the Romanist sale of indulgences that caused the disturbances.

The Apology closes abruptly with this sentence: "Now we leave it to the judgment of all the godly whether the adversaries have been right in boasting that they have actually refuted our Confession from the Scriptures."

The foregoing treatment, as the title indicates, is an outline. Attention is called again to that fact so as to emphasize the necessity of reading the Apology itself. For though an outline has the value of brevity and of reducing the topics to their essentials, it neverthe-less sacrifices something of the massiveness, the fine workmanship, and the intricate detail of the original. It is the difference between an automobile chassis and the finished passenger car.

A reading of the Apology in its entirety is certain to give an im-pression of the extensive scholarship of the author. Melanchthon showed himself to be familiar with a large amount of theological liter-ature. He knew the writings of the scholastics of the middle ages. He quoted from the fathers of the ancient church. He cited passages from the liturgies of both the East and West. He was familiar with the decisions and decrees of councils and popes. And if the results of literary criticism were not available to him in his day, so that he was unable to distinguish between the genuine and the pseudo fathers, it constitutes no valid ground for criticism of him.

Melanchthon's understanding of the history of previous centuries was sufficient to reveal the true state of affairs in the Roman Church. Like Luther, he was keen enough to see that practices then prevalent in the church under the pope had not always existed. He had had enough experience with the abuses connected with these practices to know that they were enforced with a ruthless tyranny. The Apology shows how keenly the Lutherans resented the baselessness of the Roman claims and how they smarted under the papal tyranny.

Besides his historical and theological scholarship, Melanchthon revealed that the Lutheran movement had a sound insight into Scripture. His interpretation of biblical passages was based on valid principles. A review of his explanations of scriptural passages reveals the fact that the Lutherans had found their true meaning. His discussion of the word "sacrifice" in the Bible is a case in point. The Apology, therefore, is truly a witness of what the Scriptures declare.

Chapter XII

THE ORIGIN OF THE SMALCALD ARTICLES

At the close of the Diet of Augsburg in 1530, Emperor Charles V promised to secure the calling of a general council of the church to settle the religious issues. Protestants generally desired such a council. They had some hope of reforming the church if the voice of the gospel could be heard and the restrictions imposed by the papacy could be lifted.

The popes recognized that a free council would not be to their advantage. Instead, their prestige, power, and wealth would be jeopardized. Therefore, when Charles pressed the matter, Pope Clement VII reluctantly agreed to summon a council. But he imposed conditions such that Protestants could not accept. The pope's conditions would have made reform impossible. As a result, no council was called.

Paul III became pope in 1534. He, too, felt the pressure of the emperor for the convening of a council. Accordingly he sent out a summons through the bull, *Ad dominici gregis*,[1] for the twenty-third of May, 1537. The place of meeting was to be Mantua in Italy, rather than in some German city as the Lutherans desired. What was more disconcerting was his later statement that the purpose of the council would be "the utter extirpation of the poisonous, pestilential Lutheran heresy." As it turned out, the council was repeatedly postponed until 1545 when it met in Trent.

When the call to the council reached the Lutherans, they had to make a decision as to whether or not they would attend. They had

---

[1] *Bek.*, p. 24.

to consider how their decision, whatever it was, could be interpreted. If they decided to attend, would that indicate that they were thereby showing their submission to the pope? If they refused to attend, how could they defend their position, since they had been clamoring for a council?

The difficulties of the choice are well illustrated in Luther's statements. Early in his reforming work he appealed for the assembling of a council to settle the religious issues. Yet he denied that councils were infallible and that the pope alone could summon them. Remembering John Hus, he recognized the danger in attending a council. Thus when the papal legate said to Luther, "See to it that you are prepared for the council," Luther replied, "Yes, my lord, with both this neck and head of mine." [2] More than this, Luther despaired of constructive results: "The Pope prefers to see all Christendom lost, and all souls damned, rather than that either he or his adherents be reformed even a little, and permit a limit to be fixed to their tyranny." [3]

When the elector, John Frederick, of Saxony expressed himself as favorable toward attending the council, it became necessary to make certain literary preparations. What documents should be prepared for presentation? Was the Augsburg Confession sufficient? The situation had changed since the Diet of Augsburg. A much firmer position could be taken, attacking specifically the tyranny of the papacy. Meanwhile new territories had been won for Lutheranism and they were entitled to a voice in the framing of a document. Something new must be written.

Therefore the elector requested Luther to prepare a set of articles stating the evangelical position. He was to indicate those doctrines in which no concession could be made—articles which not even peril of death would make him recant. But he was also to note those articles in which some compromise was possible. He was to report the consent or dissent of other theologians on these topics. Apparently he had been assigned the task as early as August 20. But it seems that he did nothing about it until reminded at the beginning of December.

---

[2] Julius Köstlin, *The Life of Martin Luther,* tr. J. G. Morris (Philadelphia: Lutheran Publication Society, 1883), p. 404.

[3] *Book of Concord* (Jacobs), pp. 307 f.

Luther then set to work at once, preparing a document in German rather than in Latin. When he became very sick on December 18, he had finished Parts I and II and Article 3 of Part III. The rest he had to dictate, apparently to two persons, since the original manuscript shows two handwritings. Meanwhile he summoned John Agricola from Eisleben, George Spalatin from Altenburg, and Nicholas von Amsdorf from Naumburg for a conference on the 28th. To them, together with Melanchthon, Bugenhagen, Jonas, and Cruciger, Luther submitted his Articles.

After some discussion and modification, a copy of the document made by Spalatin was signed by them and submitted to the elector on January 3. He was heartily in agreement with it, though he thought it brief. Concerning its doctrines his prayer was that God would "give grace to our brethren, to us and our descendants that we may firmly and without weakening continue and remain therein."

On February 8, the Lutheran princes and theologians from various areas met at Smalcald. The nobility convened to discuss the political aspects of the proposed Mantua council. The theologians met in separate session to agree upon the religious positions to be defended. Luther was sick again, and, though he was in Smalcald, he could not attend the sessions.

The elector had to face the problem of winning approval for Luther's document. He had hoped to have the Articles presented to the delegates by Luther, whose presence would likely have silenced opposition. But Luther's illness spoiled that plan. And besides, Melanchthon quietly worked against it. He persuaded Landgrave Philip of Hesse and others that they did not need Luther's Articles since they had the Augsburg Confession and the Wittenberg Concord. The latter document was a 1536 statement of Lutheran agreement, especially on the Lord's Supper. It was an attempt to preserve unity between Lutherans of northern Germany and those in the south under Zwinglian influence.

Moreover, Melanchthon was afraid Luther's document would stir up doctrinal controversy. The fact is that Luther's article on the Lord's Supper had been somewhat mild at first, but had been more strongly expressed in the final draft. The theologians from southern Germany were unlikely to approve this formulation. Therefore Melanchthon and the landgrave felt it unwise to present Luther's document before the assembled theologians.

Some of the delegates said that they lacked authority to act upon it. Instead they preferred to reaffirm the Augsburg Confession and the Wittenberg Concord. The theologians became acquainted with Luther's Articles, which were freely circulated among them at Smalcald. But Melanchthon's scheme apparently was successful, for there is no evidence that the Articles ever came before the assembly for formal consideration.

When the princes decided not to go to Mantua, the theologians terminated their sessions. There were three results of the meeting. First, the theologians were authorized to review the Augsburg Confession with the aim of supporting it with further scriptural and patristic quotations and of removing any contradictions between it and the Wittenberg Concord. This was not done at Smalcald because of lack of time and library materials.

Second was the authorization of a document concerning the papacy. This was prepared by Melanchthon at Smalcald. It is called the "Tractatus" from its Latin title, *De potestate et primatu papae tractatus,* and is appended to Luther's Articles in the *Book of Concord.* It was really intended to be a supplement to the Augsburg Confession. To it the theologians signed their names in approval.

The third action concerned Luther's Articles. Since they did not come up to a vote during the sessions, they did not receive official approval or signature by the princes. But they were not discarded. Instead, at the close of the sessions some of the theologians, at Bugenhagen's inducement and acting as individuals, indicated their approval of Luther's document by signing it. This is the reason for giving it the name "Smalcald Articles." The theologians of southern Germany refused their signatures, partly from lack of authority, partly from disagreement.

It is something of a puzzle why Luther wrote in the second paragraph of his preface to the Articles that they were "accepted and unanimously confessed." Two possible answers have been proposed. One suggestion is that Luther's illness, which kept him away from the sessions and in ignorance of Melanchthon's manipulations, prevented him from knowing the facts fully.

The other suggestion is that since only a few theologians withheld their signatures, the dissent could be disregarded. Those who signed were so large a majority that for all practical purposes there was unanimity. In contrast to the forty-four who subscribed, only five gave reasons for withholding their signatures. They were Bucer and Fagius from Strassburg, Blaurer from Constance, Wolfhart from Augsburg, and Fontanus from Hesse. The qualified subscription by Melander of Hesse seems to be a partial dissent.

Luther's manuscript has been at Heidelberg University. The copy made by Spalatin, which received the signatures, has been at Weimar.

Luther published his Articles (with a preface, some additional paragraphs on the mass, purgatory, invocation of saints, repentance, and confession, besides some editorial changes) in 1538. Thereafter they were frequently published. The edition issued in Magdeburg in 1553 by John Stolz and John Aurifaber was based on Spalatin's manuscript copy and includes Luther's published additions as well as the names of the signers. The Articles were included in various *corpora doctrinae*. The German *Book of Concord* of 1580 used the Magdeburg text with corrections from Luther's first edition.

A Latin translation by Petrus Generanus appeared in 1541. Apparently in ignorance of this earlier work, Nicolaus Selnecker translated the Articles again for the Latin editions of the *Book of Concord* of 1580 and 1584.

The significance of the Smalcald Articles is seen in the fact that they present a bold, clear-cut testimony of the Lutheran position in sharp distinction from that of the Roman Church. They are polemic and incisive, carrying the battle to the enemy. Since nothing is to be gained by dodging issues, the irreconcilable differences were frankly expressed. Roman Catholic practices were shown to be unscriptural, unevangelical, and tyrannical; therefore they were intolerable.

The Articles are significant also as an expression of Luther's convictions. Twenty years of reformatory activity had in no way weakened them nor caused him to retract his doctrines. The judgments of the Romish system which he made in 1520 were still valid. He was still firmly established upon the doctrine of justification by faith and was prepared to accept all that this doctrine implies. His teaching on the Lord's Supper still stands in 1536, undimmed by Zwinglian criticism. The Articles are the work of the mature Luther who was sure that the young Luther had started out on the right path.

The symbolic significance of the Articles is seen in the wide acceptance given them. At Smalcald there were forty-four signatures of theologians, including Luther's. Many who signed did so as men holding responsible official positions in their districts and having a decisive voice in directing the doctrine taught there. After the *Variata* edition of the Augsburg Confession appeared, it was Luther's Articles, rather than Melanchthon's modified phrases, which were looked upon as giving the real position represented at Augsburg.

In a sense the Articles were a private document of Luther. They did not have the formal official sanction of the Smalcald League. Yet they were highly regarded. For example, in 1541 the elector instructed his representatives at the Diet of Regensburg to adhere to the Smalcald Articles. The official book of doctrine of Brunswick in 1563 included them, as did subsequent *corpora doctrinae*. Most important was the inclusion of the Smalcald Articles in the *Book of Concord*. Such official recognition was simply the visible sign of their general acceptance, for Luther's Articles won approval almost as readily as did his catechisms.

Melanchthon's "Tractatus" has a curious history. Composed amid the anti-papal mood prevailing at Smalcald, he said of it that it was written "somewhat more harshly than is my custom." He wrote it in Latin, and in that language it was published at Strassburg in 1540 together with some other of his writings. The original manuscript is lost. A copy made by Spalatin was signed by the theologians. But at the Smalcald meeting Veit Dietrich made a German translation. It appeared in print in 1541 with the name of Melanchthon as author and with the statement that it was a translation. But when the edition of the Smalcald Articles by Stolz and Aurifaber was printed in 1553, Dietrich's translation of the "Tractatus" was printed as an appendix under the caption: "Of the Power and Primacy of the Pope. By the Assembled Theologians." That had been the title which Dietrich had written on the manuscript of his translation. In this way Melanchthon's name was omitted.

The "Tractatus" appeared in the same way in various *corpora doctrinae* and in the German edition of the *Book of Concord* in apparent ignorance of the fact that Melanchthon was the author. It was even assumed that Dietrich's German version was the original, so that for the Latin edition of the *Book of Concord* Selnecker translated it back into Latin! The edition of 1584 did recover Melanchthon's original, yet printed it with the misleading caption of 1553. Many scholars therefore believed the "Tractatus" to have been the work of the theologians at Smalcald rather than of Melanchthon, until the research of J. C. Bertram[4] in 1770 presented clear evidence of the strange confusion.

The "Tractatus" was signed by the theologians at Smalcald by formal action. In the *Recess* of the conference, signed by the princes, the "Tractatus" together with the Augsburg Confession and the Apology received mention and subscription. Therefore it had an official standing from the first—something Luther's Articles had to gain in the course of time. It had immediate practical importance since it was an attack upon the pretensions of the Roman hierarchy and a ground for rejecting the pope's summons to Mantua. Its symbolic significance is recognized in its inclusion with Luther's Articles in various *corpora doctrinae* and the *Book of Concord*.

Yet, by the strange events of its history, the "Tractatus" came to have a position subordinate to the Smalcald Articles. Intended to be a supplement to the Augsburg Confession, it came in the course of history to have the unhistorical position of an appendix to the Smalcald Articles, as Dr. Kolde has indicated.[5] But what in a strict sense is "unhistorical" has come to be the "historical" status, and is likely to remain so.

---

[4] *Geschichte des symbolischen Anhangs der schmalkaldischen Artikel.*

[5] Theo. Kolde, *Historische Einleitung in die symbolischen Bücher der evangelisch-lutherischen Kirche* (Gütersloh: C. Bertelsmann, 1907), p. 50.

Chapter XIII

OUTLINE OF THE SMALCALD ARTICLES

Luther wrote a preface for his Articles when they were to be published. He therein explained both why they were written and why they were being published. In reporting the instructions given him to prepare articles for the proposed council at Mantua he said that he was to distinguish between doctrines which were unyielding convictions, and those in which there could be compromise. The postponement of the council by the pope was ascribed to fear and to stubborn resistance to reform. Meanwhile Luther felt the necessity of publishing his Articles, since he was continually maligned and misrepresented. He wanted this to be a personal testimony of his doctrine, even though he acknowledged the public nature of the document as signed by many other theologians. This was his own avowed creed.

But he could not forget the need of a council. The distress in the church which a council could correct saddened him. He had no hopes of corrective action by any council called by Pope Paul. Yet he reminded himself that he must not be without hope, for God himself might summon a council. How much there is to reform, even in public morals! Look at all the "wantonness, lewdness, pride in dress, gluttony, gambling," etc. And all the while the church leaders are amusing themselves with matters of tonsures and cardinals' hats. May God indeed convoke a council!

Luther arranged his Articles in three groups. The first part is a group of four "concerning the divine majesty." The first of these declares the trinity and unity of God. The second indicates the distinctions in the Trinity. The third affirms the incarnation. And the fourth repeats the statements concerning Christ found in the Apostles' and Athanasian creeds. A concluding sentence states that there is no dispute in these doctrines between Romanists and Lutherans. Luther first wrote that both parties "believe and confess" these doctrines. But he crossed out the word "believe" because, remembering papal corruption, he doubted the sincerity of their faith.

But if there is no dispute in these matters, why are they named? Two reasons may be given. In the first place, Luther was conscious of being part of the church universal both in doctrine and practice. He was presenting his Articles, not as a heretic, schismatic, or sectarian, but as an ecumenical Christian. He was discussing Christian doctrines within the framework of the church. In the second place, he was certain that trinitarian faith lay at the heart of Christian theology. All other doctrines presupposed it and were built upon it. Luther wanted to be explicit about it rather than leave the assumptions unexpressed.

Part Two is also a group of four articles. In them the vehemence of the convictions of the Reformation's stalwart champion is immediately evident. The battle line between Romish and evangelical doctrine is at justification. Luther therefore promptly stated in Article I the gospel doctrine of justification through faith in Christ, and in Articles II, III, and IV showed how it is obscured by the Romish doctrines of the mass, the monastic orders, and the papacy.

He showed himself unwilling to accept a Romanism however freshly and beautifully dressed. He could be satisfied only with an evangelical church in which practice conformed to doctrine. Therefore in Part Two he presented articles concerning "The Office and Work of Jesus Christ, or Our Redemption," contrasting the righteousness of faith with that of works.

Luther stated the gospel doctrine in Article I. Christ has made atonement for us all, bearing our sins on the cross. Since we all are sinners and without merit, we are justified on the basis of his merits. They become ours through faith alone. "Of this article nothing can be yielded or surrendered."

It is worth noticing that Luther considered this a primary and chief article. It is one of two forks in the road. If it is chosen, other aspects of evangelical doctrine will be encountered. If the other fork is taken, one comes without fail into the jungle of Romish perversions. There is no way of combining the two courses. Choosing one means turning bravely, but decisively, from the other. "Nothing can be yielded." The article is so basic that some have taught that justification by faith is not simply one doctrine among all Christian doctrines, but that it is a principle fundamental to them all.

It is noteworthy also that Luther does not argue the point. He attains his purpose by incisive quotations from Scripture—Romans and Isaiah 53 and the Gospel of John. The enemies of this doctrine are therefore the enemies of God's Word. If "we must be sure concerning this doctrine, and not doubt," we can find our authority in Scripture and be assured. The quotations Luther used are few and decisive.

The designation in Article I of Jesus Christ as "our God and Lord" refers back to the articles of Part One where he is identified as a member of the Trinity. The mention of justification and of faith looks ahead to Articles II, III, and IV in which Romish substitutes for "grace alone" are considered. Hence there is an ecumenical foundation and an evangelical structure.

Article II discusses the first Romish substitute, namely, "the mass in the papacy." It is "the greatest and most horrible abomination." Instead of teaching that sins are forgiven freely for Christ's sake, the followers of the pope declared that the mass is a sacrifice which "frees men from sins." It is the teaching of Scripture against that of the pope, and there can be no compromise.

To open-minded Catholics Luther would say that the Roman mass is purely a human invention. It therefore is unnecessary. Indeed, the divinely instituted sacrament comes to us in a different and much better way. But the Roman substitute is connected with "unspeakable abuses." The chief abuse is that it is used as if it were a way "to obtain and merit the remission of sins." It obviously is in direct opposition to the doctrine of Article I.

Rabid Romanists "think indeed with entire correctness that when the mass falls the papacy lies in ruins. Before they would permit this to occur they would put us all to death if they could." For with the works-righteousness of the Roman mass there is a chain of other practices whereby forgiveness of sin can be earned. Luther named as included therein the doctrine of purgatory, superstitious beliefs, pilgrimages, cloisters selling merits, relics, and indulgences. He discussed especially the invocation of saints, which is a particularly flagrant violation of the doctrine of Christ as our only Mediator. (The section on the invocation of saints was not in his original manuscript, but appears in his printed edition.) The whole Roman system centered about the mass, which is an offensive affront to the gospel.

In the Augsburg Confession, Article XXIV says, "The mass is retained on our part and celebrated with the highest reverence." But no contradiction exists between the two articles. What is acknowledged there is the Lord's Supper, accepted and observed in an evangelical way. What is denounced here is the "Mass of the Papacy" with its false doctrine of sacrifice and merit.

Article III looks at another Roman substitute, namely, "Chapters and Cloisters." The institutions connected with monasteries and convents were originally schools. But since they are no longer conducted for educational purposes, but instead presume to be a way of earning salvation, they should be abandoned.

In Article IV is considered the Roman proposal of salvation through obedience to the pope. The bishop of Rome claimed to be head of the church by divine right. Papal supremacy had been claimed by Boniface VIII in the bull *Unam sanctam*[1] which had been reaffirmed by Leo X in 1516.[2] Luther wrote, "Such arrogance we neither will, can, nor ought with good conscience approve." In Luther's opinion a papal head of the church is unnecessary. Even if his rule was only by human right, it would still produce confusion and rivalry. It is better if Christ is the head of the church, and all the bishops are equal in rank. The distressing fact is that the pope is the Antichrist who usurps the place of Christ and who murders and tortures those evangelicals who exalt Christ. No concessions can be made to this blasphemous perversion of the gospel.[3]

---

[1] Carl Mirbt, *Quellen zur Geschichte des Papsttums und des römischen Katholizismus* (4th ed.; Tübingen: J. C. B. Mohr, 1924), pp. 210 ff. Tr. in O. J. Thatcher and E. H. McNeal, *A Source Book for Medieval History* (New York: Charles Scribner's Sons, 1905), pp. 314 ff.

[2] Mirbt, *op. cit.*, pp. 252 f.

[3] Luther made two inaccurate references in this article. In the fourth paragraph he referred to Revelation 12, when it should be 10:3. His reference to Jerome in the ninth paragraph is also inexact; and he repeats it in Part III, Article 10.

In concluding these four articles Luther remarked that the pope's council would yield nothing in these matters. Therefore when the Lutherans would meet their implacable foe, the pope, they should not ceremoniously and humbly kiss his foot, but say to him, "The Lord rebuke thee, O Satan!"

The vehemence of Luther's declarations might give the impression that he was an obstinate, lawless rebel, full of personal spite. But when all four articles are viewed together it becomes evident that here is a profound doctrine of salvation meeting the antagonism of a strongly entrenched and desperately vicious papal system. Here is a vigorous, unwavering commitment to Christ as the only Saviour. The assurance of our salvation lies in him. Luther earnestly resented anything that detracted from Christ or that jeopardized the certainty of eternal life. And in these articles he hotly says so. The heat is not only in his denunciations; it is also in his loyalty to his Saviour.

Part III consists of articles which might form the basis of discussion with "learned and reasonable" Roman Catholics. The papists care only for money, glory, honors, and power. When Luther suggested the articles as topics for discussion "among ourselves," he likely had in mind the South Germans and especially Bucer.

The fifteen articles are not in the order in which systematic theology would arrange them. They suggest the order of salvation from sin to fellowship. The orderly sequence of thought is evident enough in their arrangement. Beginning with sin (I), there follows the law (II) which reproves sin and leads to repentance (III). The forgiveness of sin comes through the means of grace, namely, the gospel (IV), and the sacraments: baptism (V) and the Lord's Supper (VI). Forgiveness is exercised in the office of the keys (VII) through confession and absolution (VIII), but the unrepentant suffer excommunication (IX). Those who exercise this office have received ordination and the call (X); incidentally, they have a right to be married (XI). They function in the church (XII) which is the congregation of the faithful who are justified by faith and are fruitful in good works (XIII), but not the spurious good works of monastic vows (XIV) and human traditions (XV). These articles present, therefore, the personal and the ecclesiastical aspects of salvation.

Turning now to an examination of each article, it is to be observed that Article I is a crisp synopsis of the evangelical doctrine of sin and a summary of opposing views. In defining the true doctrine, Luther declared that sin entered the human race through Adam, that out of this original sin arise the evil deeds forbidden in the Ten Commandments, and that "this hereditary sin is so deep a corruption of nature that no reason can understand it."

In contrast he presented seven views of the scholastics. They are either Pelagian—mankind by nature has the ability to obey God without assistance—or are Semi-Pelagian, i.e., mankind is weak and with divine help can do good works. Looking at these statements from the standpoint of the atonement, Luther declared: "If these dogmas would be right, Christ has died in vain." Both the voice of Scripture and his own soul-searching experience convinced Luther of mankind's utter spiritual inability.

The second article presents two uses of the law. The first use (to restrain men from sin) has failed of its purpose, for men remain rebellious and arrogant. The second use is to convince men of sin, so that, terrified and humbled, they would seek divine aid.

Article III, concerning repentance, is much the longest of any in Luther's whole document. Remembering the intensity of Luther's personal struggle for spiritual peace, there is little wonder at the extent of his discussion here. He had gotten to the heart of the doctrine and was prepared to expose the commercialized mockery developed by Rome.

The article does four things: it defines the scriptural doctrine of repentance; it exposes the error of the Roman doctrine; it answers the Roman arguments; and it corrects sectarian misconceptions. In doing the first of these it shows repentance in the scriptural sense to be a thorough conviction of sin by the law, and a consoling faith through the gospel. This is repentance, not in the narrow, but in the wider sense.

The false doctrine of the papists is constructed of many errors, which Luther summarized in a discriminating analysis. Since the Romanists begin with a false definition of sin and limit repentance to actual sins only, they cannot have a correct doctrine. They arbitrarily make repentance consist of contrition, confession, and satisfaction, claiming that these are works of merit and leaving no place for Christ or faith. Their definition of contrition is superficial, their practice of confession is a torment, and their plan of satisfactions leaves the individual in anxious uncertainty. The troubled soul is pointed to purgatory and indulgences and golden-jubilee-year payments of money, as if these could bring spiritual peace. Meanwhile there were monks and nuns who believed themselves in no need of repentance but thought they had an excess of holy merits to sell to others.

In answering the Roman teaching, Luther turned to the preaching of John the Baptist and the words of Paul. They taught that everyone is sinful and in need of repentance. Evangelical repentance is not a picking and choosing of good deeds and bad deeds, but it lumps them all together as tainted with sin. In acknowledging the telltale stain of original sin it makes contrition thorough, confession complete, and satisfaction certain because based on the merits of Christ. Such repentance is a daily and lifelong part of Christian life. It makes the Roman inventions utterly worthless.

Two sectarian misconceptions were noted: that the sins of true believers do not imperil their salvation; and that those who fall into sin were only apparent, and not real, believers. To the first Luther answered that saints continually feel their original sin which must be daily repented. To the second he replied that if believers fall into sin (as David into adultery), faith and the Holy Spirit were absent from them at the time. (This section on sectarian views was not in Luther's manuscript, but was inserted in the first edition.)

Looking back over this article, it is evident that Luther gave practical evidence of his convictions concerning the final authority in religion. The Roman doctrine of repentance rested on tradition and scholastic teaching. The opinions of the sects were based on revelations or inspirations. Luther held solidly to the Scriptures. They brought Christ to him. The doctrine of repentance as well as other doctrines must be related to this central fact of Christ as revealed in the Word. The difference between this and the doctrine of the Romanists amounts to a chasm.

In the brief Article IV it is stated that the gospel "gives us counsel and aid against sin" through the spoken Word, through baptism, the sacrament of the altar, and the power of the keys.

Taking up each of these separately, Luther discussed baptism in Article V. He began with a definition: "Baptism is nothing else than the Word of God in the water." Next, he rejected two errors: the teaching of Thomas Aquinas and others "that God has imparted to the water a spiritual power"; and the doctrine of the Scotists that "baptism washes away sins . . . through the will of God" rather than by water and the Word. In conclusion Luther defended the baptism of children since "they belong to the promised redemption."

Remembering Luther's disagreement with the Zwinglians on the doctrine of the Lord's Supper, we look with special interest at Article VI, "Of the Sacrament of the Altar." Before long Melanchthon was to present his doctrine, and later the Crypto-Calvinistic controversy was to develop around this doctrine. It is important to know just what Luther had to say.

Again he began with a definition. The "bread and wine in the Supper are the true body and blood of Christ." The Supper has this sacramental reality regardless of the character of the recipient, whether godly or wicked. He rejected three errors: withholding the cup from the laity; using neither bread nor wine; and the doctrine of transubstantiation.

What Luther wrote here must be seen in its historical setting. During the previous month of May a delegation from South Germany, interested in an agreement between the Lutherans of the north and south, had met with Luther and others at Wittenberg. Prominent among this delegation was Martin Bucer from Strassburg. They reached an agreement in the document called the "Wittenberg Concord" which aroused their enthusiasm. This "Wittenberg Concord" is quoted in Chapter VII of the Formula of Concord.

For Luther the central fact was the real presence of the body of Christ in the sacrament. He rejoiced that Bucer and his associates accepted this doctrine also. All agreed to the statement "that with the bread and wine the body and blood of Christ are truly and essentially present, offered and received," and "that through the sacramental union the bread is the body of Christ." In Luther's manuscript of the Smalcald Articles it appears that he wrote the first of these statements almost verbatim, but that he crossed it out and wrote the sentence which corresponds with the second statement. Melanchthon said that Bugenhagen induced Luther to make the change.

There was another point which provoked discussion between Luther and Bucer in 1536. They agreed that the body of Christ is received in the sacrament by believers, but what about others? Luther declared that it is received also by the godless (*impii*) but Bucer preferred the milder term "unworthy" (*indigni*). In Bucer's thinking there were three kinds of recipients: believers; nominal Christians who have no real faith—the unworthy; and the godless, such as the Turks. He would grant that the body of Christ is received by the first two classes only, not by the third.

At the time of their meeting Luther consented to use the term "unworthy" in their statement. Later, when Bucer published his "Explanation of the Wittenberg Concord," Luther was less pleased. In the Smalcald Articles, therefore, he used the words "wicked Christians" which in the Latin edition of the *Book of Concord* of 1584 are translated *ab impiis Christianis*. He did not expect that the sacrament would be celebrated among unconverted Turks. But he insisted that the validity of the sacrament rests on the Word of God, and does not depend upon the faith of the individual.

Aid against sin comes not only from the sacraments, but also from the power of the keys (Article VII). Luther declared that this office and power is given by Christ to the church, not simply to the Romish priests. It applies to overt sins which can be remembered, and also subtle, unconscious sins. Luther quoted four Scripture sentences which contrast sharply with Romish practice.

This brought him immediately to the doctrine and practice of confession, which is the topic of Article VIII. Before rejecting the negative phases, he presented his positive conviction. Confession and absolution should be continued in the church since it is a great consolation to troubled souls and since it is part of the office of the keys. But Christians do not need to enumerate their sins unless they wish to do so.

Luther held strongly to the Word of God as the source of authority in doctrine and as a means of grace. Absolution is the announcement of that Word to individuals. But Luther remembered the fanatics who claimed to have something better than the Word. They were "enthusiasts" in the sense that they said they had the direct guidance of the Spirit without the use of the Word. In contrast is the solemn statement of Luther: "We must firmly hold that God grants his Spirit or grace to no one, except through or with the preceding outward Word."

Even the popes are "enthusiasts" in that they claim to frame laws and doctrines independent of Scripture. Other "enthusiasts" who disparage the writings of the Apostles still publish their own writings as if the Spirit needed them. Actually, however, baptized believers become such through the Word. Though the poison of "enthusiasm" infects human nature widely, the fact remains "that God does not wish to deal with us otherwise than through the spoken Word and the sacraments." (The paragraphs concerning the "enthusiasts" were not in Luther's manuscript at Smalcald, but were inserted when it was printed.)

It is to be noted that Luther quite evidently was thinking of private confession in this article. That was the normal and customary church practice. He viewed it as something evangelical, that is, the absolution pronounced in it was a declaration of the free grace of God, rather than a judicial sentence pronounced by a Roman Catholic priest on the basis of merits. Evangelical absolution was definitely consoling because it declared God's Word to the believer.

Excommunication (Article IX) is the other side of the picture. For several centuries before Luther's day a distinction had been made between the major and the minor excommunication. In the case of a major excommunication the individual was deprived of all Christian privileges, including even a Christian burial, and he might be turned over to the civil authorities for punishment. Luther, in this article, repudiated such discipline, accepting only the minor excommunication, namely, exclusion from the sacraments.

Since absolution and excommunication are normally pronounced for the congregation by the ministers, Luther devoted Article X to the subject of ordination and the call. In the history of the church, bishops had the responsibility of ordaining ministers. Luther saw the value for fellowship and unity of continuing this policy. But the bishops had been guilty of three offenses: worldly pomp and display, complete occupation in secular affairs, and persecution of evangelical ministers. Yet the church of pure doctrine must have ministers. Since bishops will not provide them, the Evangelicals will ordain their own in accordance with ancient precedent.

The precedent which Luther cited was from the writings of Jerome. But his quotation has been called inaccurate. Quoting apparently from memory, he combined two quotations from Jerome. The first quotation, from Jerome's Commentary on Titus 1:5 did not name Alexandria when saying that the presbyters were guided by the advice of the church.[4] The second quotation is from the Epistle to Evangelus, stating that in the Alexandrian church the presbyters chose as bishop one of their own number.[5] The reference to Jerome, and the point thereby established, is better presented by Melanchthon in Part II of the "Tractatus"; therefore it will be discussed in that connection.

Since Luther was thinking of the clergy, he next turned in Article XI to the question of the marriage of priests. The Romish prohibition of such marriages he declared to be neither reasonable nor just; it results in serious immorality, and is based on no authority other than that which has been usurped. Therefore the clergy should be free to marry.

In discussing the church in Article XII, Luther made pointed what previously had been implied. He had written in Article IV about the gospel to be *preached*—a public, churchly function. He described baptism as "the *church* should administer it." In designating the Lord's Supper as the "sacrament of the altar" he indicated its place in the *church*. He wrote of the keys as an office in the *church*. Confession and absolution, he said, should not be abolished in the *church*. Excommunication is *church* discipline. True bishops and ministers serve the *church*.

Luther denied the claim of the papal organization that it really was the church. Instead, the church is the communion of saints, the body of faithful believers in Christ. The holiness of the church is found not in vestments, but in the Word and faith.

One writer has called this article (and those that follow) "marginal."[6] Yet it is not incidental to the Word and sacraments, which are

---

[4] *MSL* XXVI, 562. Cited in *Bek.*, p. 430, n. 5.

[5] Ep. 146. *MSL* XXII, 1194. Cited in *ibid.*

[6] Johannes Stier, *Luthers Glaube und Theologie in den schmalkaldischen Artikeln* (Gütersloh: C. Bertelsmann, 1937), p. 54.

central, but like the frame of a picture it provides a necessary setting for them. Without the Word and sacraments the church would have nothing to administer. Without the church the means of grace would have no human administrators.

In Article XIII Luther looked at the members of the church, their justification and new obedience. He repeated what had been the keynote of his theology. We are justified before God for Christ's sake through faith. With our faith and forgiveness there is also spiritual renewal and the developing Christian life of good deeds. The Christian life is never entirely devoid of sin and therefore must always rely upon God's grace. But neither is the Christian life, if it is genuinely one of faith, entirely devoid of good works. The life begotten through faith grows into the faithful life.

In contrast to this evangelical conception of the Christian life, Luther indicated two false ideas, namely, the life assumed under monastic vows (Article XIV), and that directed by human traditions (Article XV). The monastic life is an attempt "to earn heaven" and therefore is a denial of Christ. Since it conflicts with the evangelical doctrine of justification, the vow of monastic life should be abolished. Similarly, the life that consists in obeying a set of purely pope-made rules which have no basis in Scripture—this life also is false. Luther well knew how artificial were such human traditions.

In conclusion Luther expressed himself in words reminiscent of those he is said to have used before the emperor at the Diet of Worms. "These are the articles on which I must stand; and if God so will I shall stand even to my death. And I do not know how to change or concede anything in them."

In addition to what he had said, Luther concluded his articles with a brief ironic statement on some superstitious Romish practices too insignificant for special treatment. He called them a *Gaukelsack*, a juggler's bag of tricks. There are great numbers of consecrations with holy water or ceremonies which are simply a mockery and a fraud. Evangelical Christians will discard them all. Then follow the forty-four signatures.

The "Tractatus" of Melanchthon, which is printed as an appendix to the Smalcald Articles, consists of two parts, one concerning the pope, the other the bishops. The first part is much the longer. It was papal power which constituted the chief tyranny. It was the bulwark of the whole system of Roman abuses.

Melanchthon built his treatment "Of the Power and Primacy of the Pope" around three papal claims and discussed each of them in a separate article. The first claim was that the pope by divine right is supreme in the church. According to the second claim he is by divine right also supreme over kingdoms. And in the third place it was affirmed that Christians must believe all this and submit to the pope if they are to be saved. Melanchthon, with vigor unusual for him, called these claims "false, godless, tyrannical, and pernicious." If they are valid, the pope has the right to select or depose all bishops and to decree laws which have force equal to the laws of God.

In Article I the claim to supremacy in the church by divine right is first examined on the basis of Scripture. There are cited five passages quite damaging to the papal claim. In Luke 22:25 the contention among the disciples was over who would outrank the others. The whole point of Christ's comment was that lordship among the disciples was disapproved. The best disciples were the lowliest. The same point is made in Matthew 18:2 when Christ set a little child in the midst of them.

According to John 20:21, Christ sent forth his disciples on an equality. Paul, in Galatians 2:7, declared that he was neither ordained nor commissioned by Peter; his authority was in the ministry of the Word, not the lordship of any man. And I Corinthians 3:6 specifically shows the equality of the ministry; in fact, the church is superior to the ministers. The testimony of Scripture, therefore, is decidedly against the pope's claim to supremacy in the church by divine right.

Melanchthon next looked at the record in history. The fact was that "it was first by human law, that is, the resolution of the Council of Nicaea, that the authority of the Roman bishop arose." If his authority had been by divine right, there would have been no need for such a council action. Indeed, the pope did not even then have the right to appoint bishops. That same council decreed "that bishops should be elected by their own churches in the presence of a neighboring bishop or several. The same was observed also in the West and in the Latin churches, as Cyprian and Augustine testify."

The historical record shows that the church has been too wide-spread to have the personal supervision of the bishop of Rome. Distances were too great to have made his supreme rule possible. Church conventions were held at which he did not preside, showing that they had no thought of his alleged supremacy. Both Jerome and Gregory I were quoted in support of this fact.

When the bishop of Rome did claim supremacy, he met opposition from two sides. On the one side was the emperor (in the investiture struggle) wanting to continue his dominance of the papacy. On the other side was the patriarch of Constantinople, his rival for top rank. If the pope's title was clearly by divine right, these contests would not have occurred.

In addition to the testimony of Scripture and the historical record, there is the papal argument to be considered. It asserts that Peter had the primacy on the basis of certain passages concerning him. The typical quotations are: "Thou art Peter, and upon this rock I will build my church" (Matt. 16:18); "I will give unto thee the keys" (Matt. 16:19); "Feed my sheep" (John 21:15).

Melanchton answered that in these passages Peter is simply the representative of the other Apostles. The keys belong not to a man, but to the whole church. And the church is not built upon a man, but upon the faith which declares, "Thou art the Christ." It is not simply that Lutherans so interpret the passage; most of the church fathers, including Origen, Cyprian, and Augustine, gave it that interpretation also.[7] The papal claim clearly rests on a faulty exegesis. Article I, therefore, completely demolishes the pope's claim to be supreme in the church by divine right.

Article II much more briefly shows the intolerable injustice of the pope's claim to be supreme over kingdoms by divine right. It will be remembered that Boniface VIII made that claim in his famous bull, *Unam sanctam*, in 1302. But Christ gave the Apostles only spiritual power. He did not give them the power of the sword of government. Therefore the papal claim is "false and godless." When popes seize kingdoms (as did Alexander VI) or vex kings with excommunications and wars (as was done to Emperor Henry IV), then they are usurpers

---

[7] For sources cf. *Bek.*, p. 479, nn. 2, 4, 7.

and tyrants. It is detestable that they claim to do this by Christ's authority. It is even more detestable that they insist on Christians believing it in order to be saved. This claim certainly obscures faith and Christ's kingdom.

In Article III Melanchthon looked with deep resentment at the claim that our salvation depends upon believing the pope's claim and obeying him. Something more than personal faith is involved. Underlying the whole question is the true nature of the Roman pontiff: he has the marks of the Antichrist. He is unmasked and his revolting nature revealed in this article. Surely there is no obligation to believe in or obey such a creature!

There are three characteristics of the Antichrist which are found in the pope. First, in the church where Christ alone should be Lord, the pope has set himself up as a despotic ruler. Second, he distorts the gospel, by assuming to change Christ's doctrine of grace into a system of meritorious works, by assuming to exercise the keys both for the living and those in purgatory, and by presuming to issue decrees without the consent of the church. Third, he defends his position with cruel persecutions.

Christians surely ought to beware of the rule of the Antichrist. Doctrinal dissent and schism in the church are very serious matters. But we have no choice when the papal church is so impious and antichristian. Just look at its doctrine! It teaches that forgiveness of sin can be earned by our merits! It teaches an enumeration of sins in confession, and a system of satisfactions! It greedily teaches the people to buy indulgences! It teaches the invocation of saints—a horrible idolatry! It teaches celibacy and monastic vows contrary to the gospel! Who can consent to all this and be true to God's Word?

There can be no reform within the church when the pope persecutes those interested in reform. He will not permit a free council of the church even to consider the matter. When the church thus is shackled, "godless dogmas and godless services cannot be removed."

If no relief can be gotten from the high clergy, it should be the responsibility of the leading laymen—the nobility—to espouse the cause of reform. They should see to it that the pope does not obstruct the free action of a council, if one is assembled. They do not need to obey the pope, but ought to resist him as Antichrist when he cruelly opposes the gospel. They must not be afraid of being called schismatics or troublemakers. They must be brave in the knowledge that those who agree with the pope hinder the welfare of the church.

What Melanchthon wrote thus in Part I is much the same as Luther wrote more briefly in his Articles, Part II, Article IV. Both men rejected the pope's claim to supremacy in the church by divine right. Both repudiated the claim that obedience to the pope and faith in his claims are necessary to salvation. Both charge that he is the Antichrist, an accusation which the Spiritual Franciscans as well as Wycliffe and Hus had made against him many years before. Both remembered the papal cruelty against such men as Heinrich Vos and Johannes van den Esschen who suffered martyrdom in Brussels in 1523.

Yet Luther was more bitter in his rejection of the pope. He would consent to no pope, even by merely human right. He was completely and finally through with popes. But Melanchthon believed that under proper conditions it would be a good thing to have a good pope. So he had signed Luther's Articles with this reservation:

But of the pope, I hold that if he would allow the gospel, for the sake of the peace and general unity of Christians, who are now under him, and may be under him hereafter, the superiority over bishops which he has in other respects could be allowed to him, according to human right, also by us.

Evidently Melanchthon had some hope of reforming the papacy. Luther had no such hope.

In Part II of the "Tractatus" Melanchthon gave consideration to the power and jurisdiction of bishops. His problem lay in the fact that the Lutheran movement did not have an abundance of bishops who traditionally had the exclusive right of conducting ordinations. In some areas the bishops had resisted the Reformation; yet the need for pastors there continued. Can there be ordinations when there are no bishops? Is it by divine right, and therefore absolutely necessary, that there be bishops in the church? The answer given by Melanchthon satisfies American Lutherans, who have no bishops. In the Church of England episcopacy is still a live issue.

Recalling what he had written in Article XXVIII of the Augsburg Confession and the Apology, Melanchthon began with a statement of the primary functions of the ministry. Clerical duties involve teaching the gospel, absolving, administering the sacraments, and excommunicaing. In the divine plan these duties belong to all ministers, whether their title be pastor, elder, or bishop. The New Testament uses a varietv of terms.

It was purely a human arrangement whereby bishops became superior to the others. Jerome is Melanchthon's historical authority, the quotation being from the Epistle to Evangelus according to the text of the *Decretum Gratiani.*[8] The reliability of Jerome's statements has been questioned by such Anglican writers as Bishop Gore.[9] But Melanchthon certainly quoted Jerome correctly.

Melanchthon was using Jerome to prove that bishops have not always had the exclusive right of ordination. The evidence is clear that pastors who were not bishops have ordained other pastors. It was only in the course of history, as Jerome says, that the ordaining function was transferred to bishops. It therefore was definitely not theirs by divine right.

Nonepiscopal ordination must be recognized as valid. Since the churches must have ministers—the divine plan would have it so—the power to ordain necessarily resides in the churches. The unwillingness of the regular bishops (who continue to be Romanists) to ordain evangelical pastors must not be allowed to deprive the congregations of a ministry. The right to have a ministry is inherent in the church. This position of Melanchthon's is the rock upon which all episcopal theories break, whatever their historical or practical strength may be.

Instead of a hierarchical position, Melanchthon held a more democratic view of Christian fellowship. From Augustine's Epistle to Fortunatus[10] he quoted the story of two laymen, one of whom baptized the other, he in turn pronouncing absolution upon his baptizer. In ancient times the people elected their pastor or bishop. A neighboring bishop ratified their choice by the laying on of hands. "Ordination was nothing else than such ratification." Therefore "it is clear that the church retains the right to elect and ordain ministers."

---

[8] Ep. 146. *MSL* XXII, 1194. See above, note 4.

[9] Charles Gore, *The Church and the Ministry* (London: Longmans, Green & Co., 1911), pp. 117 ff.

[10] *Decr. Grat.* P. III D. 4 c. 36. Cited in *Bek.,* p. 491, n. 2.

Besides other duties the bishops have had two judicial tasks: one was the judging and excommunicating of obstinate offenders; the other had to do with cases of matrimony.

In cases involving excommunication, the bishops have tyrannically transferred this jurisdiction to themselves alone, and have made it a species of graft. Guilty persons had to secure release by buying a dispensation from the bishop. Innocent men were convicted on the merest hearsay and compelled to pay also. The remedy lies in restoring church discipline to the pastors and in seeing that it is used to reform individuals for God's glory.

The bishops have secured for themselves also the right to judge cases involving the laws of marriage and divorce. It is clearly by human arrangement, not by divine plan, that they have gained it, since the ancient bishops did not have it. Therefore there is no divine obligation upon Christian people to obey the bishops even when their decisions and laws are just. Moreover, gross injustice is apparent in many of their regulations. Melanchthon cited four instances of injustice, one of them being the law forbidding the marriage of persons who have served as sponsors together. The cure of the condition is to be found in establishing other courts for such cases.

In conclusion Melanchthon summarized his argument. The bishops of the Roman hierarchy refuse to ordain evangelical pastors. The bishops administer excommunication tyrannically and for personal profit. They enforce unjust matrimonial laws. These are ample reasons for repudiating such bishops, who as false prophets are sure to suffer the consequences described in II Peter 2.

A comparison of Part II of the "Tractatus" with Article XXVIII of the Augsburg Confession and the Apology is profitable. In each of these Melanchthon protested against the tyranny of the bishops. But in each document there is something distinctive. In the Confession an attack was made on the claim of the bishops to temporal power. The Confession, and more briefly the Apology, took exception to the kind of laws the bishops made, to their distortion of the gospel, and to the demand for obedience to them. The "Tractatus," however, discussed the abuses of the bishops in the matters of ordination, excommunication, and marriage.

There is a further difference. The Confession and the Apology look forward to a church cleansed and reformed, continuing an episcopal polity. In the Confession Melanchthon had said, "It is not our design to wrest the government from the bishops, but this one thing is asked, namely, that they allow the gospel to be purely taught, and that they relax some few observances which cannot be kept without sin." But in the "Tractatus" Melanchthon described a nonepiscopal church. In the earlier documents he sought to rid the church of the bishops' abuses; in this writing he would rid the church of the bishops. In the earlier documents he complained that the bishops interfered with the gospel; in the "Tractatus" he asserted that they obstructed the means of grace.

The sins of the bishops were plain enough—their tyrannical injustice, their worldliness, their greed, their utter neglect of clerical duties. Melanchthon named them all. But the gospel and its communication to the individual believer was of paramount importance to him. To obstruct that was to be guilty of the great, the intolerable sin.

He stated a principle of great importance when he declared that the demands of the gospel and the needs of the church are superior to an episcopal polity however historical it may be. Under such a principle there can be freedom, justice, and spiritual consolation.

At the end of the "Tractatus" are the signatures of thirty-three theologians at Smalcald.

Chapter XIV

THE CATECHISMS

Luther's catechisms were best sellers. The reason is that they were the best answer to an urgent demand. There were other reasons, of course, and they will be given. But the catechisms leaped into prominence when it was seen how well they filled an obvious need.

It had long been plain to church leaders that the people generally were quite ignorant in religious matters. Even before the Reformation the low level of religious knowledge in the parishes was recognized. Every Christian might properly be expected to know the Lord's Prayer and the Apostles' Creed. But even this small amount of knowledge was frequently lacking. The decrees of councils in the late middle centuries urging priests to give such instruction indicates the condition of the people.

The Reformation brought no miraculous change in the state of affairs. Religious ignorance, particularly among the peasants, was for the Lutherans a problem inherited from the past. The church visitations made in Saxony and elsewhere in 1528 and 1529 revealed distressing conditions. In one village it was discovered that the peasants refused to learn the Pater Noster because of its length. In another place there had been no Communion for several years; in another the priest could hardly repeat the Lord's Prayer or the Creed. Luther, who had taken part in the visitation, exclaimed, "Alas! what misery I beheld! The people, especially those who live in the villages, seem to have no knowledge whatever of Christian doctrine, and many of the pastors are ignorant and incompetent teachers." [1]

---

[1] Preface to Small Catechism, *Book of Concord* (Jacobs), I, 359.

It would be a mistake to assume that the Roman Catholic Church had been totally indifferent to the religious ignorance of the people. The fact that certain councils had called on the priests to increase their efforts at instruction indicates that some churchmen were alert. Besides this, there were booklets and tracts of a catechetical nature which had a wide distribution and use in the homes of the people. Priests who were faithful to their task gave instruction in connection with advice given to those who came to make confession. In some areas the priests were ordered to read catechetical materials from the pulpit. For their use manuals were issued. In the schools a certain amount of religious instruction was given. Yet, in spite of all this, only a fraction of the population was benefited.

It seemed that the problem was almost too difficult to be solved even by the enthusiasm of the Reformation. The evangelical leaders were burdened with many other duties. Yet in the midst of their labors they found time for some instruction of the people. Occasionally the subject matter of their teaching found its way into print.

Such circumstances produced Luther's catechisms. When John Bugenhagen, the pastor of the chief church in Wittenberg, was away (organizing the churches and schools of Brunswick) Luther was the supply preacher. For some time it had been customary in this church to have a series of catechetical sermons in May and another in September of each year. Luther conformed to the practice of the parish. After he had delivered the second series of sermons he set about writing out the material for publication.

He interrupted his writing in November to assist in the visitation. After his return, while he was still full of impressions of the conditions in the parishes, he preached a third series of catechetical sermons in December. He used these sermons to revise what he had previously written. In these sermons he had dealt with the Commandments, the Creed, the Lord's Prayer and the sacraments.

The growing manuscript of a catechism had much more of a background than the three series of sermons. Luther had a long experience of preaching and thinking about catechetical matters. As early as 1516 he had preached a series of sermons on the Ten Commandments, and in 1517 on the Lord's Prayer. A year later there was published in the form of a wall chart his "Brief Explanation of the Ten Commandments," as well as his sermons on that theme. His sermons on the Lord's Prayer, together with "A Short Form of the Lord's Prayer," were printed in 1519, and in the same year two tracts on the same subject. In 1520 he prepared an explanation of the Creed, publishing it together with previous material under the title, *A Short Form of the Ten Commandments; A Short Form of the Creed; A Short Form of the Lord's Prayer.*[2]

He preached again on these three topics in 1522. He repeated the series the next year, thereby beginning the custom of annual catechetical sermons at Wittenberg. Meanwhile he became acquainted in 1522 or 1523 with the catechism of the Bohemian Brethren and issued his *Booklet of Prayers* in which his "Short Form" was included. He urged the authorities to establish Christian schools. In his German Mass of 1526 he outlined a program of religious instruction in connection with weekday services.[3] His influence was such that about thirty catechisms written by other men appeared in print.

When in 1528 the "Visitation Instruction" for visitors in Saxony was written by Melanchthon in consultation with Luther, an extensive program of parish instruction was outlined.[4] Sunday afternoon classes for young people and servants were to be assembled. In the schools a certain day each week was to be used for religious instruction. In villages where there were no schools, an officer of the parish was to be responsible for the religious teaching. Everywhere a beginning must be made in removing ignorance of religion.

In the meantime Luther had expanded his catechetical field to include the sacraments as well as the three themes of Commandments, Creed, and Prayer. In the 1523 edition of "A Short Form" he added "Five Questions concerning the Lord's Supper." It may be that the Bohemian Catechism influenced him to make this addition. The *Booklet for Laymen and Children* of 1525, likely written by Bugenhagen, includes baptism and the Lord's Supper. The plan of instruction set

---

[2] Translation in the Philadelphia edition of *Luther's Works,* II, 351.

[3] W. A., XIX, 44 ff. Phila. ed., VI, 177 ff.

[4] E. Sehling, *Die ev. Kirchenordnungen des XVI. Jahrhunderts* (Leipzig, 1902), I, 149 ff.

forth in the German Mass, though it spoke of teaching the three parts used in the church for centuries, nevertheless says, "On Monday and Tuesday, early, we have a German lesson on the Ten Commandments, the Creed and the Lord's Prayer, Baptism and the Sacrament, so that these two days shall preserve the Cathechism and deepen its understanding." After 1526, therefore, it was customary to include the five parts in catechetical ideas.

With such experience and preparation Luther could proceed with his manuscript in the early weeks of 1529. But once more the work was interrupted. He realized that it was getting to be too large for the ordinary person. Therefore he prepared brief forms to be published as wall charts suitable for use with children and in the home. The charts of the first three parts were issued early in January,[5] but those of the sacraments did not appear until March 16. Soon afterwards a Low-German version of them by Bugenhagen was published in book form.

Returning to his manuscript, Luther completed it late in March. It came off the press sometime in April, the earliest evidence being a letter dated April 23. The title page reads, *Deudsch Catechismus Mart. Luther*. At that time there was no reason for calling it the Large Catechism.

With this larger work complete, Luther turned once more to his charts and had them printed in booklet form. The edition was on sale May 16, according to a letter by Roerer, the proofreader.[6] This, therefore, is the commonly accepted date of the publication of the Small Catechism. Though no copies of the first edition are extant, there survive copies of reprints made in Erfurt and Marburg. An Erfurt reprint gives the title: *Der Kleine Catechismus für die gemeine Pfarherr und Prediger. Mart. Luther.*

The first edition of the Small Catechism differed in a few items from that found in the *Book of Concord*. It omitted the introduction of the Lord's Prayer and contained nothing on confession. Its appendix included a Marriage Booklet. The edition of June 13, 1529, was intended to be used in connection with public worship, and therefore

---

[5] In connection with the K-O for Schönewald. Kolde, *op. cit.*, p. lix. Cf. Sehling, *op. cit.*, I, 1, 667.

[6] Kolde, *op. cit.*, p. lx.

included a short form of confession, the German litany with music, and three collects. The edition of 1531 was the first to include Luther's explanation of the introduction of the Lord's Prayer. With slight changes this edition is the one used in the German *Book of Concord* of 1580; but the liturgical parts are omitted, except that the section on confession is enlarged and placed between the fourth and fifth chief parts.

Two Latin translations of the Small Catechism were published in 1529. The translator of the first is unknown. It was really a booklet of prayers with the Catechism appended, and bore the name, *Enchiridion piarum precationum.* The second translation, made by John Sauerman, was more widely used and, with some corrections, was accepted in the Latin *Book of Concord* of 1584.[7]

The Large Catechism, as it is found in the *Book of Concord,* is somewhat changed from Luther's first edition. The German *Book of Concord* used a 1530 edition which included a second lengthy preface and an addition to the exposition of the Lord's Prayer, though the 1529 edition was also consulted. The Latin *Book of Concord* used a modified form of a translation made by Vincentius Obsopoeus and published in 1529.

The catechisms, being older than the Augsburg Confession, might be expected to be placed before it in the *Book of Concord.* That was actually done in one collection of symbolical books. But the catechisms, though they were widely used as teaching manuals, were somewhat slow in gaining symbolic significance. For this reason they are placed after the Smalcald Articles.

For in the *Book of Concord* the chief interest is in their confessional importance. A discussion of their great educational value must be left to the works on catechetics. The amazing story of the history, the many translations and the wide use of the Small Catechism is amply told by Reu in his *Luther's Small Catechism.*

Only gradually did the catechisms gain recognition as confessional writings. Soon after the middle of the sixteenth century the Small Catechism began appearing in *Kirchenordnungen* which set the stand-

---

[7] Cf. M. Reu, *Dr. Martin Luther's Small Catechism* (Chicago: Wartburg Publishing House, 1929), p. 67.

ard for liturgy and doctrine in their areas. The first to do so apparently was that of Pfalz-Zweibrücken in 1557. Presently the Catechism began appearing also in *corpora doctrinae* which were for the specific guidance of the preachers and teachers. The Lüneburg Articles of 1561 and the Pomeranian *Corpus* in 1564 were the first to include it. In view of this growing confessional use it was but natural that the catechisms should be included in the *Book of Concord.*

As Kolde has pointed out, the *Kirchenordnungen* specified that the Small Catechism was to be memorized and that preaching was to conform to the teachings of the Large Catechism.[8] In this way the catechisms became normative for doctrine in the parishes. It was observed that Luther in his longer preface to the Large Catechism had said that all pastors should study the Catechism because "whoever knows the Ten Commandments perfectly must know all the Scriptures, so that . . . he is qualified to sit in judgment upon all doctrines . . ." The high estimate which Luther gave to the doctrinal guidance of the Catechism for the common people was indicated in his catechetical sermons of 1528 when he spoke of a catechism as "a Bible of the laity"—a phrase applied to his catechisms in the introduction of the Epitome of the Formula of Concord.

Similarly the introduction of the Solid Declaration of the Formula of Concord could say, "Because these highly important matters belong also to the common people and laity, who, for their salvation, must distinguish between pure and false doctrine, we accept as confessional also the Large and Small Catechisms of Dr. Luther." That is true for our day as well as for the sixteenth century. Thieme declares, "For the laity the catechisms of Luther have the value of a standard of orthodoxy, of doctrinal purity." [9]

The rise of doctrinal views different from those of Luther produced controversies in many instances. The growing confessional use of the catechisms was stimulated by the controversies. When Melanchthon modified his doctrines and a controversy arose after Luther's death, the catechisms were quoted as the authentic voice of Lutheranism in contrast to the Melanchthonian form.

---

[8] *Op. cit.,* p. lxiii.

[9] Karl Thieme, *Die Augsburgische Konfession und Luthers Katechismen* (Giessen: Töpelmann, 1938), p. 25.

Some of the disciples of Luther even went to extremes in their veneration of the catechisms. Melanchthon, interested in further catechetical progress, somewhat disparagingly spoke of the Small Catechism as making only a beginning in the field. Reacting against that slight, the followers of Luther began to speak of the Small Catechism as if it were inspired and worthy of being placed alongside the ancient creeds. They even called it the "holy" Catechism. Meyer in his *Kommentar* said, "The more widespread became the conviction among Lutherans that by catechetical instruction they must guard the pure doctrine of Luther from adulterations, so much the more were they accustomed to regard the Small Catechism as a popular creedal document of true Lutheranism." [10]

The Lutherans had recourse to the catechisms not only in internal controversies but also in the conflict with Calvinism. When the Heidelberg Catechism appeared in 1563, it became the standard for the Reformed. As a result Lutheran thought turned increasingly to the Small Catechism as the banner of its faith. Each parish indicated its denominational affiliation by its choice of a catechism. The use of Luther's Small Catechism therefore became the mark of the Lutheran.

Closely related to the symbolic significance of the catechisms is their theological importance. Though they are not systematic theological treatises, they nonetheless have a solid theological base.

There are two aspects of their theology: one is ecumenical, the other is evangelical. These two are not incompatible so long as ecumenical is not taken to mean catholic in the sense of all that is common to the Roman and Eastern churches. The Catholic churches had made well-nigh catholic, i.e., universal, much that was unevangelical, Semi-Pelagian, and legalistic.

The catechisms as characteristic literature of the Reformation insisted that nothing was truly ecumenical which was not also clearly evangelical. The theological importance of the catechisms as typical of Reformation teaching is obvious. As Meyer in his *Kommentar* has said, "A scientific Luther-research dare not neglect Luther's catechism-

---

[10] Johannes Meyer, *Historischer Kommentar zur Luthers Kleinem Katechismus* (Gütersloh: C. Bertelsmann, 1929), p. 492.

ideas, for they are really understandable as being in the background of his theological ideas." [11]

The ecumenical phase of catechism theology is evident in the treatment of God and the persons of the Trinity. It was not in theology (in the strict sense) that the church had departed from that which is scriptural. The catechisms therefore had no occasion to depart from the ancient doctrines of God and the Trinity. They affirm a monotheism. The one God is both just and merciful. The holiness of his name calls forth the Second Commandment and the first petition of the Lord's Prayer.

The catechisms affirm the ancient faith that the one God is a trinity of persons whose distinctive work is recognized. The First Person is acknowledged in the Lord's Prayer as both Father and Sovereign. The Creed joins to that concept the fact that he is also Creator and Preserver.

The catechisms, in their treatment of the Creed, present the ancient faith in Christ. His incarnation and atonement are specifically affirmed. As ascended and everliving Lord he is our eternal King. The work of the Holy Spirit is specified as calling, gathering, sanctifying, and preserving us through the means of grace in the church. All this is eminently ecumenical.

It is when the catechisms come to the doctrines related to salvation that divergences begin to appear. The Large Catechism specifically attacks Roman positions. In both catechisms the need of salvation, i.e., the fact of sin, is described in Augustinian rather than Pelagian terms. In the Commandments sin is described in its ethical aspects. The explanation of the third article of the Creed defines original sin as normal and spiritual inability. The interpretation of the fifth petition of the Lord's Prayer affirms the continuance of sin in believers; and in the sixth petition the tempting incitement to sin is said to come from the devil, the world, and our own flesh.

The doctrine of salvation, the remission of sin, is also described in evangelical terms. "At the center of the presentation of the Small Catechism stands the good news—the gospel of salvation won by Christ," said Meyer.[12] The catechisms declare the forgiveness of sin

---

[11] *Op. cit.*, p. 1.
[12] *Op. cit.*, p. 504.

for Christ's sake, the bestowal of faith and the growth in grace effected in us by the Holy Spirit. They view the gospel, not as a new set of laws, but as a free gift from a loving God who bestows his grace through Word and sacraments. One can say with Meyer that these doctrines are "all grouped about forgiveness."

The evangelical character of the catechisms is shown not only in the treatment of the Creed and the sacraments, but equally so in the interpretation of the Commandments—an area in which work-righteousness can easily appear. All implication that salvation is earned by keeping the Commandments is carefully avoided.

Instead, the keeping of the law is seen to grow out of a regenerate life. The motivation of life is not simply the dread of punishment or a sense of duty and compulsion; it is especially the love and reverence for God which have been bestowed upon us by his Spirit. We do not keep the Commandments in order that we may be righteous and filled with divine love; we have the righteousness of faith and are impelled by love so that we may keep the Commandments.

When in the catechisms Luther interpreted the sacraments he once more was applying evangelical principles. Of primary concern is the fact that the blessing conveyed is God's gift; it is in no sense earned or deserved. The Word, the promise of God, is sufficient. Worthy recipients are simply those who believe what the Word and promises of God declare. Thus the element of faith is recognized.

Among Schaff's criticisms of the Small Catechism is this: "It gives undue importance to the sacraments by making them co-ordinate parts with the three great divisions." [18] When it is recognized that the Catechism was written to teach matters vital to the practice and worship of a Christian, and when the sacraments are seen as highly important elements in worship, the criticism loses its force. Considered carefully, the sacraments appear as strikingly clear applications of the evangelical principle of "grace alone." Therefore they have their rightful place in the catechisms.

The content of the Small Catechism is studied in courses in catechetics. It is too familiar to need analysis here. Let it suffice to note that in addition to the five chief parts there is a treatment of confes-

---

[18] *Op. cit.*, I, 252.

sion. It is found in the *Book of Concord* between the fourth and fifth chief parts. Luther wrote to the people of Frankfort that the section on confession was intended for those who wished to receive the sacrament. For that reason its location in the Catechism can be justified. But since it is partly catechetical and partly liturgical it might well have followed the five chief parts.

In any event, its evangelical character is above dispute. Though specific sins are to be acknowledged, there is to be no strained effort to name them all. In no sense is this confession a work of merit or a legalistic requirement. The announcement of forgiveness is "in the name of our Lord Jesus Christ." There is no mention of the fact that pardon is based upon Christ's merits, but, connected with the explanation of the second article of the Creed, the implication is clear. It is distinctly God's mercy, God's forgiveness which is announced.

It would be a mistake to think of catechism doctrines as being chiefly academic or intellectual. Instead, they are more the substance of believing than they are an outline of belief. Köllner has called attention to the fact that Luther had the gift of speaking to the common people in such a way that he appealed to their minds and their hearts. "And this speech of the heart, the product of Luther's whole theological insight, is the keynote of his catechisms." [14]

The Small Catechism, the most widely known part of the *Book of Concord*, sounds the keynote of our faith. Its positive character, its absence of polemics, its simplicity and earnestness form the melody of our faith to which the other writings add the harmony and overtones. With its larger companion the Small Catechism rightly deserves the high esteem the Lutheran Church has accorded it. For though other parts of the *Book of Concord* may in some areas have little use, the Small Catechism and the Augsburg Confession have the avowed allegiance and use of Lutherans everywhere.

---

[14] *Op. cit.,* I, 519.

Chapter XV

OUTLINE OF THE LARGE CATECHISM

There are two prefaces to the Large Catechism. The short preface, which was written for the first edition of 1529, is really an integral part of the Catechism. The longer, though not printed until the 1530 edition, appears before the other in the *Book of Concord* because of its more general nature. Of the two prefaces it has less structural relation to the text of the Catechism. But it has much more vehemence.

The longer "Christian, profitable, and necessary preface" is addressed "to all Christians, but especially to all pastors and preachers." Many of them "slight not only their office, but even the doctrine itself" because they are either too proud, too lazy, or too self-indulgent. Though they have many good books, they do not read them. They think of the Catechism as an unimportant book worthy only to be read once and tossed into a corner. Luther wrote bitingly that such men would make better hog-raisers than pastors.

In a famous passage, Luther wrote, "I am also a doctor and a preacher . . . but must remain, and that too gladly, a child and pupil of the Catechism." [1] He urged a humble and teachable spirit in the presence of God's truth in the Catechism. When it is diligently used, the Holy Spirit increases our insight and piety. It is also an important aid against temptation. Moreover, God commands us to meditate upon his Word daily.

Anyone, moreover, who knows the Commandments perfectly has learned all Scripture and is able to judge good doctrine. Therefore

---

[1] *Book of Concord* (Jacobs), I, 383.

Christians, especially pastors and teachers, should "daily exercise themselves in these studies." The storm of Luther's scorn having vented itself, he closed the preface with calm earnestness.

In the short preface, Luther stated that the Catechism was intended for instructing children and the "simpleminded." Knowledge of its contents should be a basic requirement for church membership and admission to communion. The heads of families should be responsible for its teaching. There are three things which have long been used in the church, viz., the Ten Commandments, the Creed, and the Lord's Prayer (which are then printed in full). Besides these it is important to understand the sacraments (the Scripture bases of them being printed).

Children should memorize these five things and go to church where the sermons will explain their meaning.

THE TEN COMMANDMENTS

The First Commandment is condensed to the words, "Thou shalt have no other gods before me." In general, "to have a god is to trust and believe in him with the whole heart." For the Christian this means trust in the one true God.

There are three commonly trusted false gods: money, success, and the saints. But to hold to the true God is to give to him our complete trust. This is the true worship compared with false worship—for every one worships something. Idolatry is also such worship and trust, but given to a false god. In the Romish Church there is false worship; for people are taught to trust in merits—that is, in themselves and their own works.

However, it is God who is the source of all good. Parents and rulers are merely the channels of his goodness. We therefore should accept and use his gifts according to his will. The test is always this: where is our trust placed?

It must be noted seriously that the commandment has appended to it both a warning and a promise. The warning is of God's wrath against sin, like that of idolatrous heathen and Jews. For unbelief, or lack of trust, is equivalent to hatred of God. This God cannot condone.

224

But the consolation, enjoyed by those who obey, is greater than the dread of punishment. It is a great promise because it comes from God. If it seems that good people are poor and troubled, remember that wealth-seekers are not happy. Compare King Saul who trusted in his power with David who trusted in God. God asks that we trust him. His gifts to us are entrusted to us, not to be trusted by us.

The Second Commandment is broken in many ways. When God's name is used to support falsehood, whether in business, law, or false doctrine, the commandment is violated. To lie is bad enough, but the sin is aggravated when God's name is used. God has warned of the serious consequences of such conduct.

Yet it is a common failing that people try to lie out of trouble. Therefore the young must be taught strictly that they should not use God's name in wickedness, but that they should use it in truth, praise, and prayer.

If it is objected that the saints swore, it is acknowledged that oaths in support of truth are justifiable. But God warns against misuse as earnestly as he encourages the proper use of his name. For his name used in prayer is a protection against evil; it is committing everything to his care.

Teach this commandment with kindness. The use of force is futile. Only love is effective.

The Third Commandment is explained first in terms of its Hebrew origin as a day of rest from labor. That was its pre-Christian use. In its gross sense, the Sabbath, like other Hebrew ordinances, does not apply to us. For Christians it meets the need of rest, but especially of worship. Since one day is as good as another, there is appointed the Lord's Day with its provision both for the Word and for rest.

The day is kept holy by holy words and works. The true Sabbath is marked by true worship. In contrast to Roman practice, it is not vestments and external things, but the Word which sanctifies the day. In contrast to Hebrew use, it is not mere rest, but holy exercises that hallow the day.

Luther warns against breaking the commandment by neglecting the Word, hearing it triflingly, or regarding it with boredom and sloth (which was listed as one of the seven mortal sins). For temptations are constant, and the Word therefore is needed continually.

The Fourth Commandment is introduced by the observation that the first three commandments name duties to God. The remaining commandments relate to our neighbors.

Luther saw the Fourth Commandment as applying to four groups of people. First are parents. They deserve honor for they are God's representatives. The duty thus imposed is in marked contrast to monastic ideals. Honor to parents involves esteem, respectful speech, service. That is a holy work, much superior to the spurious life of a monk, who turns his back on social obligations. Honor to parents really pleases God; his Word says so. But his Word does not command monastic vows.

Keeping this commandment is a benefit to parents, to children, and to society. It is one of the most important works possible to us. Besides this, it is our chance to be grateful for what our parents have done for us. Their goodness to us can never be sufficiently repaid. In addition, the benefit of the commandment to us is a long life and an abundant one.

On the other hand, disrespect for authority brings disaster and tragedy. In contrast to such dire results, there is the example of old families, preserved through generations, because honor has ruled in them. Under the papacy, however, this commandment was slighted.

The second group of people to whom the commandment applies is that of masters. There is need of respect for authority among students and servants. The servants have this duty toward masters as toward parents. In performing this duty they are actually receiving wages for obeying God, for they are doing God's will.

In the third group of people are the rulers. Here the commandment requires respect for government. Disrespect brings great evils, and is based on a disregard of God. Too often we complain of public evils without seeing our own guilt.

In the fourth group are pastors. Besides "fathers in blood and fathers in office" we have spiritual fathers. They too deserve honor and support, which we should gladly render.

Parents and these others in authority also need to be reminded of duties belonging to them. They are obligated to provide support and training. They must not exploit their dependents. A good society depends on it. In general, blessings follow obedience to this commandment, whereas great trouble comes of its neglect.

The Fifth Commandment is a law for individuals, not for governments. It forbids taking life. This is an evil world marked by strife, envy, malice, and murder. But God forbids all these.

In brief, the commandment means that neither (1) by deed or design, injury or anger, should harm be done our neighbor, nor (2) by failure to give help, should he be allowed to suffer. Christ pictured the last judgment as condemning those who neglected their needy fellows. We must help even our enemies. Our duty is kindness, not revenge. Holiness of this sort is superior to that claimed by the monks.

The Sixth Commandment, following the one which makes our neighbor's life safe, looks to the security of his wife. It defends the sanctity of marriage. It forbids impurity of act and thought. It requires chastity as well as help to the tempted.

Two reasons for it may be assigned. First, God honors marriage and blesses it, as his Word declares. Second, it is a natural state for normal people. In contrast, monastic celibacy produces great dangers and sins and consequently should be abandoned.

The intent of the commandment is that we should cultivate honorable marriage, that we should live chastely, and that we should love and honor our spouse.

The Seventh Commandment follows naturally, because, besides our neighbor's life and wife, his property also must be secure. Theft is defined as gaining goods without giving an equivalent return. It includes loss suffered by the wanton carelessness of servants or of workmen, or by frauds and false measures in business, or by unjust exactions by the nobility or the papacy that plunders all of Germany. The world, of course, honors great thieves, but punishes small ones.

Under this commandment Christians must not deprive their neighbors of their property but help them to preserve it. God's punishment of offenders is inescapable. In this world injustice breeds injustice and retribution comes at last, whether to malicious workmen or to profiteering merchants. In time their ill-gotten gains melt away. God punishes one thief with another, but he guards the righteous and hears the cry of the oppressed.

This should be taught the young, and let the government both rule and punish. Understand the commandment broadly: neither steal, nor permit damage to others' property, but help to improve it, and aid in need. Here is truly a good work—one approved by God.

The Eighth Commandment recognizes that connected with our neighbor's life, spouse, and goods, is his reputation. The commandment is broken in three ways. First, among the Jews it was broken by false testimony in court. Justice demands that judges and witnesses be honest; they are required to be so by this commandment. In the second place, it is broken when evangelical Christians are maligned by their enemies. Third, it is violated in our day by any injury done by the tongue, whether heresy, perjury, or slander.

Passing judgment on the conduct of others should be left to those who have the task officially. The Commandment requires that we refrain from spreading rumor, from speaking slander, and from delighting in evil report. We should not speak evil, even of the guilty, unless it can be proven in court. Without adequate evidence, do not tarnish a good name. Rather, keep silent.

There are important exceptions. Rulers, pastors, and parents have an official duty to reprove misconduct. Christians who have complaints against one another should settle their differences privately between themselves. The master of the house may deal directly with servants who are at fault. When private efforts to correct an offender fail, then use the courts rather than resort to gossip. In case the sin is a public one, the testimony also may be public.

To sum it all up, the commandment requires that we speak evil of no one, except as a necessary reproof to him. But we should excuse him and speak well of him, just as we devise clothing to conceal physical blemishes. This also is a work pleasing to God.

The Ninth and Tenth Commandments are treated together. Besides the deeds forbidden, the desires underlying them are also forbidden. Desires which injure others are sinful even when legal means are used. By nature we are greedy, but we conceal it under shrewdness. These commandments are not for thieves as much as for reputable but scheming people who use lawsuits to dispossess others, use sharp business practices to the same purpose, or estrange a woman from her husband in order to have her.

Briefly stated, these commandments warn us not to be guilty of avarice, however legal its methods, for it injures our neighbor and pollutes us. Instead we should gladly help him enjoy what is his.

Luther wrote a conclusion to his treatment of all the commandments. In it he declared that they describe what are really good works in God's sight. Keeping them, especially in their positive phases, is a large task. In the Roman Church the more dramatic works of the monks are thought to be superior. But the Commandments are never surpassed; they are not even fully kept. Hence there is need of faith as expressed in the Creed, and of petition as voiced in the Lord's Prayer. The high standard set by the Commandments calls for strenuous effort on our part.

God's wrath or mercy is related to all the Commandments. Therefore we are both warned and encouraged; we are moved by fear as well as trust. Thus the First Commandment embodies all the rest. It imparts its splendor to the others. Obedience to all of them must proceed from the fear and love of God. This must be taught diligently and exalted above all man-made rules.

With this much of the Catechism before us, we may pause in the outline for a few observations. In the first place, there is a "dated" quality to a few of the points of view. They must be seen in their historical setting and with the limitations of that day. This is particularly true of the Fourth Commandment. Luther's concept of government was paternalistic, not democratic. His insistence upon obedience to government considered the sovereign to rule by divine right. Related to this is his antipathy to revolt, as, for example, in the Peasants' War. The only way to improve conditions was to preach to the rulers. Luther's keen interest in this matter is shown by the length of his exposition; the explanation of this one commandment is a fourth of the total treatment of them all.

In the second place, and more important, is the fact that for the most part there is a timelessness about his treatment. One might have expected, for example, that in the treatment of the Sixth Commandment there would be some intimation of the inferior status of a woman to that of her husband. But it is quite lacking. Instead of the suggestion that a wife is the property of her husband, there is every indication of their equal status under the commandment and before God. The Catechism recognizes no double moral standard. This is the perennial emancipation of women under the gospel. In this matter as in many others the Catechism is not outmoded.

Third, Luther suggests directions for the social thinking of our day. We are badly in need of sound principles for social action and social service. Note particularly his treatment of the Fifth and the Seventh Commandments. In both instances the positive phase forms a basis for social service. We must be interested in the health and livelihood of others in the world.

As for social action, both Commandments set the ground for preventing injustice and of promoting benevolence. Perhaps we may disagree with Luther that the Fifth Commandment is "not for governments" when we remember murders committed by the secret police of totalitarian nations. Perhaps also we may wish that Luther had stated a principle for determining at what point the exactions of the nobility cease to be just and become unjust. His writing concerning the Twelve Articles of the Peasants recognized that there were injustices in his day.

Moreover, Luther was not so intent upon the sins against individuals that he could not see the sins against society. In this he anticipated by a long time the influential little book, *Sin and Society* by E. A. Ross.[2] Luther saw that in his day great thieves were honored as great noblemen; today they are sometimes elected to public office.

Finally, and of chief importance, was Luther's evangelical insight. It is in sharp contrast to the Roman system of merits. For example, his treatment of the Third Commandment shows the centrality of the gospel and is marked by an entire absence of legalism. There are no rules for "Sabbath observance" but only a great concern with the gospel. He related the Lord's Day to the New Testament rather than to Moses.

Whereas the Church of Rome bases conduct on obedience and duty to a just God, Luther saw the gospel portray God as also merciful. Therefore fear and love motivate our lives. Luther stressed this at some length in connection with the First Commandment. It is the keynote of all the Commandments.

---

[2] Boston: Houghton, Mifflin & Co., 1907. Cf. chap. 2.

Moreover, the evangelical insight identifies the ways in which the Christian life manifests itself, that is to say, good works. The papal church has its list of meritorious works humanly devised. Luther insisted that only those works which are commanded by God and motivated by love are really pleasing to him. This point of view was repeated in Article VI of the Augsburg Confession.

THE APOSTLES' CREED

Returning to a summary of the Catechism, we examine Luther's explanation of the Apostles' Creed. In introducing it he declared that after conduct comes faith, which aids it. For simplicity in its treatment the Creed is given in three articles grouped according to the Trinity. Stated in the briefest terms the faith of the Creed is this: "I believe in God the Father, who has created me; I believe in God the Son, who redeemed me; I believe in the Holy Ghost, who sanctifies me." [3]

The first article, as related to the First Commandment, speaks of faith in the Creator and in Providence, the source of our supply and protection. Our reaction is one of love, praise, and thanks. Where pride dwells, faith has been evicted. Faith is a humble attitude, remembering that a heavenly Father does all things for us.

The second article is one about Christ, our Lord. He is Lord because he has delivered us from the kingdom of evil under which the human race was enslaved, and has brought us under his rule and protection. "Lord" therefore means "Redeemer," for all his life and work are redemptive. He made satisfaction for our debts. A full treatment of this subject would be too much for children. This much is at least the core of the gospel.

The third article treats of the Holy Ghost, our Sanctifier. He leads us into the church and brings us to Christ. He conveys the redemption Christ has prepared, dispensing it through the church which proclaims the Word (not the papal church which obscures it).

"Church" and "communion of saints" are synonymous. "Church" means assembly, or congregation, or people, and "communion" has the same significance. (All are not agreed with Luther that *church*,

---

[3] *Luther's Small Catechism Developed and Explained*, General Synod ed. (Philadelphia: Lutheran Publication Society, 1893), p. 46.

kirche, and *curia,* are related to *kyria.*) In this holy assembly under Christ, the Holy Spirit operates through the Word.

In the church forgiveness of sin is available—a continual cleansing and comfort. Outside the church and the gospel there is no pardon. Sanctification is a gradual, lifelong process wrought by the Holy Spirit. And at last comes the resurrection, which certainly is not grossly physical.

In brief, this is the work of the Holy Spirit: to form an assembly of Christians who therein receive forgiveness and who will be raised to life at the last day.

In these three articles the Creed shows Gods essence, will, and work revealed to us through Christ. It distinguishes Christians from all others. It differs from the Ten Commandments in that it tells not what we do, but what God does for us; it is not found in us, but is revealed to us; it does not bring condemnation, but it conveys grace and power to obey.

This is enough for simple minds.

THE LORD'S PRAYER

The Lord's Prayer is the third chief part. After conduct and faith comes prayer, "resort to the ear of God." It is our duty to pray; the Second Commandment implies as much. Times of need require it. Prayer is an evidence that we are Christians. It is a resource for conquering evil thoughts. It is also an exercise of faith.

Therefore prayer should be highly esteemed since it is commanded by God. It is in no way dependent on our merit. But the prayer of every believer is acceptable. Thus there are three things to remember: prayer is based on God's command; it has God's promise of blessing in which we believe; and God has given us a model of how to pray.

Prayer offered in need has the purpose of seeking a blessing. It is unlike prayers of monks who make them as works of merit. In contrast, true prayer is earnestly offered from a sense of distress and need. Daily prayer comes from a daily sense of want. Indeed, our security rests on prayer. Let all learn to esteem prayer highly as petition offered because of our need of help.

The first petition implies that God's name is holy in its nature, but not always in our use of it. As his children, bearing his name, we want it honored by godly doctrine and conduct. It is profaned by heresy, perjury, and evil conduct. This petition simply asks what the Second Commandment requires. Such prayer is needed because many dishonor his name. Nor do any one of us honor it as completely as God desires.

The second petition is related to the first. As God's name is holy, so his kingdom is sure to come. And we pray for it to come to us. By his kingdom is meant both deliverance from the power of evil, and the increase of his righteous rule. We therefore ask for it to come to us and to all mankind.

It comes in this world through the Word and faith, and in eternity through revelation. Thus we pray that the Word may be preached everywhere and that it may effectively bring us into the kingdom.

In this we pray for an eternal, sublime treasure. God is prepared to give to us richly and expects us to pray for great things. Therefore we must pray with faith in God's great goodness.

The third petition is also in sequence. With the honor of God's name and the coming of his kingdom, is associated the doing of his will. The devil, the world, and our flesh vigorously oppose his will. We must expect that, as our enemies, they will give us no peace.

Hence we must continue to pray earnestly. These first three petitions concern the things of God, but they also affect us. Such prayer is our protection.

In the fourth petition the words "daily bread" include all that is involved in producing food, all other necessities such as clothing and shelter, peace and security, as well as good government. In the coat of arms of a prince, a loaf would be better than a lion as a symbol of the government's provision.

If all that is included in "daily bread" were enumerated, the list would be a long one. It all comes from God, and for it prayer should be made, since the devil interferes with our peace and plenty. Though God feeds the wicked as well as the good, yet he wants us to pray for food, and acknowledge it as his gift.

The fifth petition sees that the life of the Christian is not without sin. Yet even without our prayer God is willing to forgive. This prayer is to recognize and accept his pardon. Our continued need of forgiveness should humble us. This petition asks God to disregard our sins and to forgive them. As a sign of our humble repentance, we freely forgive others as God freely forgives us. Our own acts of mercy can reassure us of God's mercy.

With the sixth petition we see that, since we have all these blessings, we must pray that we may not lose them by falling into temptation. Temptations are from the flesh—its lusts and appetites; from the world—its malice, pride, power, and so on; and from the devil and his incitement to unbelief, despair, blasphemy, etc.

We pray that God would sustain us amid such grave dangers. The petition asks for strength to resist temptation, for we all feel its power and must daily expect its assault. It means, in other words, "Let me not relapse because of temptations."

The seventh petition may read, "Deliver us from the evil one"— our chief enemy. The petition is a summary, asking for deliverance from all sorts of evils, bodily and spiritual.

"Amen" indicates certainty that our prayer will be heard. It is a word of faith, as James wrote (1:6) "Let him ask in faith, nothing wavering."

BAPTISM

In addition to the three chief parts, every Christian should have an elementary knowledge of the sacraments. The first of the two is baptism.

To begin with, we must understand its nature. As a basis for baptism, whereby we enter the church, are the words of Scripture: Matthew 28:19, "Go ye . . . baptizing . . ." and Mark 5:16, "He that believeth and is baptized shall be saved." Hence it is by divine command and founding and is therefore highly important. To be baptized in the name of God means that it is God's work. It is much more valuable than the works of the monastics, no matter how spectacular they may be, for they are the works of men, not of God.

Properly defined, baptism "is not simply water, but water comprehended in God's Word and commandment and sanctified thereby." Though the sectarians despise the water, yet with God's Word it is precious; the promise of God sanctifies it. As Augustine said, "Join the Word to the element and make a sacrament." Do not judge by the mere externals, as you would not despise a nut because of its coarse shell. But esteem baptism for the Word and keep water and Word together.

Next to be considered are the benefits of baptism. Its purpose is to save us from the kingdom of sin into that of God. It does this, not by the water alone, but with the Word. Truly faith alone saves, but faith in something, namely, the Word in baptism. "It is madness to separate faith" and its object as the sectarians do. For God works through means.

Who are proper recipients of baptism? Luther answers that the believer is the worthy recipient. For it is God's work, not ours, and is apprehended by faith. They accuse us falsely who say that we preach against faith when we stress the validity of baptism as God's gift.

At this point Luther paused to summarize what he had said thus far. Baptism is established and commanded by God and is connected with his promise of grace to all who believe. Here is enough for life-long practice and increase of faith. We can always rely on our baptism—a blessing of salvation for body and soul.

The question of infant baptism also must be answered. In a sense the questions, "Can children believe?" and "Should they be baptized?" are problems for scholars. However, a simple answer is that God has actually blessed some who were baptized as infants, as, for example, the church fathers. Indeed, the church, which has had the Holy Spirit, consists mainly of those baptized in infancy, and the church cannot perish.

The central point is that the validity of baptism rests on the Word and not on faith, even when administered to someone of evil purpose and wickedness. Those who rebaptize consider infant baptism invalid. But what God does is never invalid. If you have not had faith heretofore, pray now for faith to receive what God gave you. We baptize infants on God's command in the purpose and hope that they may believe. It is a mistake to think that the abuse of baptism means that it is worthless, for worthless things cannot be abused. Baptism is always true even if it is not believed.

Finally, there is the symbolism of baptism. It signifies regeneration, as well as a daily dying to sin and a reviving to righteousness.

To leave our old nature unrestrained is to contend against our baptism. But the old nature must be increasingly submerged, as baptism signifies.

Daily dying to sin, which is repentance, is a kind of third sacrament. On the other hand, living in repentance is really walking in baptism. Actually, "our baptism abides forever," and repentance is a return to our baptism. It is not, as Jerome said, a second plank on which to swim to safety after shipwreck. For, though we may fall overboard, the ship (baptism) is never wrecked.

Luther concluded with a summary: Baptism delivers from evil, unites to God, suppresses sin, strengthens in holiness, and continues through life. Let everyone value his baptism as something to cherish. If he has fallen away, let him return to it again as an unfailing resource.

THE LORD'S SUPPER

With reference to the other sacrament, the Lord's Supper, knowledge of its nature, its benefits, and its recipients should be required of all who would partake of it.

In considering its nature, the words of institution are of greatest importance and indicate its validity. Properly defined, "It is the true Body and Blood of our Lord, Jesus Christ, in and under the bread and wine, which we Christians are commanded by the Word of Christ to eat and to drink."

The Word joined to the elements makes them the sacrament of the Body and Blood of Christ. In spite of the objections of reason, there stands the Word of Christ, "This is my body." It does not depend upon the holiness of the minister or of the recipient.

The benefits are varied. The sacrament conveys the forgiveness of sins and nourishment for the soul in its battle with temptation. It is not simply bread and wine which bring all this, but it is the connected Word which does this. If it is objected that we receive grace in the Word without the sacraments, it must be answered that the Word teaches us to use the sacraments.

The proper recipients of this sacrament also are believers. "Whoever believes it has what the words declare and bring." Faith is the means of receiving. Fasting and discipline have some value, but faith is that which truly prepared the recipient. Though some people neglect the sacrament as unneeded (since they are free of the pope's laws), yet, even though free of coercion, they should not neglect and despise God's gift. True Christians, both the strong and the weak, need frequent exhortation to believe firmly in the sacrament.

Three reasons for such exhortation may be given. First, we have Christ's command, "Do this," and we must obey, partaking often of it. We despise it if we neglect it for a long time. Under the papacy Christians went to communion out of compulsion. But we go freely out of faith and love. Neglect of it leads gradually to hardness of heart. If we look at our sins, we feel unworthy of the sacrament. But we can never be holy enough. The "shameless and dissolute" are certainly unworthy and "must be told to stay away." But those who desire to be godly should be welcomed. For the sacrament does not depend on our worthiness. The worthy are the repentant and believing who look more at the Word and command of Christ than at themselves.

The second reason is Christ's promise which is made to individual believers. This great offer should not be spurned. The unworthy receive the sacrament to their hurt, but the worthy to their benefit.

The third reason is found in our need. Besides the command and the promise is our distress, our soul-weariness and sin-sickness, though the unworthy often feel no infirmity.

If we feel none, we need to examine ourselves by Paul's list of works of the flesh (Gal. 5:19 f.). Trust Scripture to reflect your condition. Also we should scrutinize our relation to the world to detect any strain or antagonism, for the Christian is not at peace with the world. Remember next the devil's continual temptations. If none of these affects us, then we should seek counsel and prayer from others until we feel the need of mercy.

In concluding the entire Catechism Luther urged that young and old, especially the former, should learn these things so that the church may be preserved. Let the fathers teach their baptized children, thus preparing them for communion and active church life.

There are several things in Luther's exposition which deserve comment. His treatment of the Creed, being limited to the ABC's of faith, makes no effort at theological fullness. There are intimations, however, of a large theological substratum. With Christ and his salvation as a starting point, the First Person of the Trinity is believed in as the God who preserves and saves, rather than as an austere, law-enforcing monarch. The God seen through Christ is divine love. With such a point of view, theological problems have a distinctly different treatment.

If Luther's treatment of the second article is examined for a theory of the atonement, there may be seen evidences of what Aulén in *Christus Victor* calls the "classic theory."[4] The atonement was a conquest. The kingdom of evil was successfully invaded and its power broken. But the theory of Anselm, which pictured the atonement as the payment of a debt, also shows itself in Luther's treatment.

Protestantism is sometimes described (and criticized) as definitely individualistic and atomistic. Under the papacy, the church interpreted the Scriptures for the people, and only this one interpretation was permitted. It is sometimes claimed that under Protestantism every individual is free to interpret the Bible for himself; the result is sectarianism. While Luther denounced the autocratic rule of the papacy, he nonetheless had a high view of the church in which there is one faith, just as there is one Word. He believed in the corporate nature of Christianity. He had no time for sectarian individualism.

Even though it is true that what Luther affirms in the Catechism is largely ecumenical, it is also true that his explanations are confessional. The contrast to Roman or sectarian doctrines is not only implied but frequently comes to the surface. He specifically denounced the unevangelical Church of Rome but he also renounced the unchurchliness of the sects. When discussing the sacraments he could not forget the Romish scheme which both exalted and abused repentance as a sacrament. On the other hand he combated with vigor the sectarian emasculation of the sacraments. In the Large Catechism, therefore, is a simple and direct testimony of Lutheran faith aware of its tensions with unscriptural doctrines.

---

[4] *Op. cit.,* p. 20.

Chapter XVI

THE ORIGIN OF THE FORMULA OF CONCORD

In the eyes of Roman Catholics, Lutheranism is saturated with a schismatic spirit. Lutherans, in breaking the church apart, exhibited a divisiveness typical of their nature. When Lutherans avowed their devotion to the unity of Christendom, they were sneered at as hypocrites. Papal spokesmen conveniently forgot the long history of dissension in the church; they preferred to overlook the current tensions within their own ranks. They sought by every means possible to discredit the Reformation, and the accusation of "schism" came readily to their tongues. Every bit of evidence indicating disagreement within Lutheranism was eagerly exploited. This was abundant reason—even if there had been no others—for Lutherans to compose the differences which arose in their midst and to prepare a formula expressing their agreement.

POLITICAL EVENTS

The adherents of evangelical doctrine went to the Diet of Augsburg in the spring of 1530 with the emperor's assurance of his desire to reach a fair and acceptable settlement of the issues in dispute. But they went home from that diet with his threat ringing in their memories. He had accepted the Confutation as his answer to their Confession and had declared that the Protestants also must accept it not later than April 15. Otherwise he would show that he was not unmindful of his duties as the guardian of the church's welfare.

There was no doubt that the consequences of noncompliance could be quite disastrous. The signers of the Augsburg Confession recognized their danger. Accordingly the evangelical nobility met at

Smalcald, and on February 27 formed a defensive alliance called the Smalcald League. So powerful was the league that Charles V, lacking the wholehearted co-operation of the Catholic princes now jealous of him, suspected by the pope, and always menaced by France, was forced to leave the religious issue in the file of unfinished business. April 15, 1531, came and went without imperial action against the Evangelicals. Hence in 1532 the Truce of Nürnberg was proclaimed giving peace to the Protestants until a new *Reichstag* or a council could be convened. Meanwhile other German areas and cities joined the league.

But Charles V was not without aggressiveness or energy. He knew that his difficulties were of two kinds: religious and territorial. The religious problem lay within his empire. Insistence upon church reforms had become vehement in Germany and had the military support of the Smalcald League. Yet the pope gave him trouble also, for resistance to any relaxation of papal taxation or to any improvement of church conditions was the dominant attitude of the Roman curia. The two parties appeared to be irreconcilable.

His territorial problem lay without his empire. On his western front Francis I, king of France, was continually alert to every opportunity to acquire territory of the empire or even to seize the imperial throne. On his eastern front the ominous Turk was restless and belligerent. On that front there was no peace—only an armed truce disturbed by intermittent clashes. The French and the Turks were willing to form an alliance for a joint attack against Charles.

The emperor's strategy, therefore, was fairly obvious. The religious issue must be settled by compelling both the Lutherans and the pope to yield. The pope must be made to call a general council for the reform of the church. And the military power of the Smalcald League must be broken so that force could be brought to bear upon the Evangelicals to make them accept the decisions of the projected council. To make the empire territorially secure, the ambitions of the French must be rendered impossible of attainment and the Turkish threat must be removed.

The emperor's plan met with remarkable initial success. A quick campaign against France, with the help of Henry VIII of England, was so victorious that France was humbled and the Peace of Crespy, 1544, bound Francis to aid rather than attack the emperor. Circumstances were favorable to Charles also in his dealings with the Turks. Internal dissensions and troubles in Persia made the Turks amenable to imperial pressure for a treaty favorable to the security of the empire.

On the religious side also a curious combination of events played into the emperor's hands. Pope Paul III, lacking powerful allies, was obliged to yield to the demand for a general council. After considerable delay it actually convened late in 1545 in the city of Trent. Meanwhile the Smalcald League was disrupted by two unforeseen events: the bigamy of Philip of Hesse, and the desertion of Maurice of Saxony.

Philip, landgrave of Hesse, provided strong and skillful leadership for the Smalcald League, but his lust had involved him in many adulteries. He hoped that a cure could be found in a second marriage. On the basis of Old Testament polygamy, Melanchthon and Luther gave reluctant consent. When the bigamy became known to Charles, he saw his opportunity. He declared that Philip might escape severe imperial penalties only by promising to support the imperial policies. The Smalcald League thus was weakened by the limitations placed on Philip.

Serious also was the treachery of Maurice, political head of Ducal Saxony. Desiring to possess the power and position of Electoral Saxony also, he agreed to desert the evangelical cause in return for the emperor's promise of the electorate. Though he was a Lutheran, he contracted to support Charles rather than join the Smalcald League. Moreover the league failed to take adequate defense measures when imperial forces threatened.

In 1546 began the Smalcald War. The ban of the empire was pronounced against Elector John Frederick and Landgrave Philip, and armies were launched against them. The elector was defeated and captured at Mühlberg in 1547, and Philip, who submitted, was imprisoned. In accordance with the emperor's promise, Maurice for his part in the campaign became ruler of both Ducal and Electoral Saxony. The Lutheran forces thus seriously weakened were in no position to offer effective resistance to Charles. The Diet of Augsburg in 1548 issued the "Augsburg Interim" setting up a tentative arrangement of the religious issues pending their final settlement by a council. In Saxony, where the Augsburg Interim could not be enforced, Maurice issued the Leipzig Interim of 1548.

But the successes of the emperor were short-lived. It quickly became evident that the council summoned by Pope Paul was completely under papal domination, so that no thoroughgoing church reforms could be expected of it. No settlement of the vexatious church disputes could be looked for from that direction. This was a defeat for the emperor—one of a series of reverses.

For now that Maurice had secured his objectives he was cool toward the Catholic phases of the emperor's program. Irritated by the continued imprisonment of his father-in-law, Philip of Hesse, and dissatisfied with other conditions, he suddenly united with other evangelical forces and almost captured Charles, who was at Innsbruck without an army.

Meanwhile France returned to the struggle on the promise of territorial concessions. At Passau in 1552 a pact was signed terminating the struggle, and the Religious Peace of Augsburg, 1555, guaranteed to evangelical states the freedom from imperial religious domination.

THEOLOGICAL DISUNITY

However much the Reformation may have been a social movement involving economic, political, and class struggle, it was predominantly a religious event. Theological issues were basic for Luther. Yet in the doctrinal reconstruction necessitated by the rediscovered evangelical principles there were occasional differences of opinion on precise details.

Several of these crystallized into somewhat bitter controversies, which will be described in some detail in connection with each of the chapters of the Formula of Concord. At this point it will suffice to list them chronologically and recognize the state of affairs they entailed.

First was the Antinomian Controversy. The Reformation had turned attention so strongly to the gospel that some were inclined to lose sight of the law. Some persons actually went to the extreme of denying that the law has any authority over Christian believers. The controversy which ensued began in the 1530's and continued after Luther's death. Chapters V and VI of the Formula of Concord discuss the issues involved.

The Interimistic (or Adiaphoristic) Controversy arose when Maurice attempted to restore some Roman Catholic rites in the churches according to the terms of the Leipzig Interim. Some of the rites had been declared by Lutherans to be adiaphora, but a violent dispute arose in 1548 concerning the wisdom of yielding to the Interim. Chapter X of the Formula states the decision reached.

The Majoristic Controversy arose about the middle of the century when Professor George Major of the University of Wittenberg declared that good works are necessary to salvation. An opponent asserted that good works are detrimental to salvation. The Lutheran position is given in Chapter IV of the Formula.

The Osiandrian Controversy, also in the middle of the century, is so named because Andreas Osiander interpreted the doctrine of justification as involving only the divine nature of Christ and his union with the believer. An opponent went to the opposite extreme. This problem is the topic of Chapter III in the Formula.

The Crypto-Calvinistic Controversy began in the 1550's and continued into the next decade. It appeared because Melanchthon and his followers were hiding Calvinistic interpretations in their wording of the doctrines of the Person of Christ and of the Lord's Supper. Chapters VII and VIII show the difference between phrases which are secretly Calvinistic and those which are really Lutheran.

The Synergistic Controversy, which began in 1550, became acute in the 1560's when Melanchthon's followers interpreted him as teaching that man co-operates somewhat in his conversion. The opposing party asserted that unregenerate man is spiritually dead in sin. One of his opponents, Matthias Flacius, went so far as to affirm that human nature has become sin—thereby precipitating the Flacian Controversy. The Formula in Chapters I and II deals with these matters.

The controversies named involved not simply a few individuals but whole theological faculties and whole territories. The strict Luther party, known as "Gnesio-Lutherans," had its centers in Magdeburg and the University of Jena in Ducal Saxony. In points of difference between Luther and Melanchthon, it took the side of Luther. The followers of Philipp Melanchthon ("Philippists" or "Melanchthonians") were strong at the universities of Wittenberg and Leipzig in Electoral Saxony. They tended to modify Lutheran doctrine to the degree that some of them ended in Calvinism.

Between these two parties there was a large group of theologians who sought substantial Lutheran positions free of untenable extremes. Such men were found at the University of Tübingen in Württemberg and the University of Rostock in Mecklenburg.

The parties and controversies arose partly because of Melanchthon's willingness to compromise and deal in ambiguities, partly because of personal animosities, and partly by the extremes to which certain Gnesio-Lutherans went in their antagonism to the Philippists. At a time when the Lutheran Church needed to be strong, these controversies proved to be weakening and embarrassing. It was painfully evident that Lutherans needed security in the political sphere and unity in the area of doctrine.

POLITICAL EFFORTS AT HARMONY

After the Religious Peace of Augsburg, 1555, in which Lutherans had gained civil recognition, it was apparent that dissension in their ranks might lose for them all they had gained. Christopher, Duke of Württemberg, said it was urgently necessary for the Lutheran nobility to hold a meeting and reach an agreement before the next *Reichstag* convened.

Though others agreed, the Saxon rulers demurred. The duke of Saxony, with his Gnesio-Lutheran theologians, wanted as a minimum a condemnation of adiaphoristic and majoristic positions. The elector of Saxony, through Melanchthon, desired a new doctrinal formulation without retractions of past statements. These irreconcilable positions made impossible the meeting proposed by Christopher.

When the *Reichstag* met in Regensburg in 1557, the emperor expressed a desire for a colloquium in the interest of agreement between Lutherans and Catholics. To be ready for it the Lutherans held a preliminary meeting in June at Frankfort where their differences were concealed rather than removed.

The colloquium convened in September at Worms with twelve Romanist and twelve evangelical theologians in attendance. But the disunity among the Lutherans soon was evident when representatives from Ducal Saxony demanded the condemnation of certain errorists. Failing in this, they drew up their *Protestation*, and departed from the colloquium. Even the need of a common front against the Romanists was not enough to keep the Lutherans together.

In March, 1558, some of the nobility attended the coronation of Emperor Ferdinand at Frankfort. There they conferred on the problem of unity. At their direction Melanchthon wrote a union document called the Frankfort Recess,[1] which was subscribed by the leading princes. They agreed to censor all teaching and books on the basis of this document. But Melanchthon's phrases were so ambiguous that even Calvin said he could accept them. As a result other Lutheran princes rejected the document and the disunity continued.

The Frankfort Recess was not the only document in the field. Within a year there was prepared in Ducal Saxony the Weimar Confutation which both stated Lutheran doctrine and condemned by name the errors taught by some Lutherans. Meanwhile in Electoral Saxony the pupils of Melanchthon issued their *Corpus Doctrinae* (*Philippicum* or *Misnicum*) containing solely their teacher's writings.

Duke Christopher of Württemberg still had hopes of overcoming the disunity so painfully evident. Months of negotiations followed, during which time Melanchthon died, April 19, 1560. In August of that year invitations were issued to the princes for a meeting to consider unity on the basis of the Augsburg Confession of 1530.

A large number of the nobility or their representatives assembled at Naumburg late in January, 1561, in response to the invitation. Early in the proceedings the elector of the Palatinate proposed that the 1540 edition of the Augsburg Confession should be used since it represented the author's most mature expression of Lutheran doctrine. Others objected, since their instructions (in accord with the terms of the invitation) were to subscribe only the Augsburg Confession in the form published in 1531.

Finally a compromise preface was prepared approving the 1531 edition, but approving also the one of 1540 and repudiating transub-

---

[1] C. R., IX, 490 ff.

stantiation. But the Gnesio-Lutherans refused to accept the preface, which did not condemn Lutheran errorists, and soon thereafter they departed from Naumburg. The assembly was compelled to adjourn without having attained its purpose. Soon afterward the elector of the Palatinate, who had supported the Melanchthonian position, openly espoused Calvinism.

UNION EFFORTS OF THE THEOLOGIANS

As early as 1556 attempts were made to effect a reconciliation between Melanchthon, who had supported the Leipzig Interim, and Flacius, his former student, who had attacked it. There were also other disagreements, reinforced by personal feelings, party loyalties, and territorial rivalries.

Sometime later Flacius proposed the holding of a convention of all Lutherans to settle the issues in a democratic way. Melanchthon, whom many considered the leader and teacher of Lutheranism following Luther's death, was unwilling to submit his writings to such humiliating examination. Such were some of the differences between the irenic Melanchthon and the aggressive Flacius.

The conditions of peace acceptable to Flacius were sent in a letter by friends to Melanchthon, but he made no reply. Soon afterward Flacius sent to a professor at Wittenberg his thirteen "Lenient Propositions" for unity, wherein he presented the basis for Lutheran doctrine and his proposal for the condemnation of errorists. Once more a reply was withheld. When mutual friends invited Melanchthon to a meeting with his opponent he refused. Whereupon Flacius published a pamphlet, *Concerning Unity*, defending his own position.

Mutual friends still persisted and induced Flacius to write a letter directly to Melanchthon. This time Melanchthon replied. In his letter to Flacius, written September 5, 1556, he defined his position in the controversies yet admitted his mistake in the question of the Interim. But Flacius desired a public statement sharply defining the issues. This was more than Melanchthon was willing to do, especially when he heard rumors misrepresenting Flacius' motives.

Early in 1557 a group of clergymen from lower Saxony attempted to mediate between the men at the request of Flacius. They went to Wittenberg to confer with Melanchthon, but he vigorously resented their proposals as being Flacian conspiracy. Meanwhile Flacius and his friends had assembled at Coswig to hear reports of the mediation efforts. When they learned of Melanchthon's reaction, they became even more exacting in their demands upon the Wittenberg teachers.

Moreover, at Wittenberg the public and the students were greatly agitated. Flacius was criticized in publications and sermons. Four weeks later representatives of the duke of Mecklenburg, who likewise had come to Wittenberg as mediators, were angrily told by Melanchthon's son-in-law to cease disturbing the old man. The result of the attempted mediation was only increased bitterness.

The friction between the two Saxon parties continued during the next decade. The *Corpus Doctrinae Philippicum* had been published in German in 1559 and in Latin in 1560. Attacks upon it began at once and continued with unabated vigor. In an effort to settle the issue, the elector assembled the theologians of both parties for a colloquy at Altenburg. Because the discussions were carried on in writing, the sessions lasted from October, 1568, to March, 1569. Once more there was lack of agreement. The men from Jena objected to the use of the *Variata* in the *Corpus Philippicum*. They in turn were attacked as disturbers of the peace of the church.

Outside the Saxon areas there were others interested in unity among the Lutherans. In Württemberg (Swabia) there were several men who concerned themselves with the problem. First was John Brenz who had been prominent in defining Lutheran doctrines in contrast to those taught in Calvinist Switzerland. In an effort to restore Lutheranism to the Palatinate, which had become Calvinist, the Duke of Württemberg assembled the theologians of the two territories for a conference at Maulbronn in 1564. The meeting was a failure. Subsequently the theologians of each group published their points of view, Brenz writing the Lutheran documents.

When Brenz died in 1570, Jacob Andreae, professor at the University of Tübingen in Württemberg, became the leader of the consistent Lutheran movement in his area. In 1567 he wrote his *Confession and Brief Explanation of Several Controverted Articles According to Which a Christian Unity Might be Effected in the Churches Adhering to the Augsburg Confession.* The title indicates the nature of the writing.

With Martin Chemnitz he prepared for the Duchy of Brunswick a *Kirchenordnung* in 1569 which contained among other things a series of statements on the controversial issues. He also submitted to the faculty at Wittenberg a similar series of propositions as a basis for peace. Though a number of theologians elsewhere approved them, the professors at Wittenberg and Jena declined to accept the proposals.

The following year another attempt was made. Andreae hoped to gain success by a general acceptance of the Brunswick statements. At the direction of the elector, the Wittenberg and Leipzig theologians attended a meeting with others at Zerbst. Here again the result was failure because the Wittenberg and Leipzig men would agree to statements only as interpreted by the writings of Melanchthon (*Corpus Doctrinae Philippicum*). Andreae came to see that efforts to win the Melanchthonians would be fruitless.

In 1573 he published *Six Sermons on the Controversies within the Lutheran Church from 1548-73* and suggested them as a basis for union between the Lutherans in northern and southern Germany. In northern Germany, Chemnitz and the Duke of Brunswick approved the *Six Sermons,* but advised recasting them in the form of theses and issuing them through the Tübingen faculty. Andreae followed this advice. The document thus drawn up and accepted is known as the Swabian Concord. It was completed in 1573.

The articles thus prepared in the south were sent north to Chemnitz in 1574. By conference and correspondence he solicited from the Rostock faculty and from other theologians suggestions for the possible revision of the articles. He was encouraged in the replies to use phrases from some of their official declarations.

At Rostock the faculty made many changes, even to the extent of rewriting two articles. David Chytraeus was the professor chiefly responsible for the work; a Swabian with somewhat Melanchthonian sympathies, he was the chief member of the Rostock faculty and a consistent Lutheran.

The result of the revision, which had consumed a year and a half of time, is called the Swabian-Saxon Formula. Under the revisers' hands it had become lengthy and full of Latin and technical phrases. Chemnitz was busy winning the support of theologians in his own and neighboring territories for the document. The revised articles were sent south also to Andreae in September, 1575.

At Tübingen the document was laid aside for later discussion. While it was waiting the attention of the theologians, another document was being prepared. Elector Augustus of Saxony had been repeatedly warned that his theological professors were not clearly Lutheran. Finally he made known his desire for a series of statements by which he could evaluate his theologians. Late in 1575 Count Ernest of Henneberg, Margrave Karl of Baden, and Duke Louis of Württemberg commissioned three theologians to perform the task.

The topics involved were to be discussed on the basis of the Augsburg Confession, supported by quotations from Scripture, the Apology, the Smalcald Articles, the catechisms and other writings by Luther; the erroneous views were to be outlined, but no men were to be named as errorists. The document prepared in accordance with these plans was discussed and approved in January 1576 at a meeting at the Maulbronn cloister; hence it is called the Maulbronn Formula.

It came too late to be of use to Elector Augustus, who had in the meantime uncovered the deceptions of his theologians and dismissed them. Desiring to advance Lutheran unity and acting on the advice of his counselors he assembled at Torgau in May, 1576, the leading theologians of the various territories.

He asked them to discuss the controversies on the basis of the Maulbronn Formula and the Swabian-Saxon Concord. They were also to prepare a formula to be submitted to the Lutheran states for approval. They set to work, using the Swabian-Saxon Concord as the basis, inserting appropriate sections from the Maulbronn Formula and omitting or translating all Latin phrases. Their work was completed in June and observed with a service of thanksgiving.

The document prepared at Torgau—hence called the Torgau Book —was widely circulated during subsequent months in the Lutheran territories. The replies which Elector Augustus received were predominantly favorable. Those which were unfavorable came from Philippist areas; they objected to the omission of Melanchthon's name and views. On the other hand, there were those who wanted Melanchthon and others condemned by name.

After the replies had been received and their suggested emendations noted, meetings to discuss them were held at the town of Bergen in 1577. Andreae, Chemnitz, Chytraeus and others were present. Again the document underwent a thorough examination. The resultant revision is known as the Bergen Book. Because of the common criticism that the document had become too long, Andreae prepared a synopsis, which was approved also. The longer document is known as the Solid Declaration and Andreae's synopsis is the Epitome.[2]

There was every reason to expect that the Bergen Book would receive widespread approval and become actually a formula of agreement or concord. Some fifty-one princely heads of territories and a considerable number of cities officially adopted it for the direction of their churches. It was subscribed by approximately eight thousand representative persons.

In all these extensive areas it therefore actually came to be a Formula of Concord. On the semi-centennial of the Augsburg Confession there were published with the Formula of Concord the documents it approved, namely, the ecumenical creeds, the Augsburg Confession, the Apology, Luther's catechisms, and the Smalcald Articles. This compilation of symbolical writings bears the name *Book of Concord.*

The text of the Formula of Concord is German, but a Latin translation also was published in 1580. Some editions include as an appendix the Catalogue of Testimonies compiled by Chemnitz and Andreae, giving scriptural and patristic quotations in support of their doctrine "Of the Person of Christ."

THE SIGNIFICANCE OF THE FORMULA OF CONCORD

The first and most immediate significance of the Formula of Concord was ecclesiastical. As a consensus of doctrinal views it was important for church relationships and fellowship. It was an expression and a vehicle of unity among the Lutheran churches of the German territories. Though there was no organization of Lutherans on a national basis, just as there was no united German nation before the

---

[2] The *Concordia Triglotta*, p. 845, translates *Solida Declaratio* as "Thorough Declaration" in keeping with the German adjective *Gründliche.*

time of Bismarck, yet after 1577 the churches of the various states were not at serious odds with one another.

In the course of the years since 1577 there have been other controversies, such as that between the universities of Giessen and Tübingen over the question of *kenosis*. But the Formula of Concord marked the end of the major controversies in the Lutheran Church up to that time. There was now a decision in the dissensions which had stood in the way of presenting a common front against the Romanists. The Formula of Concord was a sign that agreement rather than controversy prevailed among Lutherans generally.

The Formula was not everywhere accepted. Though a decided majority of the states and cities subscribed it, there were important exceptions. In some instances, e.g., Pomerania, where another *corpus doctrinae* was in use, some time elapsed before the *Book of Concord* won its way into acceptance, replacing the other. In other cases personal animosity toward the authors of the Formula or their princes stood in the way of accepting this new document, even though there was no doctrinal disagreement with it.

But in the case of the Melanchthonians who were Crypto-Calvinists there could be only rejection of the Formula. A halfway position was no longer tenable for them, and presently they were within the fold of the Calvinists. A defense of the Calvinist position was issued in 1581 at Neustadt by Zacharias Ursinus under the title, *De Libro Concordiae Admonitio Christiana* (Newsted Admonition). Since the Formula of Concord made clear the defection from Lutheranism of the Melanchthonians, it was discussed in 1607 by the Calvinist theologian, Rudolf Hospinian, as the *Concordia Discors*. The reply was made in 1614 by the Lutheran theologian, Leonard Hutter, in his *Concordia Concors*.

A second significance of the Formula of Concord is symbolical. It was accepted as an expression of convictions and as a doctrinal guide. The fact that it was subscribed by approximately two-thirds of the Lutherans of Germany meant that it had the status of a symbolical writing. Since then there have always been large numbers of Lutherans who give official recognition to its normative character. Those who do not enumerate it in their church constitutions usually consider

it an important interpretation of the doctrines set forth in the Augsburg Confession.

It is part of the progress of sixteenth-century Lutheranism which
it would be unhistorical to ignore. Amid the circumstances of that
day it was a necessary development. Lutherans were under the
necessity of giving witness to their faith. No other outcome was possible to those faced with personal convictions, political requirements,
and a desire for peace. The common agreements of Lutherans encom-
passed by controversies needed to be given expression, both as a
declaration of their faith and as a commitment for future fellowship.
Weary of timid ambiguities, the subscribers gladly supported a document of forthright Lutheran doctrine.

Thirdly, the Formula of Concord has theological significance. It is
important as indicating how the second generation of Lutheran theologians understood Reformation doctrine. It shows them accepting
Luther as their guide and discarding the later positions of Melanchthon. It demonstrates that they accepted from Melanchthon the impulse to give doctrinal and scholastic formulation to evangelical faith.
But it also indicates that the doctrinal ore which they refined was
Luther's rather than Melanchthon's. They used Melanchthon's methods to propagate not his, but Luther's views. The theological position
is that of a consistent, if scholastic, Lutheranism.

It is to be noted also that the thought forms and types of argument are typical of the theological scene of that day. Walker says of
the Formula of Concord that "it is minute, technical, and scholastic, in
marked contrast to the freshness of the Augsburg Confession." [3] Such
characteristics by no means make the Formula useless as a symbolic
writing in the Lutheran Church. Fault is to be found only if it is
assumed that Lutheran theology must always have those characteristics, that it must use only those thought forms and phrases. Since
the twentieth century makes use of different concepts in its thinking,
it is necessary, for an appreciation of the Formula, to have an understanding of the philosophical distinctions current in that day.

A fourth significance is political. Under the Religious Peace of
Augsburg of 1555 Lutherans enjoyed certain political and religious

---

[3] W. Walker, *A History of the Christian Church* (New York: Charles
Scribner's Sons, 1937), p. 444.

rights in the empire. There was always the possibility that they might lose those rights. A prince was responsible for the peace and good order of his territory. If disorder over religious matters arose in his state, or if heresy appeared, the emperor could hold him responsible, and might compel him and his people to return to the Roman Church. The Jesuits were alert to this possibility and were prepared to exploit it.

In a day, therefore, when the ruler was responsible for the religion of his people, the controversies in the Lutheran Church had a political significance. This fact was recognized in that day. At the colloquium at Worms in 1557 the Gnesio-Lutherans from Ducal Saxony challenged the right of the Melanchthonians to be considered Lutherans and therefore to be included in the provisions of the Religious Peace of Augsburg. It immediately becomes apparent why the Formula of Concord as officially adopted by states and cities had political significance in the empire. With the coming of modern religious toleration, that political significance disappeared.

Chapter XVII

OUTLINE OF THE FORMULA OF CONCORD
(CHAPTERS I-VI)

In the subtitles assigned to the Epitome and the Solid Declaration several points are to be noticed. First, a connection with the Augsburg Confession is affirmed; either the articles are those of the Confession (as in the Solid Declaration), or the theologians are those so designated (as in the Epitome). The theological and political reasons for this claim have already been noted.

Second, the articles discussed are those controverted. Other dogmatic topics may be expected to be omitted. Third, an agreement has been reached. Fourth, the basis of the agreement "in a Christian way" was the Word of God. The Solid Declaration more specifically names "the analogy of God's Word," to which is added "the summary contents of our Christian doctrine."

The Formula is introduced by a statement of position and purpose. It is acknowledged that the final authority in doctrine is found in the Scriptures alone. Comprising the Old and New Testaments, they are "prophetic and apostolic" and are otherwise referred to as "God's Word." This is a clearly evangelical, rather than a Roman, position.

Next, the three ancient creeds—Apostles', Nicene, and Athanasian—are accepted as valid testimonies against heresies. The Solid Declaration applied to them the designation "ecumenical," introducing the use of that term in connection with these creeds. In addition the Lutheran writings are named and accepted as testimonies against the errors of Rome and the sects. But it is made quite clear that in examining doctrines the Scriptures are the only judge, while the creeds and confessions are merely testimonies.

In addition to these points made in the Epitome, the preface of the Solid Declaration reviews briefly the occasion of the Augsburg Confession, indicates the reasons for the rise of the Lutheran controversies, and shows how important they were. Though "useless wrangling" is repudiated, reasons are given why the church from apostolic times has had to define its doctrine. There is involved also the necessity of delineating the teachings not in accord with the Lutheran confessions; erroneous doctrines are to be "censured" and "reproved."

The specific loyalty to Luther is noticeable. Melanchthon is not named, even when his writings—the Augsburg Confession and the Apology—are mentioned. Remembering the antipathy to Melanchthon by the authors of the Formula, it may be that they had him with others in mind when, in noting errors, they warned that "no one be misled herein by the reputation of any man." Therefore the 1540 edition of the Augsburg Confession is ignored and the 1530 form distinctly specified.

The theological rather than the popular nature of the discussion is also emphasized. Several times the controversies are mentioned as being "of the theologians." The catechisms of Luther are distinguished from the other writings as being intended for the laity; the Epitome speaks of them as "the Bible of the laity." In contrast thereto the Formula is acknowledged to be frankly theological.

The unity of the church is kept constantly in view. Christians are united by their faith. Departures from the faith disrupt fellowship. When Christians present a common testimony before the world, there is strength in their harmony. As the ecumenical creeds "were regarded as the unanimous, universal Christian faith," so the Lutheran writings are "the unanimous consensus and declaration of our Christian faith and confession."

Such doctrinal unanimity is declared to be necessary for "thorough, permanent unity in the church." The doctrinal positions are presented in official documents "which always and everywhere were received in all the churches of the Augsburg Confession"—reminding one of the rule of Vincent of Lerins: *semper, ubique, et ab omnibus.*

CHAPTER I. OF ORIGINAL SIN

The historical occasion for this chapter is found in the synergistic and, more specifically, the Flacian controversies. It has already been noted that following the writing of the Frankfort Recess there was prepared by the Gnesio-Lutherans in Ducal Saxony the Weimar Confutation. It was a document stating not only the approved positions but also listing and condemning alleged errors. All the clergy and theologians of the duchy were ordered to subscribe it.

Professor Victorin Strigel refused to sign it because it condemned a certain statement. It had been declared by some that a man cooperates to a degree in his conversion. Such a statement was condemned as a Philippist error. Strigel disagreed with the condemnation.

In consequence of the professor's refusal to sign, a disputation between Strigel and Flacius (the author of the Confutation) was held in the Duke's presence in 1560. Strigel in his discussion affirmed that sin is an attribute, an "accident" (in the sense used by scholastic philosophy), and that it does not replace the essence or substance of human nature. Furthermore, original sin must be regarded as a suspension of man's righteous nature and not a total corruption of it.

Flacius, eager to assert the terrible and extensive distortion of human nature known as original sin, went so far as to say that the very essence and substance of man has become sin. In the years which followed, the pupils of Flacius propagated his view literally. But his colleagues in the faculty rejected it, producing a controversy in 1567.

It must be noted that Flacius distinguished between *substantia materialis*—the stuff of which a thing is composed—and *substantia formalis*—the form it takes. He seems to have meant the latter when he said that sin is *substantia*. Yet he steadily refused to abandon this misleading phraseology, even though he was willing to use also other phrases which had the approval of such men as Andreae. Not long afterward when there was a change of rulers, Flacius lost his professorship at Jena, was declined residence in Strassburg and Frankfort, and after some years of wandering died in 1575.

The question at issue in the controversy, therefore, concerned a precise definition of original sin. The Augsburg Confession in Article

II had affirmed and briefly defined original sin. But is original sin the essence of human nature, or is it merely an attribute? Is it proper to distinguish theologically between man's nature and original sin as corrupting that nature?

Lest anyone think this is "unnecessary wrangling" the Solid Declaration promptly points out the importance of the problem. For if the undisturbed goodness of human nature is affirmed, the result is Pelagianism—a serious perversion of the gospel as the church generally recognizes.

On the other hand, if out of a dualistic idea of the existence of good substances and evil substances (light and darkness), it is held that sin is merely the evil stuff oozing into sight, we are confronted with a Manichaean conception—something quite foreign to Christianity and vigorously opposed by the ancient church.

The discussion makes use of thesis and antithesis, the affirmative and the negative. The Solid Declaration makes three affirmative points: that mankind's inherited spiritual malady is truly sin; that nature comes from God but sin from the devil; that the corruption of human nature is complete and total. These points are followed by a summary of the declarations of the Apology with reference to the results, extent, terribleness, penalty, and cure of original sin.

The Epitome, however, asserts the necessity of a distinction between nature and sin, the reasons for that distinction, and the total corruption of human nature which original sin entails.

It is obvious that the doctrinal position here set forth is coherent with the other symbolical books. The Apology is referred to by name and its connection with the Augsburg Confession, "the common confession of our Christian doctrine," acknowledged. The Smalcald Articles also are named and quoted. Every effort is made to stress this confessional harmony, which would be adversely affected if the peculiar views of Flacius were to prevail. In all the previous symbolical writings the discussion of original sin used language which implies that original sin is a quality of nature. There is no quotable basis for the Flacian perverted view.

It is noteworthy also that a well-rounded conception of doctrine prevails. Original sin and its implications are discussed in their connection with the other doctrinal loci, rather than in isolation. The great basic doctrines of creation, incarnation, sanctification, and the resurrection are examined for their reference to original sin and human nature. Taking a comprehensive view of theology, a decision is reached in the dispute whereby is attained a declaration marked by perspective and balance. As might be expected of an ecumenical approach, there is doctrinal cohesion within the Lutheran systematic theology.

The antitheses form two groups: the positions of the Pelagians and their synergistic relatives; and those of the Manichaeans together with the Flacianists.[1] In the first instance, there is rejected the view that mankind since Adam is by nature good, either wholly or partially. The corollary is that what is called original sin is really not sin, but is a debt, or a purely natural quality of life, or a slight defect, or simply an impediment to holiness. In the second instance the position rejected is that original sin is a foreign substance which has entered the soul, like poison put into wine. If that were true, human nature would not be to blame, but only the intruded substance would come under God's judgment.

Arguments in rebuttal to these antitheses are given. The Manichaean (Flacian) doctrine cannot be true because God created and perpetuates human nature, not sin. Christ in the incarnation assumed human nature, not sin. God sanctifies human nature and raises it from the dead, but this cannot be true of sin. Hence a distinction between nature and sin is truly necessary.

Luther's terminology, which recognizes the thorough involvement of original sin in human nature, is justified. Likewise among scholars the scholastic distinction between "substance" as essence and "accident" as a quality is acceptable and useful. However, the discussion of theological details must not obscure the central fact taught in Scripture that original sin is a thorough, horrible, and deadly corruption of the soul.

CHAPTER II. OF THE FREE WILL

Again, as in Chapter I of the Formula, the doctrinal dispute is a phase of the Synergistic Controversy. It is commonly recognized that

---

[1] Those to whom the antithetical statements are attributed are named in footnotes to the Epitome in Volume I of the Jacobs edition of the *Book of Concord*.

evangelical theology found much that is compatible in the writings of Augustine. Luther certainly was Augustinian in the doctrines of sin and grace; and in Chapter II of the Formula it is the bishop of Hippo who is quoted from among the church fathers.[2] Augustine surely was not synergistic.

Though there are differences of opinion among scholars as to the extent to which Luther agreed with Augustine on the doctrine of predestination, the situation with regard to the freedom of the will is much clearer. Luther in *de servo arbitrio* and Melanchthon in the first edition of *Loci* used very strong expressions to describe man's bondage.

Luther's insistence on the monergism of God's grace appears in another connection, when, writing against the enthusiasts who taught the immediacy of the Spirit, he affirmed the importance of the grace conveyed by the divinely appointed means of grace. Luther's view was that man does nothing in conversion, but the divine agency operates in him through the means of grace. But when man's will resists, grace is not conveyed.

In the course of the years Melanchthon wrote on these topics in such a way as to make less sharply clear the monergism of God's grace. He used broader and somewhat more ambiguous terms. Instead of viewing conversion only from God's side, he tried to see it from man's side also.

Hence he sometimes wrote of conversion, using the word in the broadest sense to include contrition plus faith plus good works. He spoke of three concurrent factors in conversion: the Spirit, the Word, and man's will as not resisting. This is Melanchthon's well-known three-factor theory.

The question at once arises: Did Melanchthon depart from, or modify, Luther's view? Chemnitz, who was close to the whole situation and was not a Philippist, wrote that Melanchthon did not advocate synergism. Yet modern writers, such as Kolde and Tschackert, note how much Melanchthon wrote in an Erasmian vein, showing dissatisfaction with the phrases of Luther.[3]

---

[2] *Contra duas epp. Pelag. ad Bonif.* I, 19, 37. *MSL* XLIV, 568. Cited in *Bek.*, p. 780, n. 1.

[3] T. Kolde, *Analecta Lutherana, Briefe und Aktenstücke* (Gotha, 1883), p. 266. P. Tschackert, *Die Entstehung der luth. und der ref. Kirchenlehre* (Göttingen, 1910), p. 520. Cited in *Conc. Trig.*, Hist. Intro., 128.

Whatever may be our opinion of the position of Melanchthon, there can be no doubt of the fact that some of his students gave a decidedly synergistic interpretation to his phrases. In speaking of the third factor in his theory, they said that man's will is not merely not resisting but actually adapting itself to the working of the Spirit in conversion. It is clear, therefore, that there were Philippists who were synergists and that there were phrases of Melanchthon which, though not clearly synergistic, were capable of such an interpretation.

It was a phrase of this sort, condemned in the Weimar Confutation, which Professor Strigel in 1560 refused to repudiate. It was discussed in the colloquy with Flacius held in the presence of the duke, as noted in connection with Chapter I of the Formula. The result of the colloquy was indecisive.

Sometime later the Gnesio-Lutherans protested against some of the duke's decisions and regulations and were dismissed from office. Philippists were appointed in their place. Before long another change was made and all the Gnesio-Lutherans except Flacius were reinstated. Whereupon the controversy was renewed. The colloquy held at Altenburg October, 1568, to March, 1569, also was indecisive, and from it the Philippists withdrew. The positions of the two parties were irreconcilable.

The question to which the Formula gives an answer is concerned with mankind since the fall and prior to regeneration. What spiritual ability does such unregenerate human nature have? Can an unregenerate person prepare himself for God's grace? Can he without regeneration even move to accept that grace? The question is carefully framed so as to exclude the condition of mankind before the fall, or after regeneration, or after the resurrection; it excludes also human abilities in nonspiritual matters even in the unregenerate state. For a certain freedom in nonspiritual matters is acknowledged. Luther said, "In worldly and external affairs, which pertain to the livelihood and maintenance of the body, man is intelligent, reasonable, and very active." [4]

It at once becomes apparent in the discussion that the positions taken rest upon scriptural and confessional grounds. On each point

---

[4] Solid Decl., II, 20; (Jacobs) I, 556. The problem of the origin of this quotation is given in *Bek.*, p. 879, n. 4.

the Scripture is carefully examined and pertinent passages are quoted freely. Thereafter the testimony of the Lutheran writings is presented, all of them being quoted. In addition, there are quotations from other writings of "Dr. Luther of godly and holy memory." The thoroughly Lutheran character of the doctrine discussed in this chapter of the Formula is incontrovertible.

The thetical or affirmative part of the chapter affirms the bondage of the will in spiritual matters. Indeed, the understanding as well as the will is involved in the slavery to sin. The "heart" is mentioned only incidentally in the Epitome, though more prominently in the Solid Declaration, indicating the ancient psychological distinction of the intellectual, the volitional, and the affective phases of the mind.

The complete incapacity of unregenerate human nature to understand with appreciation the gospel, to guide in holy living, or to love God, is vigorously asserted. More than this, man cannot in any way begin or assist in the process of his conversion. The Holy Spirit must even give him the power to accept the grace of God; he is utterly incapable of doing so otherwise.

These theses are affirmed and defended from Scripture and the confessions. First, human nature is turned away from God. The condition is described by several figures of speech, viz., blindness, darkness, deadness. Second, human nature is turned toward evil; it is marked by lust. Third, conversion is solely the work of the Holy Spirit. He regenerates the spiritually dead. Next, the Formula explains how conversion occurs. "God does not force man to become godly . . . yet God the Lord draws the man whom He wishes to convert . . ." [5] Since God desires the salvation of all—none are predestined to perdition—he has arranged that when individuals are hearing the Word a spark of faith is enkindled by the Spirit, and presently the spark bursts into flame. The life newly begotten has spiritual powers not formerly possessed; but they are Spirit-given.

The antithetical or negative declarations are presented under nine heads (according to the numbering in the Epitome): determinism, Pelagianism, Semi-Pelagianism, synergism, perfectionism, enthusiasm, Flacianism, certain inexact phrases of the theologians, and Melanchthon's three-factor view.

---

[5] Solid Decl., II, 60; (Jacobs) I, 564.

In the eighth section is examined the statement that since human nature always resists God, therefore the Holy Spirit is given to those resisting him. Concerning this, though a lifelong trace of "refractoriness" is conceded, yet through the Word faith is aroused, resistance is overcome, and a willingness to receive the Holy Spirit is engendered. Since all this is entirely the work of the Spirit, it is incorrect to say that "God draws the willing" or that "in conversion man does something." In the ninth section it is affirmed that only two efficient causes in conversion are to be named, viz., the Holy Spirit and the Word.

CHAPTER III. OF THE RIGHTEOUSNESS OF FAITH BEFORE GOD

The Osiandrian Controversy was the historical occasion for the doctrinal statements contained in the third chapter of the Formula. The controversy gained its name from its chief figure—Andreas Osiander (1498-1552). He was a prominent pastor in the city of Nürnberg. Because of his ability and his leadership he was a representative of his city at the Marburg Colloquy (1529), the Diet of Augsburg (1530), the conference at Smalcald (1536), and other gatherings.

In 1548 because of his vigorous opposition to the Augsburg Interim, he was compelled to leave Nürnberg. Duke Albert of Prussia secured his services as superintendent and as professor in Königsberg with double salary. But he was soon involved in more trouble.

He is said to have been "as proud, overbearing, and passionate as he was gifted, keen, sagacious, learned, eloquent, and energetic." [6] The fact of his double salary, together with his lack of academic degrees and his haughtiness caused trouble with his colleagues. The friction almost led to physical violence, so that on one occasion some firearms were said to have been carried in an academic procession.

It is small wonder, therefore, that his statements were closely scrutinized and anything unusual in them challenged. His view of justification became the target for attack and a controversy ensued. The duke, distressed by the discussion, asked for an opinion on the controversy from Melanchthon, Flacius, and Brenz. It was the judgment of both Melanchthon and Flacius that Osiander had definitely

---

[6] *Conc. Trig.*, Hist. Intro., p. 153.

departed from Lutheran doctrine, though Brenz took a milder view of the situation.

Osiander's death soon afterward largely put an end to the trouble. A reverberation of the controversy was heard when his son-in-law, John Funck, who had loyally supported him in the controversy, became involved in political intrigue, was convicted of high treason and executed. There seem to have been no others to propagate the Osiandrian doctrine—one which is reminiscent of medieval mysticism and an emotional approach to God.

The point at issue in the controversy involved the doctrine of justification. It was acknowledged that we are justified by faith in Christ. But is it by his divine nature or is it by his human nature that the necessary merit is provided? Osiander had said that Christ, who dwells in the believer, by his divine nature provides an abundant righteousness in comparison with which a man's sin is like a drop in the ocean. Hence the man is justified by infusion rather than imputation, by the sanctifying presence of Christ instead of his saving merits. In contrast, Francesco Stancaro, an Italian professor at Königsberg, had said that Christ is our righteousness according to his human nature.

The Formula proceeds promptly to the thetical statement that (1) Christ is our righteousness according to both natures. (2) No merit of ours can be considered, but (3) we apprehend Christ's merit through faith, which (4) is trust, and not mere knowledge. (5) To "justify" is to "declare righteous" and is distinguished from "regeneration" or "renewal"; (6) it involves also the nonimputation of the believer's sin. (7) Faith produces works of love, but they are part of sanctification, not of justification. (8) Human merit is excluded, hence use is made of the exclusive particles: "of grace alone," "without merit," "without works," "not of works," etc. In the Epitome the order of sections (7) and (8) is reversed.

The thetical discussion clearly leans heavily on the Apology from which it frequently quotes, and with which it is thoroughly in accord. Luther is quoted to the same effect. The topic is seen in reference to the order of salvation: first comes the Word, then is begotten faith which lays hold on the merits of Christ, whereupon the person is justified, and good works follow. But in this discussion justification is carefully distinguished from what precedes and from what follows.

The doctrine thus defined serves two purposes, viz., to console the believer and to honor Christ. Moreover, it is clearly recorded that the righteousness of Christ whereby we are justified is not the pre-incarnation righteousness of his divine nature but is that of his active and passive obedience during his earthly life.

The antithetical statements of the Epitome may be grouped as follows: 1 and 2—inadequate ideas of the incarnation and atonement; 3 and 4—inaccurate definitions of justification; 5, 6, 7, and 8—mistaken conceptions of faith; 9, 10, and 11—confusion of justification with sanctification. Statements 5 to 11 arose out of the ambiguities of the Interims. None of these is in accord with the chief evangelical doctrine, viz., justification by faith.

CHAPTER IV. OF GOOD WORKS

The controversy which made this chapter necessary is called Majoristic because it centered around George Major (1502-74), a professor at Wittenberg. His prominence is shown by the fact that he was a participant in the preparation of the Leipzig Interim.

In this connection he defended the statement that good works are necessary to salvation. Melanchthon had this statement in later editions of his *Loci*: "The acceptance into eternal life or the gift of eternal life is joined to justification, i.e., to remission of sins and reconciliation which is joined to faith. Hence eternal life is not given because of the worth of good works, but freely because of Christ. And yet good works are thus necessary to eternal life because they must necessarily follow reconciliation." [7] Melanchthon's students taught this doctrine, though Luther objected. In later years Melanchthon rejected the phrase as misleading.

The sentence in the Leipzig Interim is: "As now this true knowledge (faith) must shine in us, so it is assuredly true that these virtues, faith, love, hope, and others must be within us, and are necessary unto salvation." [8] When Major was criticized by Flacius and Amsdorf for this statement, his defense was, "Nobody is ever saved without good works."

---

[7] *C. R.,* XXI, 429; quoted in Schaff, *op. cit.,* I, 275.
[8] Quoted in Schaff, *op. cit.,* I, 275.

In 1552 and later he declared that his statement was to correct those who continued in evil ways, and that he did not mean that works earn salvation but merely that they follow faith. He consented in 1558 to cease using the phrase. Yet he was always accused of this error; as was also Justus Menius, superintendent in Gotha, against whom Amsdorf declared that "good works are detrimental to salvation" because they are assumed to be a ground of merit.

The Formula therefore set itself to answer the question, "Are good works necessary to salvation or are they injurious thereto?" Connected with it are two other questions: "Do good works come from necessity or from free will?" "Should men be urged to good works from the law or from the gospel?"

Here again the relation of faith and works is analyzed. A mistake at this point can undermine the whole evangelical position. The differences in phraseology are slight but decisive, just as a slight angle of deviation in aim can result in missing the target. The Formula once more takes up the biblical *sedes doctrinae*, reviews the declarations of the Augsburg Confession and the Apology, and sets a straight course to avoid salvation by works.

The Solid Declaration treats the issue under four heads. In the first section is presented a summary of the declarations upon which the Lutheran theologians were unanimous. They agreed that good works are expected of the Christian; that these good works are those commanded by God and empowered by the Spirit; that these good works, though imperfectly motivated and performed, are accepted by God for Christ's sake; and that such good works grow only out of the matrix of faith.

It is obvious that anyone who is a believer will not intentionally continue in sinful deeds. The use of the word "necessary" to describe this invariable connection between faith and conduct cannot therefore justly be criticized. For no component of coercion is included. In the regenerate, the new obedience is gladly rendered. The Epitome covers this ground in the ten affirmative statements.

The second section insists on the doctrine of justification by faith alone. Good works dare not be considered as *meriting* salvation unless the comfort of the gospel is to be removed, doubts be raised, and pride be cultivated. To say that "good works are necessary to salvation" is to open the door to papists, Anabaptists, and others who preach salvation by works. The teaching of the churches must be accurate to be true. In the Epitome, the first negative thesis specifies the inaccurate statements to be avoided.

The third section faces the assertion that good works *preserve* salvation. It is certain that something must be done to preserve it. They are in error who say that salvation cannot be lost, even by willful crimes; Scripture teaching is against them. They also are in error who make the preservation of salvation a human work.

In the latter group were the papal theologians who in the Confutation defended their position by quoting II Peter 1:10, "Give diligence to make your calling and election sure." In the Vulgate is added the phrase, "by your good works." Hence they argued that good works preserve salvation.

But the Lutheran theologians saw clearly that salvation is not by works, either those done before justification or those to be performed in the future. Salvation is always a gift of God. Yet it may be lost by willful sin. The words in II Peter 1:10 must therefore be interpreted in this sense. Other passages of Scripture are in harmony therewith.

The opinion that good works sustain salvation was approved by the Council of Trent. Therefore Evangelicals should express pure doctrine in discriminating language. In the Epitome it is the third negative thesis which corresponds to this third section of the Solid Declaration.

The fourth section discusses the statement of Amsdorf at the other extreme of the controversy, viz., that good works are injurious to salvation. It is true that good works are a hindrance if the Christian thinks them meritorious and a way of earning salvation. But Amsdorf's statement is too sweeping. It would assume that true faith can exist without corresponding ethical life. It ignores God's express command to cultivate Christian virtues. Hence the Epitome in the second negative thesis declares Amsdorf's unqualified statement to be "offensive and detrimental to Christian discipline."

This entire chapter is another evidence of the balance and soundness of Reformation doctrine. Many minds had considered the evangelical and the ethical to be alternatives, even antitheses, in Christian life. The partial theology of antinomians took one alternative, that of Romanism took the other. One emphasized faith without works, the other, works without faith. Lutheranism found faith and works to be co-ordinate in the doctrine of the Apostles and the church.

But the position of the Lutherans was attacked from both sides. When within their ranks there were some who imperfectly understood it, a clear and incisive reaffirmation was imperative. The Lutheran Church has therein an ethical principle compatible with the material principle of the Reformation.

Tested in history, the Lutheran position has provoked criticisms. It has been said that the doctrine of justification by faith has been phrased too much with an eye to excluding Roman doctrine, hence is somewhat negative. The movement of Pietism was a protest against what seemed to be a weak emphasis on good works.

Efforts to give an adequate account of the connection between justification and regeneration have at times been under suspicion. Standing between Roman moralism and antinomian moral laxity, Lutheranism has seemed immobile. Dr. Kawerau declared, "The Formula of Concord closed the controversy by avoiding both extremes, but failed to offer a final solution of the question demanded by the original motive of the controversy."[9] The problem of a vigorous ethical emphasis connected with *sola gratia* is still engaging the attention of theologians.

CHAPTER V. OF THE LAW AND THE GOSPEL

The Antinomian Controversy was the occasion which called forth Chapters V and VI of the Formula of Concord. It began with John Agricola[10] (1492-1566) who was envious of Melanchthon. He criticized in the Saxon Visitation Articles (1527) Melanchthon's advice that pastors should preach the law to produce repentance. Luther mediated and silenced the controversy. Yet in Agricola's catechism of 1528 there appeared the view that Old Testament law was God's ineffective attempt to produce repentance. Once more Luther quieted

---

[9] G. Kawerau "Philippists," *NSH* IX, 32 f.

[10] His name was *Schneider*, corrupted to *Schnitter*, i.e., *reaper* or *farmer* which in Latin is *agricola*.

the issue. He repeated his declaration that the law still produces contrition and the gospel arouses faith.

In 1536 Agricola became a resident of Wittenberg and was befriended by Luther. Rumors of his persistence in his old views reached Luther, who discussed the matter with him privately and was reassured of his theological soundness. But when Agricola was about to publish a treatment of the gospel pericopes, his antinomian views were evident, and Luther publicly discussed the issues. When Agricola proved obstinate, he was placed under virtual arrest by the elector. He fled to Berlin from which he sent back a recantation. But before the settlement of his case was complete, he accepted the position of court preacher in Brandenburg.

The controversy was revived in 1556 in the discussions concerning the attitude of Justus Menius toward Majoristic doctrines. Pastor Andrew Poach of Erfurt, Pastor Anton Otto of Nordhausen, and others expressed opinions hostile to the law. Poach considered the law as bringing only condemnation. The works of the law, even if perfect, have no reward since they are a duty. Otto was more extreme in his position. According to his teaching the law has no value for directing Christian conduct. The law belongs to the kingdom of Moses and of the pope.

Against such statements Flacius, Moerlin, Wigand, and Westphal protested. They insisted on the three uses of the law: *usus legis politicus; usus legis paedigogicus;* and *usus legis didacticus.* The purposes of the law have been to restrict, convict, and direct. It is also true that Melanchthon had often used the word "gospel" to mean the Word of God; hence he spoke of teaching the gospel which calls to repentance. Some of his disciples, using the term "gospel" in the narrow sense (*vs.* law), made antinomian statements.

The question at issue is a precise one concerning the distinction between law and gospel. The Apology had clearly indicated the distinction in the discussion of Article VI of the Augsburg Confession. Yet in the defense of Article XII the Apology said, "Contrition thus occurs when sins are censured from the Word of God, because the sum of the preaching of the gospel is this, viz., to convict of sin, and to offer for Christ's sake the remission of sins and righteousness, and the Holy Ghost, and eternal life, and that as regenerate men we should do good works" (chap. V, 29). If, strictly speaking, it is the law which convicts and terrifies, while it is the gospel which consoles with the assurance of forgiveness, may the distinction be discarded in preaching?

The Formula of Concord promptly declares its decision. "The distinction between the law and the gospel is a very brilliant light, which is of service in rightly dividing God's Word." It is acknowledged that the Evangelists and Paul sometimes used the terms "gospel" and "repentance" in an inclusive as well as a specific way. The broader usage is justifiable when salvation in its entirety rather than its parts is considered.

In reality, repentance and faith are co-ordinate. For the law by itself begets either pride or despair. The comfort of the gospel needs to be added. As Luther had said, whatever terrifies the conscience is law and whatever consoles is the gospel. The necessity of both was indicated by quotations from the Smalcald Articles and from the Apology.

Yet the distinction between law and gospel must not be obliterated. "The law is properly a divine doctrine wherein the true, immutable will of God is revealed as to how man ought to be, in his nature, thoughts, words, and works, in order to be pleasing and acceptable to God; and it threatens its transgressors with God's wrath and temporal and eternal punishment." Prominent among the sins reproved is unbelief. "But the gospel is properly a doctrine which teaches what man should *believe*, that with God he may obtain forgiveness of sins."

This distinction, which Luther earnestly advocated, is found in the Old Testament Scriptures as well as in the New Testament. Therefore it should be observed in the churches so that both the law and the gospel shall continually be preached. If they are confused, the result is an obscuring of Christ and a transforming the gospel into law as was done in Romanism. To avoid such dangers, the proper distinction between law and gospel must be diligently observed.

The controversy discussed in this chapter was no mere theologians' quibble. The evangelical position so strenuously won must not be lost by carelessly slipping back into unevangelical concepts. Against the legalism of Rome an extreme reaction naturally became antinomian, which nonetheless also endangered the evanglical position. Ranges of opinion often lie not on a straight line but on a U-shaped curve, so that the extremes approach each other. Evangelical doctrine had been revived by discerning minds which differentiated between law and gospel. In that distinction pure doctrine is safeguarded and many practical applications are provided, as Dr. C. F. W. Walther has abundantly shown in his book.[11]

CHAPTER VI. OF THE THIRD USE OF THE LAW

As indicated above, it was the Antinomian Controversy which was the occasion for this chapter also. However, there was another phase of it which needed settlement. Chapter V expressed the doctrine that the law should be preached to convict of sin and arouse contrition. That is the second use of the law. It is applied to the unregenerate and unbelieving. But is the law needed for those who are regenerate and believing? Has the gospel not freed them from the law, so that they do not need to be directed by it? It was this third use of the law for Christian believers which was in dispute.

It must be recognized at the outset that the law delineates the will of God. The Christian delights in God's will (Ps. 1:2), being willing to perform it without coercion. He could dispense with the law if he had attained perfection in his knowledge of God's will and in his spiritual impulses. But such perfection is not attained; concupiscence remains in this life, even in the regenerate. Believers therefore still need the law both to instruct them further in God's will and to reprove their imperfections.

If the law is obeyed by the unregenerate, it is because of fear of punishment or hope of reward and not from a love of the good. Hence it is an hypocrisy. But in the regenerate obedience is given freely out of love for God and therefore is a fruit of the Spirit. Yet in believers there continues a struggle between flesh and spirit.

The Christian needs the law as a check to his pride. He needs it to indicate ideals as yet unreached in his life. With all this he must remember that God accepts his good works, though imperfect, for Christ's sake. Until the resurrection day, when neither law nor gospel will be needed any longer, there will be the necessity of restraining

---

[11] *The Proper Distinction between Law and Gospel*, tr. W. H. T. Dau (St. Louis: Concordia Publishing House, 1929), pp. 77 ff., 94 ff., 112 ff., etc.

fleshly lust in human nature. Therefore it is a mistake to omit the third use of the law.

It will be observed that this chapter is in harmony with the doctrine of original sin as presented in the other confessional statements. It is also accordant with the formal principle of the Reformation which accepts the Scriptures as God's Word for faith and life. It repudiates a perfectionism which both denies continuing concupiscence in the believer and also professes to find spiritual guidance within one's self rather than in Scripture. For perfectionism is fanaticism.

Chapter XVIII

OUTLINE OF THE FORMULA OF CONCORD
(CHAPTERS VII-XII)

CHAPTER VII. OF THE HOLY SUPPER

This chapter was made necessary by the Crypto-Calvinistic Controversy. Subtly or ,secretly Calvinistic interpretations and phrases had been introduced into the statements of Lutheran doctrine. Melanchthon at first had not opposed Luther's doctrine of the Lord's Supper. , He wavered when Oecolampadius showed him that some of the church fathers had held a symbolic view. By 1540 he was using phrases more moderate than those employed by Luther. He ,found the views of Zwingli offensive but accepted those of Calvin.

Calvinistic views, of the Lord's Supper largely triumphed over those of Zwingli in areas outside Lutheranism. Such was the case, for ex-ample, in the *Consensus Tigurinus* (Zurich) of 1549. It taught, that in the Supper the glorified Christ gives spiritual influence to the believer (the predestined). Efforts were made to propagate these views in Germany in subtle ways. It will be remembered that adherents of the Augsburg Confession had political privileges not given to others.

The controversy arose in 1552 in Hamburg when Joachim Westphal, a pastor there, published a pamphlet proving from their publications that the ,Reformed denied the real presence but used phrases similar to Lutheran terminology. Calvin replied with three treatises (1555, 1556, 1557) somewhat abusive in tone, referring to Westphal as "this foolish venerable doctor." Westphal answered in more moderate language. He had the approval of other Lutherans.[1]

---

[1] A list ,of the tracts is given in Schaff, *op. cit.*, I, 279, n. 1.

The Westphal-Calvin debate set off a controversy in Bremen in 1555. A preacher, Albert Hardenberg, was suspected of Calvinism by a colleague. In defending himself he attacked the doctrine of the ubiquity of the body of Christ. Lutheran theologians elsewhere warned against his views. It seems that he sought to avoid controversy and to decline colloquies. Nonetheless his views led to his dismissal from office in 1561.

The controversy made its appearance in the Palatinate in 1558. Tilemann Hesshusen (Heshusius), a professor at Heidelberg, who was also a preacher and a superintendent, attacked the Calvinist doctrine. He clashed verbally and physically with his colleagues. When the elector died, the new elector, a Crypto-Calvinist, required Hesshusen to subscribe the *Variata*, but he refused and was deposed from office in 1559.

More important was the controversy in Saxony. Elector Augustus (brother and successor of Maurice) was a moderate Lutheran. He considered Flacius extreme and made trouble for him whenever he could. The Philippists, utilizing the elector's dislike of the Gnesio-Lutherans, were able to deceive him and advance their own cause.

After Melanchthon's death in 1560, Augustus inquired of his theologians concerning their views. Their statement obscured the issue by attacking Zwingli and Flacius; Calvinism was not attacked—a fact which Augustus was not shrewd enough to detect. Caspar Peucer, Melanchthon's son-in-law, later confessed that these theologians who knew that their views were Calvinist intentionally planned this subterfuge to keep their jobs.

The Philippists continued to gain in strength and boldness. When their Wittenberg Catechism of 1571 was attacked, they were again summoned by the elector. They presented as their statement the *Consensus Dresdensis* constructed of quotations from Luther and Melanchthon, but always interpreting Luther's statements by Melanchthon's indistinct phrases. Augustus was convinced that his professors were the victims of Flacian agitation.

When he became the guardian of the sons of the duke of Saxe-Weimar, he expelled the Flacianists from Jena. The Philippists now felt secure. About this time there appeared a publication entitled,

Exegesis perspicua et ferme integra controversiae de sacra coena, which was attributed to them. It repudiated the *communicatio idiomatum,* affirmed a spiritual presence in the Supper, and declared that Luther must be interpreted by Melanchthon.

Friendly Lutheran princes warned the elector of the deception, sent him the Maulbronn Formula as a guide, and informed him of the true state of affairs. The discovery of an incriminating letter among Peucer's personal papers completed the unmasking. In the light of all this the Philippists were expelled from office.

The question at issue concerned the acceptance of a Lutheran or a Zwinglian-Calvinistic doctrine of the Lord's Supper. Is it true, as Lutherans teach, that in the Supper the body of Christ is present in essence, is distributed with the bread, is orally received by the believers to their consolation and by the unbelieving to their condemnation? Or is it true, as the opponents taught, that the body of Christ is absent in essence, that the elements are merely signs, that Christ is present only spiritually and according to his divine nature, and that the words of institution are to be interpreted symbolically? The gross sacramentarians (Zwinglians) gave a purely symbolic interpretation, denying any presence of Christ in the sacrament. The subtle sacramentarians (Calvinists) affirmed a presence, but a spiritual presence only, involving merely the divine nature of Christ.

The Formula first turns to typical Lutheran statements concerning the real presence. It quotes from the Unaltered Augsburg Confession and the Apology, from both catechisms of Luther, from the Wittenberg Concord, the Smalcald Articles, Luther's Large Confession, and other writings. The unanimity of their testimony is impressive.

The thesis common to them all is that in the Supper there is a sacramental union of earthly elements and the real presence. The Scriptures do not teach transubstantiation but simply the sacramental union. Many eminent church fathers held this view, comparing the sacramental union with the union of Christ's natures. It is the view of the Lutherans set forth in the Augsburg Confession, as a comparison with Luther's writings shows. It is the view implicit in Christ's words of institution.

The words of Christ are to be accepted, not in an allegorical or metaphorical sense, but in their natural meaning. As Abraham accepted God's promise really and not allegorically, we also should accept his clear word. For Christ's words are not figurative; they have a realistic context. The four scriptural accounts show no figurative aspects. The passage in I Corinthians 10:16 speaks of a bodily, not a spiritual, presence. Paul's warning against communion unto condemnation excludes the idea of a mere spiritual presence. It is most fully in accord with Christ's words to teach the doctrine of the real presence.

An attempt had been made to interpret Paul's words by saying that the "body of Christ" of which he spoke is the church. But this is evidently untenable. For the unworthy receive the sacrament, not as a fellowship, but as a judgment.

In the Christian life there are two kinds of eating. There is a spiritual eating described in John 6:54, which is nothing else than faith. But there is also a sacramental eating which is supernatural and incomprehensible. The ancient church recognized and taught both kinds of eating. The sacramentarians, however, deny the existence of the sacramental eating.

There are also two kinds of eaters: the worthy and the unworthy. Unworthiness actually is simply unrepentance and unbelief. Those who have repentance and faith, even though weakly, are the worthy.

The essential point is that the sacrament is God's gift. All of its value rests on the merit of Christ. The real presence is not produced by man's act, but by God's power. The words of Christ are always efficacious—both at the time of the institution of the Supper in the upper room as well as ever since. This is the view which Luther firmly held. The declaration in the administration of the sacrament, "This is the body of Christ," is by divine command. The words of institution ought to be recited in obedience to Christ's command and to confirm faith in what God does.

Man's part in the sacrament is to use it, for it is not a sacrament without use. The sacramental action includes consecration, distribution, and reception of the elements. The sacramentarians speak only of the believer's act of faith. Yet it is not man's action, but God's Word which makes the sacrament efficacious. Hence it is a mistake to stress faith too much and God's gift too little.

Luther's view rested upon four propositions: the personal union of two natures in Christ; the ubiquity of God's right hand; the dependability of God's Word; there is more than one mode of being in any place. He developed the fourth point to show that there are three kinds of presence: the comprehensible or local; the incomprehensible or spiritual, as of sight, sound, heat, or light; and the heavenly or omnipresence. The sacramentarians spoke of a "spiritual" presence, meaning a spiritual communion by faith. But Luther used the word "spiritual" to mean a real supernatural presence in the sacrament based upon the truth and omnipotence of God.

The Formula concludes with an enumeration of errors. First are named three Roman errors: transubstantiation, the sacrifice of the mass, and communion in one kind only. Next are listed sixteen errors, most of which are sacramentarian: (1) a purely symbolic interpretation of the words of institution; (2) a merely spiritual presence in the Supper; (3) bread and wine are simply signs of fellowship; (4) the elements are only signs of the absent body of Christ; (5) the elements are merely signs to confirm our faith; (6) the believer receives by faith only the power of Christ; (7) the only mode of receiving Christ is spiritually by faith; (8) Christ's body is locally present in heaven alone; (9) a real presence in the Supper is impossible; (10) faith produces Christ's presence, and the words of institution may be omitted; (11) believers receive Christ, not in the Supper, but in heaven; (12) the unworthy do not receive Christ in the Supper; (13) worthiness consists, not in faith, but in man's own preparation; (14) lack of such preparation brings condemnation; (15) the consecrated elements should be adored; (16) Capernaitic eating.

The Epitome reduces the discussion to ten affirmative statements. With one exception, each statement is declared to be what "we believe, teach, and confess." The long quotations from other Lutheran confessions are, of course, omitted. The Epitome presents twenty-one negative statements which are almost, but not quite, identical with the errors listed in the Solid Declaration.

In the history of Lutherans in America this chapter of the Formula of Concord received special attention. It was charged by some with being a bit of unnecessary scholastic speculation in an area where only simple faith can function. It was condemned as being the peculiar theory of one man, Martin Luther, rather than the inclusive faith of the whole Lutheran Church. Oral manducation was regarded as a repulsive vestige of incomplete emancipation from Romanism. In rejecting this chapter these men were prepared to reject the entire Formula of Concord.[2]

But four things need to be noted. First of all, it is a mistake to think of this doctrine in the Formula as being the product of a Lutheran scholasticism developing after Luther's death. Instead, it is the doctrine taught by Luther in his Large Confession of 1528 and his catechisms of 1529. Moreover, it is less scholastic than it is scriptural.

In the second place, it should be rememberd that the doctrine of the real presence was not so much the prejudice of one man as it was the conviction of the church he led. There was objection to this doctrine from non-Lutherans. But the only really serious objection to it from within the Lutheran group came from the Philippists who were influenced by Calvinism.

It is notable, thirdly, that the doctrine of the real presence in the Formula represents the confessional consensus of the Lutheran Church. Its harmony with the other Lutheran confessions is too prominent to be overlooked. Those who deny its relation to the Augsburg Confession do so on the basis of the *Variata*, never the *Invariata*. It is not hyper-Lutheran in the sense of out-Luthering Luther. It is rather the common conviction and teaching of the Lutheran Church.

Finally, the historic occasion which called forth the declaration must not be forgotten. It was controversy over the doctrine of the Lord's Supper which made necessary careful thinking and precise statements. Lutherans believed that the words of our Lord indicate in his Supper a special union of Christ with the elements so that Christ is received with the bread in the mouth. In the midst of controversy, therefore, oral manducation was the statement distinguishing Lutherans from those who wanted to enjoy the social benefits of the Augsburg Confession while modifying its doctrine. The latter group

---

[2] Richard, *op. cit.*, chap. XXVIII. S. Sprecher, *The Groundwork of a System of Evangelical Lutheran Theology* (Philadelphia: Lutheran Publication Society, 1879), p. 35.

held a view different from the Lutherans on the doctrine of the person of Christ, as discussed in the next chapter of the Formula.

CHAPTER VIII. OF THE PERSON OF CHRIST

It may seem that in the controversy on the Lord's Supper the Lutherans had an excessive interest in the body of Christ. Their central interest, however, was in the whole Christ, both divine and human. Their opponents in denying a bodily presence in the sacrament were teaching a doctrine of a half-Christ. Christological considerations were primary; with Luther they antedated his defense of his doctrine of the Lord's Supper.

The historical occasion for Chapter VIII of the Formula of Concord was the Crypto-Calvinistic controversy described at the beginning of the treatment of Chapter VII. Luther had dealt with the topic in his discussion of the Zwinglian positions. But the earlier Lutheran confessions gave only a brief statement on Christology because no longer statement seemed necessary. The activity of the Philippist party among the Lutherans, however, made a declaration on this doctrine urgent. Thus in 1559 the Württemberg Confession, written by Brenz and adopted by a synod at Stuttgart, contained a declaration of the doctrine of the ubiquity of Christ's body.[3]

The question at issue had two phases. Is the union of the two natures of Christ a union in name only? Do the qualities of each nature communicate anything to the other? The Zwinglians had said that no truly human body of Christ could be in heaven and in the Lord's Supper at the same time. The Crypto-Calvinists declared that nothing should be ascribed to Christ's human nature "which is above or contrary to its natural, essential property."

The Formula first states six theses which "we believe, teach, and confess." (1) The eternal Son of God became incarnate. (2) In the incarnation there was a union of human and divine natures without confusion or separation. (3) Each nature retains its identity. (4) Each nature has its appropriate qualities (which are named). (5) The one person of Christ now exists in two natures inseparably. (6) In this personal union the human nature of Christ is exalted.

---

[3] Cf. Schaff, *op. cit.,* I, 293.

The ancient church had dealt with this topic. The Nestorian view had been that the two natures are merely in contact, like boards glued together.[4] The orthodox view expressed in the Creed of Chalcedon affirmed a mutual interpenetration of the attributes of the two natures. Zwingli in his teaching was repeating the old mistake of separating the two natures, even though the church has taught a union of them.

Certain corollaries follow logically from the doctrine of the personal union; hence Christ in both natures is at God's right hand; hence Mary's Son was the Son of God; hence he worked miracles; hence he was raised from the dead and exalted; hence he ascended according to both natures and is present in the Holy Supper in both natures.

The Formula next presents the doctrine of the *communicatio idiomatum,* or interplay of qualities, in the form developed by Chemnitz. The *communicatio,* which in the last analysis is a sublime mystery, has three evident phases. In the first phase or genus, the attributes of each nature are ascribed to the Person. Zwingli had made use of this when naming the Person by erroneously meaning only the divine nature; the human nature was included only as a figure of speech, an *alloeosis.* Zwingli said that anything, such as suffering and death, which affected the ,human nature, did not affect the divine. Luther objected to the view that not Christ, but his human nature, died for us. Zwingli's view would seem to make two Christs. Luther, stressing the union of the two natures, insisted that it was correct to say of the crucifixion, "God died."

The second phase or genus is that in which Christ's work is performed through both natures which co-operate therein. In the third genus, the attributes of the divine nature are ascribed to the human. Thus the human nature shares in his glory. In Scripture many divine attributes and works, such as power and judgment, are assigned to the man, Jesus Christ.

The Formula presents in evidence three arguments. First, the ancient orthodox church taught that Christ in the incarnation received human attributes. Second, the Scriptures teach that Christ is to

---

[4] Until recently Nestorianism was known imperfectly from writings of opponents. For works discovered and assembled cf. J. F. Bethune-Baker, *Nestorius and his Teaching* (Cambridge, 1908).

exercise judgment for the very reason that he is incarnate. Third, the Scriptures clearly show Christ's redemption as based on his incarnation.

It has been orthodox doctrine to believe that Christ's human nature was affected by his divine nature. Orthodox theology did not confuse the essential attributes of the two natures, nor yet denied their *communicatio*. If the properties of the two natures were not confused, neither were they equalized. It must be recognized, therefore, that the *communicatio* is real and not merely verbal—an actual interplay of qualities without changing the essence of the two natures.

The personal union is the central fact of the incarnation. In the person of Christ the fullness of the divine dwelt in human body (Col. 2:9). The divine majesty was concealed during the humiliation but revealed in the exaltation. The divine shines through the human as fire in glowing iron, without loss of essential identity. The indwelling of God in all believers is not comparable to the incarnation. Only Christ could say, "All power is given unto me" (Matt. 28:18). The divine nature is not weakened nor is the human made equal to the divine. The incarnation did not remove the Son's omnipotence, omniscience, or majesty.

On the basis of this personal union and *communicatio* the omnipresence of his body must be affirmed. For there is ascribed to his humanity (body and blood) a quickening power in all believers everywhere. Hence he is with us, not only by his divine nature, but also by his human nature. He is not half present but fully so.

The importance of this for the real presence is obvious. On this the Formula quotes Luther's *Large Confession Concerning the Holy Supper*,[5] and his little book, *The Last Words of David*.[6] It is an error to deny majesty to Christ's humanity. In our daily lives we are consoled by the presence of the incarnate Christ.

The Formula concludes with a list of seven errors: that Christ's human nature is fused into the divine; that his human nature has a new essence; that it has become equal with the divine; that his ubiquity is by a local mode; that only his human nature suffered; that Christ is present with believers only in his divine nature; that there is

---

[5] W.A., XXVI, 261 f.
[6] W.A., LIV, 49 f.

no *communicatio*. These errors are contrary to God's Word. Yet in the last analysis we face a mystery which is beyond reason and speculation.

The Epitome presents the Formula's propositions in twelve affirmative theses. Its twenty negative theses are an expansion of the errors listed in the Solid Declaration. The Epitome enumerates the Christological errors of ancient heresies as well as those espoused by the sacramentarians.

In a theology so strongly Christocentric as is the Lutheran, it is to be expected that the doctrine of the incarnation would have such a full and careful treatment as is here given in the Formula. The Lutheran theologians were convinced that here they were on solid scriptural and ecumenical ground—a ground significant for their personal assurance of salvation.

CHAPTER IX. OF THE DESCENT OF CHRIST TO HELL

This chapter deals with a controversy which arose in 1544. John Aepinus, the superintendent of Hamburg, in his lectures that year to the clergy of his district said that the *descensus* is part of the atonement and humiliation of Christ. He declared that Christ's body remained in the grave, while his soul entered Hades to share the common human fate.

Opponents quoted against him the words on the cross, "It is finished!" to indicate the end of his humiliation. Some of the opponents who were rude and insolent were deposed from office in 1551. Melanchthon was asked for an opinion on the controversy but avoided a clear-cut answer. When Aepinus died in 1553 the controversy in large measure ended, though echoes of it were heard elsewhere.

The problem involved is related to the Christology of the previous chapter. The Epitome shows the question at issue to have been speculation concerning the *descensus*: Was it before or after Christ's death? Was the descent in soul only, or by divine nature alone, or both in body and soul? Was it part of his passion or of his triumph?

The chapter in the Solid Declaration, which is actually shorter than that in the Epitome, makes four brief points. First, the *descensus* involved Christ according to both natures (in keeping with the previous chapter). Second, it was a triumphant act after his burial. Third, it should be accepted by faith, without speculation concerning the details. And, fourth, it is a ground of consolation for the Christian. The Epitome gives only the second and third of these points.

The doctrine is based on I Peter 3:18, 19. It is in contrast to the Romish notion that in the *descensus* Christ released the Old Testament saints from the *limbus patrum*. It was in contrast also to the Calvinist view which on the basis of Psalm 16:10 and Acts 2:24, 27, interpreted the *descensus* as part of Christ's humiliation.

CHAPTER X. OF CHURCH RITES WHICH ARE CALLED ADIAPHORA, OR MATTERS OF INDIFFERENCE

This chapter was made necessary by the controversy provoked by the Augsburg and Leipzig Interims of 1548. The text of the Augsburg Interim had been prepared by several Romanists together with John Agricola of Brandenburg. It followed roughly the outline of the Augsburg Confession. The *Catholic Encyclopedia* says, "The points of doctrine were all explained in the sense of the Catholic dogma, but couched in the mildest and vaguest terms; and wherever it was feasible, the form and the concept approached the Protestant view of those subjects. In matters of ecclesiastical discipline two important concessions were made to the Protestants, viz., the marriage of the clergy and the communion under both kinds." [7] The Leipzig Interim, prepared by Melanchthon and others for Electoral Saxony, preserved Lutheran doctrine but required conformity to Roman rites in confirmation, ordination, extreme unction, most of the canon of the mass, and so on.

In some areas the Interim was enforced; elsewhere it was resisted. Melanchthon detested it. But his policy was, "Save what you can." He felt that resistance would mean the loss of everything. He advised Maurice to make such concessions to the emperor as seemed necessary.

The young professor, Flacius, who then was but twenty-eight years old, pleaded with Melanchthon to resist the Interim. Failing in this he published anonymously Melanchthon's "opinions" contained in the advice to Maurice. He also published pamphlets anonymously against the Interim. When it became known that he was the author

---

[7] F. J. Schaefer, "Interims," *op. cit.*, VIII, 77 f.

of these publications, he had to resign and go to Magdeburg. There he continued his literary war.

A considerable literature resulted. The controversy was conducted with some bitterness, as evidenced by one tract entitled, "Against the Vile Devil Who Now Again Transforms Himself into an Angel of Light." The opponents of the Interim considered the pope the Antichrist with whom no compromise was possible. The defenders of the Interim pointed out that they were saving the church from destruction, protecting those too weak to stand persecution, and choosing the lesser of two evils. They said that Flacius exaggerated the issue, sounding a fire alarm when he saw just a little smoke in the Wittenberg chimney. Later, in a letter to Flacius, Melanchthon confessed his mistake in not resisting the Interim. But he was unwilling to say so publicly. Melanchthon as a collaborationist was the target of much attack by the uncompromising Gnesio-Lutherans.

The question at issue in this Interimistic (or Adiaphoristic) Controversy was this: Should Christians yield under pressure of persecution and restore the use of rites and ceremonies which in themselves are adiaphora, i.e., are neither divinely commanded nor forbidden?

The Formula of Concord first marks out the boundaries of genuine adiaphora. True adiaphora are never contrary to God's Word, never unionizing, never Romanizing, never useless, foolish spectacles, never essentially constitute the worship of God.

Concerning their status, it is said that adiaphora may be changed by the church in the interest of good order, discipline, and edification. But there is always the necessity of a clear doctrinal confession by word and deed. Adiaphora are matters of freedom. Compulsory adiaphora involve a contradiction of terms. When they cease to be free they must be resisted. An example is cited from the period of the Apostles. Circumcision was an adiaphoron and Paul refused to yield to those who wanted to make it compulsory. He took the same position in matters of food, times, and days.

The results of coercion are seen in the fact that compulsory rites obscure the gospel and restrict Christian liberty. When there is external conformity under pressure, without doctrinal agreement, then error is strengthened and believers are confused.

The Lutheran position, as made clear in the Augsburg Confession, is one of unity of doctrine with liberty in ceremonies. The Smalcald Articles also declared that the church in its true nature consists of the believers with their ministers who are faithful to the gospel. The true church needs neither pope nor human traditions nor papal cruelties. With such principles, as Dr. Luther said, the church will know how to deal with adiaphora.

Five errors are listed: that human ordinances are services of God; that human ordinances are compulsory; that adiaphora may be admitted under persecution; that under persecution consent may be given to unevangelical doctrines or practices; and that adiaphora should be prohibited at all times. In conclusion, it is reaffirmed that there may be diversity of practice so long as there is unity in doctrine. The Epitome summarizes this whole discussion in five affirmative and four negative theses.

By this chapter Lutherans repudiated the leadership of the vacillating Melanchthon. Rather than make discretion the better part of valor, they accepted the sturdy courage of Luther. A vestment or a genuflection may seem a small thing for which to suffer martyrdom. But they knew that adiaphora should not be imposed as Rome demanded, nor should they be prohibited as Puritans insisted later, but they should be free. And for freedom martyrdom might be necessary.

CHAPTER XI.
OF GOD'S ETERNAL FOREKNOWLEDGE AND ELECTION

Though there had been no great controversy, yet there had been some debate and discussion. Calvin's views had been published in the *Consensus Genevensis* of 1552. They therefore were widely known and discussed. Lutheran theologians also had published treatments of predestination which might easily have broken into active controversies, for the two parties approached the problem from different premises. Calvin developed his doctrine as an aspect of the sovereignty of God. Lutherans, however, arrived at their declarations from the universality of sin and the monergism of God's grace.

Such controversial literature as appeared was not the product of difference of opinion among Lutherans. Instead, it made evident the disagreements between Calvinists and Lutherans. Thus Hesshusen in 1560 attacked the Calvinist position and was answered by Theodore Beza.

More important was the conflict between John Marbach and Jerome Zanchi at Strassburg, 1561-63. In that city where a mild, unionistic theological atmosphere prevailed, Marbach from his pulpit led an aggressive, decidedly Lutheran movement. He tried to republish there the work of Hesshusen. In this he was opposed by Zanchi, a converted Italian and professor of theology at Strassburg.

The dispute involved the doctrine of the Lord's Supper as well as that of predestination. In each case Zanchi took a position which had the support of Calvinist theologians. But Marbach was able to win the support of the people so that his movement was dominant in the city.

The first paragraph of the Formula of Concord is introductory to the discussion. It indicates the topic to be discussed, viz., the eternal election of the children of God. The reasons for the chapter are not the settlement of a prevalent controversy but the avoidance of future dissension and the exposition of what is an important scriptural doctrine.

First, a distinction must be made. God's foreknowledge of all things good and bad is not the same as his election to salvation. His foreknowledge of evil is not a desire for evil, but is used to limit and overrule evil. It is never the cause of evil. But election has to do only with good, and is the cause of salvation.

A basic thesis must constantly be kept in mind. It is not that election is part of God's inscrutable will. Such a doctrine leads either to despair or false security in the godly, or at least to painful doubts. Scripture never leads to despair or pride, but always to repentance, godliness, faith, and assurance. Therefore the thesis is this: election is to be understood always in the light of Christ.

Election analyzed on this basis includes eight items: redemption through the merits of Christ; the offering of his merits to the individual through the Word and sacraments; the activity of the Holy Spirit through the means of grace; the justification of all who repent and believe; the sanctification of the justified; their preservation; the increase of their spiritual gifts; eternal life for them. Such election is both general and particular. All of this, and not parts only, is included in election.

Who then are the elect? The answer is not to be found in reason, or the law, or in external appearances, much less in investigating divine secrets. The elect are called through the Word and preaching. God's summons is for everyone and his call is earnest. The elect are those who heed the call. To them the Spirit gives the assurance of salvation and will preserve them therein if they do not turn from him.

Revelation is the basis for this doctrine. Election is to be known, not from God's secret will, but from his revealed Word, e.g., the Epistle to the Romans. In it is found no contradiction between God's will in the general call and his will in election. Otherwise consolation is lost to the believer. But the promise of the gospel is individualized in the sacraments and in the application of the Word in private absolution. We can trust that promise as an evidence of election to eternal life.

From man's side the evidence of election is seen in his faith. The elect are not those who resist the Holy Spirit in the means of grace but those who through faith yield to him. The cause for the rejection of the call is to be found in man's perverse will. And when men fall from grace, their willfulness, and not God's will, is the cause.

The mystery of predestination, as far as it is revealed, bears the pattern of *sola gratia*. Since our salvation rests solely on the purpose and power of God, it is both consoling and completely dependable. It is a doctrine which consoles individuals in the midst of trouble. It also assures the purity and the perpetuity of the church. In addition, it warns us against the deadly peril of rejecting the call of God.

The Formula warns against going beyond revelation. The Christian is urged to be satisfied with what is revealed and not to speculate on the mystery which is not revealed. God foreknows the elect, but to us it is a mystery. God alone knows the hour when each one will be converted.

Attention must be given to what is revealed. In Scripture there is a description of those whose hearts are hardened; therein we may see God's judgment and our duty. Scripture portrays the consequences of human actions; repelling God's grace brings judgment, while accepting it arouses praise. Scripture teaches that God's grace is entirely unmerited. Beyond his grace, the ways of God are unsearchable.

It is a Christocentric doctrine which is here presented. Election must be considered with Christ, not without or beyond him. The way of election is repentance and faith; and God wishes all men to know it. But more knowledge than that is not needed. Therefore we should not harass our minds with questions about God's secret counsel. It is enough that we trust Christ.

Through it all the application of redemption is the work of the Holy Spirit. It is he who gives the power to repent and believe, if he is not resisted. The believer, in whom he dwells, has the assurance of his election by his exercise and increase of Christian virtues. Those who fall from grace may by him be restored.

This is the divine program. God draws men through the means of grace. If some repel those means, it is not because God did not desire their salvation. The cause of condemnation is not God, but the will of the devil and man. God's desire is simply that all should repent and believe. The unrepentant and unbelieving guiltily incur his punishment. A hardened heart, such as Pharaoh had, is part of God's punishment of sin.

But there is good news. The merits of Christ, not our works, are the ground of our election. Hence there is no basis for despair or for a dissolute life; such results come from false doctrine. On the contrary, the true doctrine of the Scriptures offers consolation. Therefore we do well to accept the Scriptures and avoid speculation concerning the divine mysteries.

The Formula concludes with the declaration that this discussion is intended to provide common doctrinal agreement. No truth is yielded for the sake of compromise. But true unity in doctrine gives glory to God, supports the truth, and converts sinners. The Epitome summarizes this discussion in fourteen affirmative and four negative theses, concluding with a prayer for Christian unity.

This chapter goes beyond the limit set in the title of the Solid Declaration, namely, that of discussing "certain articles of the Augsburg Confession concerning which there has been controversy." No article of the Augsburg Confession could be quoted by the authors of this chapter. Chemnitz and Andreae here venture out upon theological discussions of their own. Luther is mentioned only once when three sentences are quoted from his preface to the Epistle to the Romans.[8] It is evident, therefore, that this chapter of the Formula has less direct connection with the other symbolical writings than the previous chapters have had. It rather is a combination of the exegetical and homiletical conclusions of its two authors.

It is true that they might have quoted much from Luther—much more from him than from Melanchthon. Luther's *de servo arbitrio* and his treatments of Exodus, the Psalms, and Romans would have provided ample quotations. In quite Augustinian fashion Luther had advocated a divine determinism. But he taught that predestination must be understood in terms of revelation and the work of Christ, and discouraged speculation concerning the unrevealed will of God.

The logic of the doctrine involves difficulties. The doctrine of *sola gratia* means that God alone, without any human help whatsoever, produces conversion. But since not all are saved, God's grace must function irresistibly on those whom he has selected. This logic avoids synergism but ends in Calvinistic predestinarianism.

On the other hand we may begin with the universal grace of God who wishes all rather than a few to be saved. Since, however, all are not saved, there must be some difference between human individuals to account for the fact. This avoids the dangers of predestinarianism but opens the way for synergism.

Thus Philip Schaff said that "there is an obvious and irreconcilable antagonism between Art. II and Art. XI."[9] It was his view that Lutherans must choose between *sola gratia* and *gratia universalis.* "The Lutheran system, then, to be consistent, must rectify itself, and develop either from Art. II in the direction of Augustinianism and Calvinism, or from Art. XI in the direction of synergism and Arminianism."[10]

Nothing is to be gained by evading this issue. It will not do to write of "alleged inconsistencies," or to put "logical contradictions" in quotation marks to suggest that the accusation is false. Logic is the

---

[8] Sec. 33; (Jacobs) I, 655. *Erlangen Ausgabe,* LXIII, 135. Cited in Bek., 1073, n. 3.

[9] *Op. cit.,* I, 314.

[10] *Ibid.,* I, 315.

human method of knowledge. What does not fit into its pattern is clearly illogical or paradoxical.

The point of the criticism is removed when it is frankly acknowledged that the Lutheran doctrine includes logical incompatibles. The Formula of Concord paradoxically includes both *sola gratia* and *gratia universalis* because both of them are taught in Scripture. The Formula specifically refuses to make reason superior to revelation in such a way that grace alone is accepted and universal grace is rejected. It knows of no way of solving the logical problem and therefore calls it a mystery, just as Luther did. Even Schaff had to admit the paradoxical nature of several theological doctrines, for he ended his discussion with this sentence: "The human mind has not been able as yet satisfactorily to set forth the harmony of God's sovereignty and man's responsibility." [11]

CHAPTER XII. OF OTHER FACTIONS AND SECTS, WHICH NEVER EMBRACED THE AUGSBURG CONFESSION

Since the Formula addressed itself chiefly to the problems within Lutheranism, it had ignored the sects on the fringe of the Reformation. The Formula was itself an effective answer to the sectarian accusation of Lutheran disunity. It closes with this chapter consisting of Andreae's list of sectarian errors which Lutherans wish to disavow.

First are seventeen erroneous doctrines of the Anabaptists, though it is acknowledged that the Anabaptists differed much among themselves. The Epitome took the first nine and the last two articles of the Solid Declaration and grouped them as "articles that cannot be tolerated in the church." These are statements that Christ's flesh and blood did no come from the Virgin Mary; that he was only a highly endowed man; that justification is based on man's piety; that unbaptized children are not sinners; that only adults should be baptized; that children of Christian parents are holy; that there are no sinners in the true church; that no church building in which Roman mass had been said should be used for worship; and that adherents of the Augsburg Confession should be shunned.

Those numbered eight to twelve are grouped by the Epitome as "articles that cannot be tolerated in the government." These articles

---

[11] *Ibid.*, I, 316.

deny that civil office is pleasing to God, that Christians may hold office, or use the services of public officers, or take a judicial oath, or inflict capital punishment.

The remaining three articles "cannot be tolerated in domestic life." They deny to the Christian the right to hold property, or to be a land-lord, merchant, or cutler (maker of arms). They allow Christians to divorce spouses of another faith in order to marry those of their own faith.

Next are seven erroneous doctrines of the Schwenkfeldians. The Epitome by dividing the first article makes the list consist of eight arti-cles. Concerning Christ the Schwenkfeldians taught that his human nature was not distinct after the resurrection but was absorbed into the divine nature. They rejected the Word, baptism and the Lord's Supper as means of grace. They taught the possibility of Christian perfection, the necessity of church discipline to attain congregational perfection, and the requirement of perfection in the ministry if preaching and the sacraments are to be valid.

A brief article disposes of the New Arians. They rejected the Nicene doctrine and taught a subordinationist view.

Finally, the errors of the anti-trinitarians are listed as two, though the Epitome combines them into one. The views which the Formula condemns are those which reject the Nicene and Athanasian creeds and which teach a tritheism in which the three divine persons are separate and equal, or in which one is supreme over the other two.

All errors listed in this chapter are rejected as contrary to God's Word, the ecumenical creeds, and the Lutheran symbolical writings. But the whole declaration of the Formula "is our faith, doctrine, and confession, in which we also will appear, by God's grace, with unterri-fied hearts before the judgment-seat of Christ, and for it will give an account." In this sense the document was subscribed as a pledge of future faith and doctrine.

ESTIMATE

The Formula of Concord creates in the reader an impression of its extensive, if somewhat repetitious, scholarship. Krauth called it "the amplest and clearest confession in which the Christian Church has ever embodied her faith." [12] Schaff, who wrote both with eminent scholarship and with the critical position to be expected of a Calvinist, gave the following as his opinion: "It sums up the results of the theological controversies of a whole generation with great learning, ability, discrimination, acumen, and, we may add, with comparative moderation." [13] Guericke, who spoke of the Formula as the "keystone" and the "chief creed" of the Lutheran Church, called it "the most scientific, the most developed, and the most comprehensive of all the symbols." [14]

Those who prefer indefiniteness and lack of distinctness in theological doctrines will always be dissatisfied with the Formula of Concord. It makes its appeal instead to those who have a taste for clear thinking, careful exegesis, and as much logical consistency as Scripture affords. It must not be forgotten, however, that it was made necessary by controversies, and controversy is not a normal condition of Christian life. Its method if used amid normal Christian conditions can run the danger of becoming pedantic and scholastic, rather than dynamic and confessional. It is both a true and a living faith which we desire.

For our day, therefore, the value of the Formula of Concord for living faith should continue to be recognized. As has been noted in Chapter I, there is an earnestness and deep conviction in the Formula of Concord. It does not seek controversy; it desires peace. It is not marked by indifferentism; it has ardent doctrinal convictions. Amid the raucous and skeptical clamor of men's voices, it dares to have a faith. Christ is central. What man is, what the function of the law is, what righteousness is—answers to all these questions are given in terms of the Evangel. The Formula of Concord therefore is a witness out of Reformation days whose voice Lutherans will continue to re-echo.

---

[12] C. P. Krauth, *The Conservative Reformation and Its Theology* (Philadelphia: J. B. Lippincott & Co., 1875), p. 302.

[13] *Op. cit.*, I, 338.

[14] H. E. F. Guericke, *Allgemeine christliche Symbolik* (Leipzig: Adolph Winter, 1861), pp. 123 f.

BIBLIOGRAPHY

SOURCES

The Ante-Nicene Fathers, edited by Alexander Roberts and James Donaldson. Buffalo: The Christian Literature Publishing Co., 1885.

A Select Library of the Nicene and Post-Nicene Fathers, edited by Philip Schaff. Buffalo: The Christian Literature Co., 1886.

Corpus Reformatorum, edited by C. G. Bretschneider and H. E. Bindseil. Halle: C. A. Schwetschke & Son, 1835-59.

D. Martin Luthers Sämmtliche Werke. Erlangen: Carl Heyder, 1826-98.

D. Martin Luthers Werke. Weimar: Herman Böhlau, 1883-.

Works of Martin Luther. Philadelphia: United Lutheran Publication House, 1915-32.

Mirbt, Carl. *Quellen zur Geschichte des Papsttums und des römischen Katholizismus.* 4th ed.; Tübingen: J. C. B. Mohr, 1924.

Thatcher, O. J. and McNeal, E. H. *A Source Book for Medieval History.* New York: Charles Scribner's Sons, 1905.

TEXTS AND TREATISES

Aulén, Gustaf. *Christus Victor.* London: S.P.C.K., 1931.

Badcock, F. J. *The History of the Creeds.* London: S.P.C.K., 1938.

Cohrs, Ferdinand. *Die Evangelischen Katechismusversuche vor Luthers Enchiridion.* Berlin: A. Hofman & Co., 1900.

Concordia Triglotta. St. Louis: Concordia Publishing House, 1921.

Die Bekenntnisschriften der evangelisch-lutherischen Kirche. Göttingen: Vandenhoeck & Ruprecht, 1930.

Fendt, Leonhard. *Der Wille der Reformation im Augsburgischen Bekenntnis.* Leipzig: H. G. Wallmann, 1929.

Guericke, H. E. F. *Allgemeine christliche Symbolik.* Leipzig: Adolf Winter, 1861.

Hill, Charles L. *The Loci Communes of Philipp Melanchthon.* Boston: Meador Publishing Co., 1944.

Jacobs, H. E. *The Book of Concord.* Philadelphia: United Lutheran Publication House, 1882-83.

Johnson, F. E. *The Church and Society.* New York: Abingdon Press, 1935.

Kolde, Theo. *Analecta Lutherana, Briefe und Aktenstücke.* Gotha, 1883.

————————. *Historische Einleitung in die Symbolischen Bücher der evangelisch-lutherischen Kirche.* Gütersloh: C. Bertelsmann, 1907.

Köllner, Eduard. *Symbolik der lutherischen Kirche.* Hamburg: Friedrich Perthes, 1837.

Krauth, C. P. *The Conservative Reformation and Its Theology.* Philadelphia: J. B. Lippincott & Co., 1875.

McGiffert, A. C. *The Apostles' Creed.* New York: Charles Scribner's Sons, 1902.

Meyer, Johannes. *Historischer Kommentar zu Luthers Kleinem Katechismus.* Gütersloh: C. Bertelsmann, 1929.

Neve, J. L. *Introduction to the Symbolical Books of the Lutheran Church.* 2nd ed.; Columbus: Lutheran Book Concern, 1926.

Nygren, Anders. *Agape and Eros.* London: S.P.C.K., 1932-39.

Plitt, Gustav. *Einleitung in die Augustana.* Erlangen: Andreas Deichert, 1867-68.

Rauschenbusch, Walter. *A Theology for the Social Gospel.* New York: Macmillan, 1917.

Reu, M. *Luther's German Bible.* Columbus: The Lutheran Book Concern, 1934.

————————. *Dr. Martin Luther's Small Catechism.* Chicago: Wartburg Publishing House, 1929.

Richard, J. W. *The Confessional History of the Lutheran Church.* Philadelphia: Lutheran Publication Society, 1909.

Schaff, Philip. *The Creeds of Christendom.* New York: Harper & Brothers, 1899.

Schmauk, T. E., and Benze, C. T. *The Confessional Principle and the Confessions of the Lutheran Church.* Philadelphia: General Council Publication Board, 1911.

Second Lutheran World Convention. Philadelphia: United Lutheran Publication House, 1930.

Seeberg, R. *Text-book of the History of Doctrines.* Tr. by C. E. Hay. Philadelphia: Lutheran Publication Society, 1905.

Sehling, Emil. *Die evangelischen Kirchenordnungen des XVI Jahrhunderts.* Leipzig, 1902.

Selected Sermons and Addresses by the late Samuel Alfred Ort, D.D., LL.D Seattle: H. C. Stafford, 1914.

Stier, Johannes. *Luthers Glaube und Theologie in den Schmalkaldischen Artikeln*. Gütersloh: C. Bertelsmann, 1937.

Thieme, Karl. *Die Augsburgische Konfession und Luthers Katechismen*. Giessen: Töpelmann. 1938.

Tschackert, P. *Die Entstehung der lutherischen und der reformierten Kirchenlehre*. Göttingen: Vandenhoeck und Ruprecht, 1910.

Walker, W. *A History of the Christian Church*. New York: Charles Scribner's Sons, 1937.

Williams, Chas. D. *A Valid Christianity for Today*. New York: Macmillan, 1909.

INDEX

NAMES AND SUBJECTS

Absolution, Private, 91
Adiaphoristic Controversy, 243, 282f.
Admonitio Christiana, 251
Aepinus, John, 281
Aerius of Sebaste, 181
Agricola, John, 189, 267f.
Albert (Duke of Prussia), 262
Albrecht of Mansfeld, 136
Alexander of Hales, 41, 119
Alexander VI (Pope), 207
Altenburg Colloquy (1568), 247, 260
Alva, Duke of, 51
Ambrose, 20, 21, 23, 42, 149, 157, 180
   Explanatio symboli of, 23, 24, 27
Ambrose, pseudo-, 112
Ambrosiaster (pseudo-Ambrose), 77
Amsdorf, Nicholas von, 189, 264, 266
Anabaptists, 73, 75, 84, 85, 87, 94, 98, 102, 106, 160, 289f.
Andreae, Jacob, 247f., 250, 288, 289
Anglican Church, The, 209
Anselm, 238
Antinomian Controversy, 242f., 267f., 270f.
Apollinaris (Apollinarianism), 34(n.)
Apology, The, 6, 10f., 15, 51f., 70, 124, 136, 145–186, 249, 257, 263–268

Apology, The,
   confessional character of, 144
   on baptism, 160
   on bishops, 184f.
   on the church, 158–160
   on clerical celibacy, 175–177
   on confession, 161, 164f.
   on ecclesiastical orders, 169
   on good works, 151ff., 172
   on the invocation of saints, 172f.
   on justification, 151–157
   on the Lord's Supper, 160, 174ff., 274
   on the mass, 177–182
   on monastic vows, 182ff.
   on the nature of faith, 149f.
   on original sin, 145f.
   on repentance, 161ff.
   on the sacraments, 168f.
   on sacrifice, 178ff.
   on traditions, 169–171
   origin of, 137–144
   publication of, 140f.
   quality of, 141ff., 185f.
Apostles' Creed, The, 17–30
   Badcock on origins of, 22ff.
   catechetical use of, 24f.
   "catholic" in, 28
   Christology of, 27f.
   communion of saints in, 29
   doctrine of the church in, 28f.
   doctrine of God in, 26f.
   ecclesiastical use of, 25
   evaluation of, 30
   Harnack on origins of, 19ff.

Apostles' Creed, The,
  Large Catechism on, 231f.
  liturgical use of, 24
  Old Roman Symbol, 23, 26, 27,
    29, 34
  polemical use of, 25
  regula fidei as basis of, 19
  resurrection of the flesh (body)
    in, 29
Arius (Arians, Arianism), 30f., 61,
  290
Athanasian Creed, The, 40–45
  authorship of, 42f.
  Christology of, 44
  doctrine of God in, 43f.
  doctrinal use of, 43
  evaluation of, 45
  liturgical use of, 41, 43
  origin of, 41f.
Athanasius, 41f.
Atonement, Doctrine of the, 67f.
Augsburg Confession, *passim,* xi,
  46–136, 188f., 245, 249, 254,
  268, 284
  Christology of, 65–69
  doctrine of the atonement in,
    67f.
  doctrine of God in, 59–62
  doctrine of justification in, 69–
    72
  doctrine of the Lord's Supper in,
    87–89, 118–120, 122–125,
    274
  doctrine of the means of grace
    in, 82–84
  doctrine of original sin in, 62–
    65
  ecumenical aspect of, 52f.
  editio princeps of, 52
  evangelical character of, 53f.
  official character of, 55
  on baptism, 85–87
  on Christ's second coming, 105–
    107

Augsburg Confession,
  on the church, 78–82
  on civil affairs, 101–105
  on clerical celibacy, 120–122
  on confession, 90–92, 125–127
  on ecclesiastical orders, 97–99
  on faith and good works, 111–
    113
  on the freedom of the will, 107–
    109
  on good works, 75–77
  on the invocation of saints, 113–
    116
  on the means of grace, 73–75,
    82–84
  on the ministry, 73
  on monastic vows, 129–132
  on the origin of sin, 109–111, 257
  on the power of bishops, 132–136
  on repentance, 92–94
  on rites and usages, 99–101
  on traditions, 127–129
  on the use of the sacraments, 95f.
  origin of, 46–57
  political character of, 56
  preface to, 58f.
  preparation for, 50ff.
  presentation of, 51
  variata edition of, 10, 52f., 90,
    119f., 123f., 247, 273, 277
Augsburg, Diet of, 46f.
Augsburg Interim (1548), 242,
  256, 282
Augsburg, Religious Peace of
  (1555), 144, 242, 252f.
Augustine, 23, 33, 37, 42, 60, 61,
  62, 64, 86, 110, 112, 128, 146,
  148, 149, 151, 155, 157, 168,
  206, 207, 210, 234f., 259
Augustine, pseudo-, 108f., 167
Augustus (Elector of Saxony), 248,
  273f.
Aulén, Gustav, 67, 70, 238
Autun, Council of, 42

Badcock, F. J., xi, 22ff., 31, 42
Baptism,
  benefits of, 86
  in the Apology, 160
  in the Augsburg Confesson, 85–87
  in the Large Catechism, 234ff.
  in the Smalcald Articles, 201
  necessity of, 85f.
  of children, 86f.
Baptists, 87
Die Bekenntnisschriften usw., x, 13
Bergen Book (Formula of Concord), 250
Bernard of Clairvaux, 163
Bertram, J. C., 193
Bethune-Baker, J. F., 279(n.)
Beyer, Dr. Christian, 51
Beza, Theodore, 285
Biel, Gabriel, 123, 163
Bishops,
  the Apology on, 184f.
  the Augsburg Confession on, 132–136
  the Tractatus on, 209ff.
Blaurer, Ambrosius, 191
Boniface VIII (Pope), 133, 197, 207
Book of Concord, *passim,*
  ecumenical character of, 12
  evangelical character of, 14
  in American Lutheranism, 3
  Latin translation of, 2
  publication of, 1f.
  subscription to, 2f.
  theological character of, 12
Brenz, John, 74, 247, 262f., 278
Brück, Dr. Gregory, 51, 58f., 140, 142
Bucer, Martin, 78, 191, 198, 201
Buehring, P. H., 81
Buffalo Synod, The, 98f.
Bugenhagen, John, 47, 189, 202, 214

Caesarius of Arles, 20, 42
Calvin, John, 65, 88, 109, 272, 284
Campbell, Alexander, 16
Campegius, (Cardinal) Lorenzo, 165
Carlstad, Andreas, 75, 171
Carpzov, John Benedict, ix
Cassiodorus (*Historia tripartiva*), 124, 129
Catechism, The Large, 168, 223–238
  and modern social issues, 229ff.
  evangelical insights of, 230f.
  on baptism, 234ff.
  on the Apostles' Creed, 231f.
  on the Lord's Prayer, 232ff.
  on the Lord's Supper, 236f.
  on the Ten Commandments, 224–229
  preface to, 223f.
Catechism, The Small,
  content and use of, 221f.
  Latin translations of, 217
  publication of, 216f.
Catechisms, Luther's, xii, 11, 213–238, 249, 274
  confessional status of, 217ff.
  in various *Kirchenordnungen*, 217f.
  origin of, 213ff.
  theological importance of, 219ff.
"Catholic"
  in the Apostles' Creed, 28
  in Ignatius, 28
Celibacy, Clerical,
  the Apology on, 175ff.
  the Augsburg Confession on, 120–122
Celsus, 171
Chalcedon, Council of, 32, 41, 66
Charlemagne, 37f., 41
Charles the Bald (of France), 42
Charles V (Emperor), *passim,* 79, 120, 133, 137, 187f., 239ff.

Chemnitz, Martin, 2, 248, 250, 259, 288
Chiliasm, 106f.
Christology,
of the Apostles' Creed, 27f.
of the Athanasian Creed, 44
of the Augsburg Confession, 65–69
of the Formula of Concord, 278–280
of the Nicene Creed, 31f., 35ff.
of the Smalcald Articles, 195ff.
Christopher (Duke of Württemberg), 244, 245
Chrysostom, 124, 126
Chrysostom, pseudo-, 167
Church, The,
in the Apology, 158–160
in the Apostles' Creed, 28f.
in the Augsburg Confession, 78–82
in the Nicene Creed, 39
in the Smalcald Articles, 204f.
marks of, 80
unity of, 81f.
Chytraeus, David, 248ff.
Civil affairs, The Augsburg Confession on, 101–105
Clement of Rome, 18
Clement VII (Pope), 133, 187
Cohrs, Ferdinand, xi
Commandments, The Large Catechism on the, 224–229
Communicatio idiomatum, 5, 279f.
Communion of saints, The, 29, 79
Concordia concors, 251
Concordia discors, 251
Concordia Triglotta, x, 45, 54, 62, 139f., 143, 150, 250
Confession,
the Apology on, 161, 164f.
the Augsburg Confession on, 90–92, 125–127
the Smalcald Articles on, 202f.

Confessional subscription, 8f.
Confessions, The,
as historical documents, 10f.
importance of, 5
Scriptural basis of, 5ff.
Confutation (of the Augsburg Confession), 51f., 59ff., 133ff., 145, 155, 161, 173, 178, 239
Consensus Dresdensis (1576), 273
Consensus Genevensis (1552), 284
Consensus Tigurinus (1549), 272
Constantinople, First Council of, 32, 41
Corpus Christi observance, 120
Corpus Doctrinae Christianae Philippicum, 2, 245, 247, 248
Creeds, The Ecumenical, 16–45, 254f.
universal character of, 16
Cruciger, Casper, 189
Crypto-Calvinistic Controversy, 243, 272f., 278f.
Crypto-Calvinists, 52, 201, 251
Cyprian, 29, 118, 119, 155, 157, 206, 207
Cyprian, pseudo- (Arnold of Bonneval), 180
Cyril of Alexandria, 160
Cyril of Jerusalem, 32

Damasus (Pope), 23
Decretum Gratiani, 126, 210
Denk, Hans, 94, 106
Dietrich, Veit, 192
Dionysius (Pope), 20
Disciples of Christ, 16
Docetism, 66
Donatism (Donatists), 84, 160
Duns Scotus, 163

Ecclesiastical orders,
the Apology on, 169
the Augsburg Confession on, 97–99

Eck, John, 51, 63, 137
  Four Hundred Theses, x, 10, 48, 59, 62, 65, 69, 73, 75, 78, 82f., 85, 87f., 90, 93, 95, 97, 99, 102, 106, 109f., 111, 114, 118, 121, 123, 125, 127, 130, 133, 135, 161
Election, Doctrine of, 285–289
Elert, Werner, 80
Ephesus, Council of, 41
Epiphanius, 32
Erasmus, Desiderius, 117
Ernest (Count of Henneberg), 249
Eucharist, *see* Lord's Supper
Eunomius (Eunomians), 61
Eusebius of Caesarea, 31, 36, 37
Eutychians (Eutychianism), 66
Ex opere operato, 95f., 148f., 163, 169, 177, 178, 179, 181
Exegesis perspicua, 274

Faber, Johannes (of Leutkirch), 137
Fagius, Paulus, 191
Faith,
  the Apology on, 149f.
  the Augsburg Confession on, 112f.
  the Formula of Concord on, 262ff.
Faustus of Riez, 20
Feine, Paul, 19
Fendt, Leonhard, xi, 64, 113, 132
Flacian Controversy, 243, 256ff.
Flacius, Matthias, 243, 246f., 256ff., 260, 262, 268, 273, 282f.
Fontanus, Johannes, 191
Formula of Concord, The, 4, 5, 7ff., 11, 82, 88, 94, 160, 254–291
  Catalogue of Testimonies, 250
  Christology of, 278–280
  confessional significance of, 251f.

  ecclesiastical significance of, 250f.
  Epitome, 250, 254, 261, 276, 281, 289f.
  evaluation of, 290f.
  on the *descensus*, 281f.
  on freedom of the will, 258–262
  on good works, 264–267
  on justification by faith, 265ff.
  on the law and the gospel, 267–270
  on the law (third use of), 270f.
  on the Lord's Supper, 272–278
  on original sin, 256ff.
  on predestination, 284–289
  on the righteousness of faith, 262ff.
  on sects, 289f.
  origin of, 239–250
  political significance of, 252f.
  preface to, 254f.
  theological significance of, 252
Formula missae (Luther), 125
Francis I (of France), 240f.
Franciscans, The Spiritual, 117, 209
Frank, F. H. R., xii
Frankfort Recess (1558), 245, 256
Fritschel, G. J., xii
Funck, John, 263

Garrison, W. E., 12
Gelasius I (Pope), 119f.
Generanus, Petrus, 191
Gerson, John, 123, 128
Gnesio-Lutherans, 243f., 246, 253, 256, 260, 273, 283
Gnosticism, 22, 27, 29
God, Doctrine of, *see* Trinity, The Holy
Good works,
  the Apology on, 151ff., 172
  the Augsburg Confession on, 75ff.

Good works,
   the Formula of Concord on, 264–267
Gore, Charles, 210
Gottschalk of Orbais, 130
Grabau, J. A. A., 98
Gratia universalis, 288f.
Gregory I (Pope), 129, 207
Gregory VII (Pope), 121, 133
Guericke, H. E. F., 291
Gussman, Wilhelm, xi

Hardenburg, Albert, 273
Harnack, Adolf von, 19ff., 32f., 38
Henry IV (Emperor), 207
Henry VIII (of England), 29, 240f.
Hesshusen (Heshusius), Tilemann, 273, 285
Hilary, 173
Hill, C. L., 69, 147
Hilten, John, 182
Hippolytus' *Church Order,* 19
Hospinian, Rudolf, 251
Hus, John, 209
Hussites, 118
Hutter, Leonhard, 251

Ignatius, 17, 28
Irenaeus, 18, 21, 27

Jacobs, Henry E. (*Book of Concord*), x, 8, 15, 47, 66, 90, 143, 146, 150, 157(n.), 164, 223, 258, 260, 288
James I (of England), 133
Jerome, 119, 151, 157, 204, 207, 210, 236
John the Steadfast (Elector of Saxony), 47, 49, 136
John Frederick (Elector of Saxony), 188f., 241
Jonas, Justus, 47, 113, 137, 189
Jovinian, 128, 177

Julian the Apostate, 171
Justification by faith,
   in the Apology, 151–157
   in the Augsburg Confession, 69–72
   in the Formula of Concord, 265ff.
Justin Martyr, 18

Kantonen, T. A., 4
Karl (Margrave of Baden), 249
Kawerau, Gustav, 267
Kenosis (Gniessen-Tübingen) Controversy, 251
Keys, Power of the, 132f., 162f., 202
Kolde, Theodore, xi, 193, 216, 218, 259
Köllner, Edward, x, 25, 222
Köstlin, Julius, 188(n.)
Krauth, C. P., 290f.

Lateran, Fourth Council of the, 119
Law, The Formula of Concord on the, 267ff., 270f.
Leipzig Interim (1548), 242, 243, 246, 264, 282
Leo X (Pope), 197
Lietzmann, Hans, 42
Loofs, Friedrich, 41, 42, 43
Lord's Day, The, 135
Lord's Prayer, The Large Catechism on the, 232ff.
Lord's Supper, The,
   communio indignorum, 202
   concomitance, 119
   consubstantiation, 89
   in the Apology, 160, 174f., 274
   in the Augsburg Confession, 87–89
   in the Large Catechism, 236f.
   in the Formula of Concord, 272–278
   in the Smalcald Articles, 201f.

Lord's Supper, The,
  real presence, 88f., 124f., 160,
    274ff.
  transubstantiation, 89
Louis (Duke of Württemberg),
  249
Lüneberg Articles (1561), 218
Luther, Martin, *passim*
Luther, Works of,
  Erlangen edition, LXIII, 135–
    288
  Philadelphia edition, II, 177–
    168; II, 291f.–168; II, 351–
    215; III, 228ff.–103, 104; IV,
    341–54; V, 32ff.–103; VI,
    177ff.–215
  Weimar edition, VI, 243–101;
    VI, 501–168; VI, 572–168;
    XI, 245ff.–103; XII, 215–125;
    XVIII, 742–64; XIX, 44ff.–
    215; XIX, 623ff.–103; XXIII,
    133, 143–66; XXVI, 261f.–
    280; XXVI, 449ff.–49; XXVI,
    500–59; XXVI, 502–68;
    XXVI, 504, 505–73, 103;
    XXVI, 506–80; XXVI, 507–
    120f.; XXVI, 508–114; XXVI,
    509–107; XXX(2), 89–54;
    XXX(3), 336–140; XL(1),
    441–67; XL(1), 603–72; XL
    (2), 347–80; LIV, 49f.–280;
    Briefe V, 319–50; V, 496–
    114; V, 578–139; *Tisch.* I,
    90–98

Macedonians, 34(n.), 38
McGiffert, A. C., xi, 23, 26, 29
Major, George, 243, 264f.
Majoristic Controversy, 243, 264f.
Mani (Manicheans), 60f., 258
Marbach, John, 285
Marburg Articles (1529), 49, 59,
  65, 68, 74, 75, 86, 87, 89, 91,
  92, 95, 101, 107

Marcellus of Ancyra, 20
Marcion (Marcionism), 22, 27
Marriage, 103, 161
Mass, The,
  abuses of, 122–125, 196f.
  derivation of the term, 180f.
  for the dead, 181
Maulbronn Conference (1564),
  247f.
Maulbronn Formula (1576), 249,
  274
Maurice (of Saxony), 241f., 282
Means of grace, The, in the Augs-
  burg Confession, 73–75, 82–84
Melanchthon, Philip, *passim*
Melander, Gustaf, 191
Menius, Justus, 265, 268
Mennonites, 87
Meritum condigni, 148, 154, 155
Meritum congrui, 148, 154, 171f.
Meyer, Johannes, xi, 219f.
Ministry, The,
  call to, 98f.
  in the Augsburg Confession, 73f.
  in the Smalcald Articles, 203f.
  moral character of, 84
  parity in, 210
Mirbt, Carl, 197(n.)
Missale, Old Gallican, 20, 22
Moerlin, Johannes, 268
Mohammedans, 61, 170
Monasticism,
  the Apology on, 182ff.
  the Augsburg Confession on,
    129–132
  the Smalcald Articles on, 205
Monophysites, 66
Morrison, C. C., 77
Münzer, Thomas, 110

Naumburg Conference (1561),
  245f.
Nazarites, 184
Nestorians (Nestorianism), 66, 279

Nestorius, 32, 279
Neve, J. L., 9, 64, 110
Nicaea, Council of, 31, 206
Nicene Creed, The, 30–40
  Badcock on origin of, 32f.
  catechetical use of, 34
  Christology of, 31f., 35ff.
  doctrine of the church in, 39
  doctrine of God in, 35
  doctrine of the Spirit in, 37f.
  ecclesiastical use of, 34
  evaluation of, 39f.
  filioque, 16, 33, 38, 41
  Harnack on origin of, 32
  liturgical use of, 34
  Niceno-Constantinopolitan form, 32ff.
  polemical use of, 34
Nicetas of Remesiana, 20
Nicholas of Cusa, 119
Nicholas of Lyra, 159
Ninety-Five Theses, Luther's, 90
Novatians, 94
Nürnberg, Truce of (1532), 240
Nygren, Anders, 72(n.), 80(n.)

Obsopoeus, Vincentius, 217
Oecolampadius, Johannes, 13, 272
Ordination, 210
Origen, 207
Ort, S. A., 9
Osiander, Andreas, 243, 252f.
Osiander, Lucas, 2
Osiandrian Controversy, 243, 262ff.
Otto, Anton, 268

Patripassianism, 27
Paul III (Pope), 187, 194, 241
Peasants' War, 102f.
Penance, Romanist doctrine of, 90f., 126, 161f.
Pelagians (Pelagianism, Semi-Pelagianism), 63, 69, 109, 146ff., 171, 258, 261

Peucer, Caspar, 273
Philip of Hesse, 189, 241f.
Philip II (of Spain), 51
Philippists, 244, 249, 253, 256, 260, 273, 278
Pietism (Pietists), 77, 267
Pirminius of Reichenau, 21
Pius II (Pope), 121
Platina, Bartolomeo, 121
Plitt, Gustav, xi, 64, 77, 110
Poach, Andreas, 268
Pope, Supremacy of the, 206f.
Protestation of Worms (1557), 245

"Quietism" in Lutheranism, 77, 113

Ramiro II (of Aragon), 131
Rauschenbusch, Walter, 38, 64f.
Rechabites, 184
Regensburg, Diet of, 244
Repentance,
  the Apology on, 161ff.
  the Augsburg Confession on, 92–94
  the Smalcald Articles on, 199f.
Resurrection, Human,
  in the Apostles' Creed, 29
  in the Nicene Creed, 39
Reu, J. M., xi, xiii, 6, 217
Richard, J. W., xi, 50, 277
Rituale Romanum, 17
Ross, E. A., 230
Rufinus of Aquileia, 20, 21, 23, 26

Sabellius (Sabellianism), 27
Sacraments, The,
  the Apology on, 168f.
  the Augsburg Confession on, 95f.
Sacrifice, The Apology on, 178ff.
Saints, Invocation of,
  the Apology on, 172f.
  the Augsburg Confession on, 113ff.
Samosatenes, "New," 61f.

Sauerman, John, 217
Savonarola, Girolamo, 117
Schaefer, F. J., 282
Schaff, Philip, xi, 1, 30, 41, 141, 221, 264, 272, 278, 288, 289, 291
Schmauk, T. E., and Benze, C. T., xi, 4, 50
Schwabach Articles (1529), x, 49, 59, 65, 68, 74, 75, 79, 81, 86, 88, 89, 91, 92, 95, 101, 103, 107
Schweinfurth Conference (1532), 144
Schwenkfeld, Caspar von (Schwenkfeldians), 75, 94, 290
Scotists, 133
Seeberg, A., 19
Seeberg, Reinhold, 13
Sehling, E., 216
Selnecker, Nicholas, 2, 191, 193
Siegbert of Mainz, 121
Sin, Original,
   the Apology on, 145f.
   the Augsburg Confession on, 62–65, 109–111
   the Formula of Concord on, 256ff.
   the Smalcald Articles on, 199
Smalcald Articles, The, xi, 15, 119, 124, 136, 160, 194-205, 249, 257, 284
   confessional status of, 192
   Latin translation of, 191
   on baptism, 201
   on the church, 204f.
   on confession and absolution, 202f.
   on the divine majesty, 194f.
   on excommunication, 203
   on the Lord's Supper, 201f., 274
   on the ministry, 203f.
   on monastic vows, 205

Smalcald Articles,
   on the office and work of Christ, 195ff.
   on the power of the keys, 202
   on repentance, 199f.
   on sin, 199
   origin of, 187–193
   polemical character of, 191
Smalcald League, The, 240ff.
Smalcald Recess (1537), 144
Smalcald War, 241f.
Socinians, 61
Sola gratia, 267, 286, 288
Spalatin, George, 189, 191
Sprecher, Samuel, 277
Stancaro (Stancarius), Francesco, 263
Stier, Johannes, xi, 204
Strigel, Victorin, 256, 260
Stuttgart, Synod of (1159), 278
Swabian-Saxon Formula (1576), 248f.
Symbolum quicunque, See Athanasian Creed
Synergistic Controversy, 243, 256ff., 258–262

Tauler, John, 123
Tertullian, 18, 20, 27, 37, 62
Theophylact, 160
Thieme, Karl, xii, 218
Thomas Aquinas, 6, 14, 128, 147, 201
Thomists, 133
Toledo, Council of, 33, 37
Torgau Articles (1529), x, 47, 82, 111, 113f., 117, 120f., 123, 125, 127, 129f., 132f.
Torgau Book (1576), 249
Tractatus, The, 190, 205–212
   history of, 192f.
   on bishops, 209ff.
   on papal claims, 206ff.

Traditions, Human,
the Apology on, 169ff.
the Augsburg Confession on, 99–
101, 127–129
Trent, Council of, 51, 119, 187,
241
on justification, 72
Trinity, The Holy,
in the Apostles' Creed, 26f.
in the Athanasian Creed, 43f.
in the Augsburg Confession, 59–
62
in the Nicene Creed, 37f.
in the Smalcald Articles, 194f.
Tschackert, Paul, 259

Unitarians, 61
Ursinus, Zachary, 251

Valentinians, 61
Vincent of Lerins, 13, 42, 255
Virgin Mary, The, 27, 36f., 100,
113, 173
Visitation Articles (1528), 101,
125, 214
Voss, Gerhard, 41
Voss, Heinrich, 209
Vulgarius, See Theophylact

Waldenses, 117
Walker, Williston, 252
Walther, C. F. W., 270
War, Lutheran attitude on, 105
Weimar Confutation (1558), 245,
256, 260
Westphal, Joachim, 268, 272f.
Wigand, John, 268
Will, Freedom of the,
the Augsburg Confession on,
107ff.
the Formula of Concord on, 258–
262
Williams, C. D., 4
Wittenberg Concord (1536), 144,
189f., 201
Worms, Conference of (1540), 144
Württemberg Confession (1559),
278
Wycliffe, John, 117, 160, 171, 209

Zanchi (Zanchius), Jerome, 285
Zerbst Conference (1570), 248
Zwingli, Ulrich, 63, 65, 66, 68, 75,
88, 89, 99, 109, 146, 273
on the Person of Christ, 279f.
on the sacraments, 95, 272
ratio fidei of, 90

SCRIPTURE REFERENCES

Genesis
1:1 27

Psalms
1:2 270
16:10 282
19:13 126
32:5 165
38:4 162
51:4 165
51:16, 17 178

Proverbs
10:12 152
27:23 165

Isaiah
28:21 163
58:7, 9 153

Jeremiah
17:9 126

Daniel
4:27 153

Malachi
1:11 178
3:3 . . . . 178f.

Tobit
4:11 154

2 Maccabees
15:14 172

Matthew
3:8 165
5:3, 7 153
7:15 133
11:26 162
15:3, 9 128
15:14 135
16:16 17
16:18, 19 207
18:2 206
19:11 121
19:17 153
19:21 . . . . . . 183f.

Matthew
19:29 183
20:28 69
23:3 185
25:45 45
28:18 280
28:19 . . 17, 26, 234
28:20 79

Mark
1:15 163
5:16 234

Luke
6:37 153
7:47 151
11:41 154
17:10 75
22:25 206

John
6:54 275
8:44 110
16:12, 13 133
20:21 206
21:15 207

Acts
2:24, 27 282
5:29 47
8:37 17
10:43 163
15:10 128
15:29 133
19:5 17

Romans
1:7 26
1:24 110
2:6 155
4:5 154
4:9 169
4:13 154
5:12 62
7:7, 23 146
10:9 17

Romans
13:1, 2 104
14:17 . . . . . 128, 160
14:23 164
15:6 26

I Corinthians
1:4 77
2:14 108
3:6 206
7:2, 9 121
8:6 18
10:16 . . . . 160, 275
11:27 88
11:31 167
11:33 124
12:3 17
13:2 152
13:13 152
14:33 29
15:3, 4 17

II Corinthians
13:14 . . . . . . 17, 26

Galatians
2:7 206
3:22 63
5:19f. 237

Ephesians
2:8 . . . . . 112, 169
4:6 26
4:9 28
5:25, 26 . . . 29, 158
5:30–32 29

Philippians
2:5–11 17

Colossians
1:15 35
2:9 280
2:11, 12, 14 . . 163
2:15 28
2:16 . 128, 135, 159

Colossians
2:20 128
3:14 152

I Timothy
2:5 115
3:2 121
3:16 168
4:1, 3 128
4:3 122
5:9–11 184

II Timothy
4:1 18
4:8 155

Titus
3:5 86

Hebrews
5:1 179
10:10–14 ..124, 178
11:6 .....153, 155
12:23 29
13:15 178
13:17 185

James
1:6 234
2:24 153
5:16 165

I Peter
2:9 29
2:13, 14 104

I Peter
3:18–22 ...17, 282
3:19 28
4:8 152

II Peter
1:10 .....172, 266
1:21 38

I John
2:1 115
4:15 17
5:5, 10 17

Revelation
10:3 .....197(n.)

Type used in this book
Body, 10 on 13 and 9 on 11 Caledonia
Display, Bodoni

p. 86 — "not lack but contempt of
baptism that damns"— Augustine

p. 92 — "people should go to communion
sometimes without confession"— Luther

p. 96 — Faith — analogy of dollar bill

p. 49 — "Marburg Articles" — Zwinglians

p. 80 — "God has nothing to do with holy
men. A holy man is a fiction"

p. 83 — "all pastors are either Christian
sinners or hypocritical saints"

p. 112 — "pilgrimage vs. duties at home"

p. 122 — abuses of mass

p. 131 — Celibacy — "frustrated tower of Babel
trying to reach God"

p. 168 — sacraments & sacramental signs